Nobody's Child

SUSAN VINOCOUR

Nobody's Child

A Tragedy, a Trial, and a
History of the Insanity Defense

W. W. NORTON & COMPANY
Independent Publishers Since 1923

The names and identifying details of many people who appear in this book have been changed. Dialogue has been reconstructed based on the author's contemporaneous notes, her recollection of events, interviews, and trial evidence.

For information about permission to reproduce selections from this book, write to Permissions, W. W. Norton & Company, Inc., 500 Fifth Avenue, New York, NY 10110

For information about special discounts for bulk purchases, please contact W. W. Norton Special Sales at specialsales@wwnorton.com or 800-233-4830

Manufacturing by Lake Book Manufacturing
Book design by Ellen Cipriano

Library of Congress Cataloging-in-Publication Data
Names: Vinocour, Susan Nordin, author.
Title: Nobody's child : a tragedy, a trial, and a history of the insanity defense / Susan Vinocour.
Description: First edition. | New York : W. W. Norton & Company, 2020. | "The names and identifying details of many people who appear in this book have been changed. Dialogue has been reconstructed based on the author's contemporaneous notes, her recollection of events, interviews, and trial evidence." | Includes bibliographical references and index.
Identifiers: LCCN 2019050530 | ISBN 9780393651928 (hardcover) | ISBN 9780393651935 (epub)
Subjects: LCSH: Insanity defense—United States. | Insanity (Law)—United States. | Competency to stand trial—United States. | Trials (Murder)—New York (State)
Classification: LCC KF9242 .V56 2020 | DDC 345.747/04—dc23
LC record available at https://lccn.loc.gov/2019050530

W. W. Norton & Company, Inc., 500 Fifth Avenue, New York, N.Y. 10110
www.wwnorton.com

W. W. Norton & Company Ltd., 15 Carlisle Street, London W1D 3BS

1 2 3 4 5 6 7 8 9 0

This book is dedicated to Dorothy and Raymie,
to Paul and Eric, and to the many others like them

Tell me, ye judges of our mortal sins,
Where madness ends, and sanity begins?

—Dry Nurse, *Monomania*

Crimes are not to be measured by the issue of events but from
the bad intentions of men.

—Cicero

CONTENTS

A NOTE TO READERS

THIS IS A WORK of nonfiction and is richly documented. Its aim is not to point a finger at specific individuals involved in a particular case of injustice, or to expose its central subject to possibly unwanted attention, but to make a larger point about all such cases. For that reason, the names of the individuals central to this story, other than my own, have been changed.

My sources include more than seventeen hours of face-to-face interviews with the woman I am calling Dorothy Dunn, as well as extensive psychological testing; interviews with her defense attorney, teachers, and social workers; trial transcripts; and review of a multitude of documents, including police reports, depositions, the medical examiner's report, medical and psychiatric records, school records, Department of Social Services records, media accounts, and a long list of wonderful books in the fields of history, law, and mental health. It also comes from my years as a law guardian, a defense attorney and prosecutor, a specialist in child abuse and trauma, and a clinical and forensic psychologist.

The terms *psychiatric evaluation* and *psychological evaluation* are legally equivalent in New York State and are used here interchangeably. Likewise, the term *mental health expert* as used in this book refers interchange-ably to both psychiatrists and psychologists.

The terms *mental retardation* and *mentally retarded*, discarded in the most recent *Diagnostic and Statistical Manual* of the American Psychiatric Association in favor of the term *intellectual disability*, were the formal psychiatric terms for indicating developmental intellectual disability at the time of Dorothy's case and so are used here. No pejorative judgment about a person's overall worth or other capabilities is intended.

It is important to note that the vast majority of people who suffer from mental illness are not dangerous and do not engage in criminal activity. Most of the harm done to others is done by people who are perfectly well.

PROLOGUE

W HAT FOLLOWS IS a story about how the insanity defense
works, and does not work, in our country in the early twenty-
first century. It illustrates our confusing and ambivalent attitudes about
mentally ill defendants, about guilt and punishment, and about the difficulty of applying fourteenth-century legal concepts of insanity to modern
understandings of the human mind. It is about a legal system that is unreliable in its attempts to ascertain truth or offer justice to impoverished
defendants, especially those of color. And it is about the failures of our
schools, hospitals, communities, and social service agencies—our failures as a society—to respond to those with serious mental illness before
someone dies.

PART I

The Crime

CHAPTER 1

A THICKSET BLACK WOMAN in a faded housedress hung up the pay phone and stepped out of the graffiti-scarred phone booth at the Public Market. With her head down and her shoulders slumped, she trudged past the live chickens in their wooden crates and past the Vietnamese woman selling twisted shoots of lucky bamboo, limping slightly; her knee was bothering her more than usual. It was September; there was a chill in the air, which smelled of decomposing leaves and wet earth, though it is unlikely that she noticed any of this. Her name was Dorothy Dunn.

Mrs. Dunn slowly made her way the ten blocks back to her home, her eyes fixed on the sidewalk, which was heaved in places by Rochester's cold winters. Her neighborhood was not high on the list for urban renewal. Arriving at the house, with its peeling green paint and porch spindles leaning like loose teeth, she hobbled up the front steps, unlocked the three locks on the door, and let herself in. The interior was shabby and dark, and chairs were stacked up against the front windows like barricades.

She seemed not to notice the three young children huddled together on the threadbare couch in the front room, their eyes wide as owls'; she did not speak to them, nor they to her. She went into the kitchen and slumped down onto a chair, chin on her chest.

A few minutes passed before the stillness was broken. Its siren wailing, a rescue squad van pulled up in front of the house; paramedics spilled out and scrambled up the rickety porch steps. They pounded on the door and called out, but the woman didn't move. One of the children, her ten-year-old daughter, Alice, cracked the door open and peered out.

"Where's the child?" they asked, pushing their way in. Spying the woman, they went to her, but she gave no answer. She had on a dime-store wig, perched awry so that it looked as if her head wasn't on straight.

"I guess he must've fell," Dorothy said, as if to herself. "He'll be awright, won't he?" She looked up at them for the first time. "You can fix him, can't you?" she asked.

And then they saw him: her three-year-old grandson, Raymie, sprawled on his back in the pantry, his milky eyes wide open. He had a large, bloody bruise on his forehead, his skin was cold to the touch, and he was clearly dead.

POLICE AND HOMICIDE detectives arrived, followed soon after by the medical examiner's investigators. Curious neighbors gathered outside, abuzz with speculation, while a crime scene technician cordoned off the property with yellow crime scene tape. A police photographer entered the house and made his way to the pantry, where he busied himself documenting the position of the small body, with its bloated belly and matchstick-thin arms, the heaps of soiled clothes piled like the nests of some filthy beast in the corner of the room, the bare cupboard shelves, and even the refrigerator, door open, empty but for a brick of government-issue cheese and a package of wrinkled hot dogs.

The woman began to wander through the house, rinsing some food-crusted dishes stacked up around the kitchen sink, then stopping and drifting into the living room, where she moved the furniture about aimlessly. She seemed not to notice the growing number of people in her home. She pulled herself heavily up the stairs, muttering softly, and went into the children's bedroom, where she started to make the beds, tugging fitfully at the stained and tangled sheets.

One of the police officers went over to the children, who were still sitting on the broken-down couch in the living room, silently watching.

"Who's the little boy in the pantry?" she asked.

"That's Raymie," Alice said, her voice barely a whisper. "Precious's boy."

"Precious?"

"That's my sister."

"Where is she?"

"I don't know. She don't come by here no more."

"And who's the lady that was in the kitchen when we got here?"

"Mama," she said.

Alice's gaze shifted to the pantry, where the technician was photographing the child's body as it lay on the floor.

The homicide investigator standing beside them made a note on his pad. Then he walked to the foot of the stairs and called up to Mrs. Dunn.

"I need you to come down here," he said. Mrs. Dunn let herself be led down stairs without protest by an officer who'd gone up to do a search of the bedrooms. "Sit down, Ms. Dunn. I need to ask you some questions," the investigator said. She sat.

"Will it take long?" Dorothy asked. "My babies is hungry. I gotta feed them."

And she stood up again, went to the sink, filled a kettle with water, and put it on to boil. She laid out bread dusted with delicate green and yellow mold, picked up a knife, and began to spread jelly on the bread.

"Ms. Dunn," the officer said, "I need you to sit down now and answer some questions about the boy."

As he spoke, he stepped up behind her, carefully took the butter knife out of her hands, and set it down on the counter. He held her firmly by the shoulders and guided her back down into the chair.

He began to question her: Had she ever hit the child? What had she hit him with? He did not inform her of her right to remain silent or that whatever she said could be used against her. Nor did he tell her that she had a right to counsel.

Later, sitting in a cell with her public defender, she said, "The man was talking to me, asking questions all the time about Raymie. Was he this, and was he that. How could I explain 'bout Raymie to this man? He never even knew that child. The man kept asking me what happened to Raymie. My thoughts was going around, all in a mess. I couldn't sort it out. The questions, they was too fast. They all runned together. My mind was empty, like it went out for a walk and hadn't brought itself back yet."

She heard the man say that she didn't have to talk anymore if she said she wanted a lawyer.

"I want the lawyer," she said.

Maybe now they would stop asking her questions and let her rest, she thought. But she was wrong. The questioning continued until, finally, the officer gave a slight nod to his partner and unhooked the handcuffs from his belt.

"Am I going to prison?" Dorothy asked.

"Why do you say that?" said the officer.

"I'm going to prison," she whispered softly to herself, looking at the men with their hats and their guns. "Oh, my babies, my babies." And she looked back over her shoulder at her three young children, with their liquid eyes, as the handcuffs clicked shut and the police led her away.

CHAPTER 2

DOROTHY DUNN spent the weekend in jail, and on Monday she was transported to the courthouse in shackles, an armed deputy at each elbow, for her arraignment. As she stood mute, eyes fixed on the floor, the judge informed her of the charge against her: child endangerment, a class A misdemeanor punishable by up to a year in jail. He asked if she had an attorney and, when he could not decipher her mumbled response, took it that she did not. He asked if she could afford to hire an attorney and inferred from her silence that she could not.

The Sixth Amendment to the U.S. Constitution guarantees an accused person "the right . . . to have the Assistance of Counsel for his defence," and the Supreme Court held in 1963, in the case of *Gideon v. Wainwright*, that if a defendant is indigent and can't afford an attorney, one must be appointed at the state's expense.

The judge's eyes cast around the courtroom; he was looking for an attorney he could assign to represent Mrs. Dunn. His gaze lit on Karen Hughes, a public defender who happened to be present in the courtroom on another case.

"Miss Hughes," he called out, "I'm assigning this case to you."

He didn't ask—and it wouldn't have mattered—how many other cases young Ms. Hughes already had. She was relatively new at the job and already had more cases than she could handle. But all her colleagues in the defender's office were similarly overwhelmed; they were each assigned more than two hundred felony cases a year—far above national standards for maximum caseloads. And their clients were often the most difficult to represent: people with few resources, limited education, and no friends in high places; most often, they were people of color.

As journalist Andrew Cohen has pointed out about the ruling in the Gideon case,"There is a vast gulf between the broad premise of the ruling and the grim practice of legal representation for the nation's poorest litigants." The Brennan Center for Justice calculated that vastly underpaid and overworked public defenders across the country spend, on average, less than six minutes per case in hearings where clients plead guilty and are sentenced: six minutes to interview the defendant, review the evidence, and advise their client that their best bet is to plead guilty. This is only getting worse over time, as public defender budgets are cut. The Brennan Center noted that public defenders' caseloads were so high in Missouri in 2004 that the trial public defenders had an average of only 6.6 hours to prepare each felony case. It observed, "The present M.A.S.H. style operating procedure requires public defenders to divvy effective legal assistance to a narrowing group of clients," forcing them "to choose among clients as to who will receive effective legal assistance."

Public defenders have a high attrition rate because of the stress and the impossible ethical bind they are in. Many suffer from depression and feelings of helplessness that drive them out of the law entirely. But Karen Hughes wasn't there yet; she still had hope that she could bring a measure of justice to most of her clients. And there was no point protesting the assignment of the Dunn case; she had no authority to decline. She could only sigh audibly.

"How does your client plead, guilty or not guilty?" the judge asked.

Karen and her new client, about whom she knew nothing, had a brief, whispered conference, during which, Karen later recalled, Mrs. Dunn stared down at the floor and mumbled unintelligibly. Karen skimmed the charging instrument, which gave her the bare bones of the what, where, and when of the crime charged. Then she flipped quickly to the demographic sheet and gave it a quick glance: defendant's name, age, race, address. No phone. Five children, three of whom lived at home.

"Not guilty, Your Honor," Karen said on the woman's behalf. There would be time to discuss guilt and innocence with her client later.

She made her standard request that the defendant be released on her own recognizance, pending trial. After all, she argued, the purpose of bail is to ensure that a defendant will show up for trial and not skip town—where and with what money could this woman flee? There were also the woman's three young children, currently in temporary foster care, to consider; they needed their mother.

"Denied," the judge said, without looking up. "I don't know that they need *this* mother, counselor. Bail is set at fifty thousand dollars." This sum meant that the woman would have to remain in jail until her trial, many months away, unless she could come up with five thousand dollars in cash for a bail bondsman. Her children would be farmed out to foster care for the duration, unless there was some qualified relative willing to take them in.

"Remanded to the county jail," the judge said, rapping his gavel down smartly. "Next case."

With that, Mrs. Dunn, who seemed oblivious to it all, was hoisted up by her elbow by a burly deputy and taken away, the six-minute proceeding at an end.

CHAPTER 3

LATE IN THE DAY, after most people had gone home to supper, Karen managed to get over to the jail to see her new client. The woman was locked in a special segregation cell on the women's unit—five feet by seven, bare except for a metal toilet and a thin foam mattress set on a cement shelf. She'd been segregated from the general population so the other women wouldn't harm her; no one likes a child murderer.

Mrs. Dunn looked up at Karen with empty eyes, seeming to have no memory of her. This struck Karen as odd; most of her clients clung to her the way a drowning man clings to flotsam. She introduced herself again and briefly explained her role as the woman's defense attorney, but Mrs. Dunn's face registered little reaction, and she made no eye contact.

"Do you understand that you are charged with endangering your grandson, Raymie, and that I'm your attorney?" Karen asked.

"Yes, m'm. Raymie, that's my little grandbaby," the woman said. A fat tear swelled in the corner of her eye and brimmed over, rolling down her full cheek. "I should've kept him with me, but he got a mark on his leg. I didn't want to have to tie him no more," she said, shaking her head.

"I don't know, I just don't know. . . . He must've got into something. That boy didn't never sleep, seemed like. He just out-stayed me up. I tried to keep him safe. I didn't want my kids thinking that something happened to him, right there in my own house. I thought he'd be all right." She sighed. "It's hard. It's just real hard. My daddy died in that house."

Karen couldn't follow; what was the woman talking about? A mark on his leg? Tying him? Her father dying? What did any of this have to do with the dead child?

Dunn belched a great, roiling burp.

"Sorry," she said. "I'm not feeling so good. Must be my stomach's not used to the food here yet."

"It's okay," Karen said. "I'll come back in a few days, when you're feeling better." As she spoke, she skimmed through the police report, where the arresting officer had noted the woman's oddly disconnected state and aimless wandering during questioning. And then she saw something else. As the emergency responders had knelt over the child's cold, limp form, Mrs. Dunn had said, "He'll be all right, won't he? You can fix him, can't you?"

"I be all right, I guess," Mrs. Dunn said.

But Karen didn't think she would be all right. She thought there might be something very wrong with the woman. It occurred to her that she should get a psychiatric evaluation of Mrs. Dunn, who didn't seem coherent. Maybe she was incompetent to stand trial. Or maybe, just maybe, she had been legally insane when the child died and, therefore, "not guilty."

KAREN HAD NEVER raised an insanity defense before, though she'd represented hundreds of defendants, many of whom had had mental health issues. The odds of success with the insanity defense are so poor; it is used in only 1 percent of all criminal cases and succeeds less than one time in four of those, contrary to popular belief; it is a complex, time-intensive defense to prepare.

But first things first: for now, she just needed to find a psychologist willing to do a psychiatric evaluation in an unpopular case for a third of the usual compensation—there wasn't much money in the public defender's budget to pay expert witnesses—and to give an opinion about whether this woman was currently competent to stand trial.

When Karen got back to her office, she asked around and came up with a name. My name.

"I'm no expert," she said later. "But something obviously wasn't right. That's when I decided to call you."

Thanks for nothing, I thought.

CHAPTER 4

AND SO DOROTHY DUNN'S story began for me. I am a clinical and forensic psychologist; I was formerly a legal aid defense attorney and law guardian for abused children, then a special assistant district attorney specializing in child abuse and domestic violence, before returning to school for my doctorate in psychology. In addition to working with patients and heading the mental health team for juvenile probation, I perform mental health evaluations for the court.

I was padding around the kitchen in scuffed moccasins on a Saturday morning, nursing a mug of coffee, while my husband, Jacob, did his rendition of a short-order cook, burning bacon and toast as only he can. When he'd come to the United States from Israel, years before, barely speaking English and with fifty dollars to his name, he'd gotten a job working the midnight-to-dawn shift at a greasy spoon, going to college during the day. Everything he learned about cooking he learned there: he'd never met a food he couldn't fry.

We'd met in Ann Arbor, while we were both in graduate school, and moved from there to Detroit. In those days, Detroit was infamous for its homicide rate of almost three a day. Neighborhoods destroyed during the '67 riots still lay in ruins and rubble. Unemployment was over 20 percent, higher among young African-Americans. Poverty was rampant. We'd been eager to start a family, but in some cleaner, calmer place, and had been happy to move from the heavy industry of Detroit to Rochester, in upstate New York.

Rochester is a pretty town on the shores of Lake Ontario, nestled among the hills and valleys of the Finger Lakes, with Niagara Falls to the west and New York City a few hundred miles southeast. A medium-sized city, it boasts of better-than-average schools and lovely suburbs for folks working in medical and high-tech jobs or teaching at one of the several colleges clustered nearby. Traffic isn't bad, there's a good symphony orchestra, and the local wines are eminently drinkable.

But there are downsides: long, dreary months of deep winter when the sun remains hidden for weeks at a time, and high poverty rates in the inner city, especially for black and Hispanic families, and particularly for children. As in so many American cities, most middle- and upper-income white residents have very limited exposure to the grittier parts of the city or its inhabitants; one lifelong resident I met had never been downtown and had no idea there was an impressive waterfall right in the middle of the city. The city government is business-friendly, traditionally more enthusiastic about renovating the relatively new airport once again than hiring extra teachers or child protective workers. In other words, it is a city much like most other midsized cities in the Northeast.

I yawned, tossed place mats on the table, and flicked on the television to a recap of Friday's news.

On the screen was a woman reporter standing in front of a ramshackle house. Behind her, two policemen had a sullen-faced black woman pinioned between them and were shoehorning her into the back of a squad car. Her eyes were dull, and there was something odd-looking about her.

"Moments ago," the reporter said, "police took Dorothy Dunn into custody after finding the body of her dead three-year-old grandson, Raymie, in the house. According to unnamed sources, the boy was severely malnourished and had signs of multiple physical injuries. This same source indicated that the child had been dead for several days when paramedics arrived on the scene. He was in the care of his grandmother because his mother is ill. According to the police chief, Ms. Dunn is being charged in connection with his death."

Multiple injuries. Three years old. Dead.

"Fry the bitch!" I said, feeling a rising anger.

Jacob gave me a look but knew enough not to comment. I sat down with my burnt toast. The phone rang and I picked it up, my thoughts still on the dead child.

"Hello?" I said.

"This is Karen Hughes," said an unfamiliar woman's voice. "I'm an attorney with the public defender's office. I've just been assigned a new client, and I think there may be something wrong with her. I'm looking for someone to perform a psychological evaluation, and your name came up."

I knew why she had called me. There aren't many mental health experts in town who'll take on cases involving legal issues, and of the few who do, some work only for the prosecution, where they will be well reimbursed for their trouble. But I've acquired the reputation of being willing to work for both the prosecution and the defense, wherever the psychological evidence leads, sometimes pro bono. As an old legal aid attorney, I know how difficult it is for indigent defendants to obtain expert opinions. And how are the indigent to have the equal protection of the law if mental health experts won't make themselves available to evaluate them? The integrity of our legal system is only as sound as the justice we provide to the poorest among us.

"Who's the client?" I asked, my attention split between the woman on the phone and the woman on the television screen.

There was a pause.

"Dorothy Dunn," she said.

"Shit," I said.

I didn't want to do it. The woman could go to hell, as far as I was concerned.

"There's something you need to know," I said. "I just told my husband they should fry the bitch. I don't know if I can be objective; I don't have a lot of sympathy for child abusers."

Doing a psychological evaluation is not a neat, tidy business. You don't do it from afar, keeping your hands clean. You must roll up your sleeves and reach into a person's soul, like a kind of psychological laying on of hands. What is this person made of? How do *they* see the world? It is a matter not of standing dispassionately off at a safe distance but of crawling up inside the accused and accomplishing a kind of empathic mind meld. Then you must step back into yourself and use psychiatric models to build the unique puzzle that is them.

But I did not want to get that close to this woman.

MY THOUGHTS WENT BACK to when I was fifteen, to the kitchen breakfast table on a school day like any other. Sunlight streamed in through the mullioned windowpanes, leaving bright bars of light and dark on the green plastic tablecloth.

My father, a doctor, sat at the head of the table, my mother to his left. I was opposite him, and my eight-year-old brother, Paul, was beside me. My other brother, Eric, who was five, had been called to the table but dallied a moment. The room smelled of coffee and toast, and we each had a plate of scrambled eggs. In my memory, they are an unnatural, glistening yellow. I am on heightened alert; my father's tight-lipped silence alerts me that my parents aren't getting along. Paul and I studiously regard our eggs, careful not to do anything to set him off. But Eric hasn't yet learned to sense the danger, in spite of a broken arm the year before when my father, in a rage, threw him against a wall for speaking out of turn.

Eric arrives at the table with a broad grin, his blue eyes twinkling. My father says something to him in a low, ominous growl. "What?" Eric says. This is a mistake. My father's fist strikes out, quick as a hooded cobra, punching Eric hard in the chest. Eric's eyes roll back in his head and he keels over backward, stiff and straight. His color drains away.

My father jumps out of his chair and feels for a pulse. Feeling none, he begins CPR, sweat breaking out on his forehead as he pumps Eric's chest furiously. Eric's skin begins to take on the bluish cast of old tin that I had seen on corpses in the hospital. My mother, Paul, and I are frozen in place, afraid to speak or move, even to breathe, as if a spell has been cast. After two or three minutes—it seems much longer—Eric's eyes flutter open in his gray face.

He takes a ragged breath, and my father returns to his seat at the head of the table without a flicker of emotion.

"I don't feel so good," Eric says in a weak, small voice. He looks nauseated and green. "May I be excused?"

"Sit down and eat your goddamn eggs," my father hissed.

I still can't bear the sight of eggs in the morning.

This was neither the first nor the last time my father hurt one of us. I had been kicked down a flight of stairs as a child and backhanded hard enough to knock out a tooth. And Paul used to be so terrified when my father came into the bedroom at night that he would hide between the mattress and the box springs to escape notice. Child abuse is one of the great secrets behind the closed doors and perfect white picket fences and neatly starched choir robes of suburbia.

I left home for college as soon as I could, barely seventeen, beset by guilt at abandoning my brothers unprotected but knowing I had to get away. I cried that first night, not homesick but heartsick, afraid that my father might kill one of them without me there to run interference. I cried, but I didn't go back. Later, I learned that the abuse continued after I left.

Paul survived, though he's thrice divorced and estranged from most of the family. Eric wasn't so lucky; he took his own life at twenty-two, sitting in the garage with the car running, holding the guitar he loved. I became an attorney, a psychologist, and a child advocate, and I have a particular dislike for child abusers.

KAREN HUGHES'S VOICE intruded on my consciousness: "Will you do it?"

And I heard my own voice say, "Okay, as long as you know what you're getting into." I regretted it as soon as the words were out of my mouth.

CHAPTER 5

Acourier from the public defender's office arrived at my office at the hospital early Monday morning, delivering a bulging accordion file full of documents on the Dunn case. I grabbed a doughnut from the secretary's office, dumped the contents of the file out on top of my desk, and began to sort through them.

Who was this Dorothy Dunn, and what had she done to little Raymie? Karen needed to know whether the woman was mentally ill and, if so, whether she was competent to stand trial; could she assist counsel in preparing a defense? And if she *was* competent to stand trial, one crucial question remained: had she been legally insane—that is, unable to know what she was doing or that it was wrong—at the time of the child's death? Whether she had killed the child was a matter for the jury to decide. But her state of mind at the time was crucial, and that was a psychological question, calling for mental health expertise.

I began by scanning police photos of the Dunn house: filthy, broken-down furniture piled up in front of the windows, heaps of dirty clothes in a corner of the living room floor, the kitchen sink and counter overflowing with dirty dishes and pots, the refrigerator nearly as empty as a yawning, toothless mouth, cupboards bare except for a bottle of ketchup and a sticky jar of jelly. A child's small body on the pantry floor next to an empty bag of sugar. And then there was a picture I didn't initially see the relevance of: a small wooden cutting board with a handle, like a pizza shovel.

Next, I listened to the recording of the 911 call Mrs. Dunn had made from the phone booth at the Public Market:

Hello, 911 operator. What is your emergency?

My baby . . . my little grandbaby, he fell.

The voice was low and slow, like a person walking through thigh-high mud.

What is your emergency, ma'am?

It's . . . my baby's not moving so good . . .

There was a pause.

Is he conscious?

I don't know . . . I think he might of fell and hurt himself. . . . Maybe you all ought to come.

Is he breathing? the operator asked.

He was in the kitchen, in the pantry room, and he fell, the woman said, as if to herself, her voice halting and uneven.

Is he alert and able to talk?

There was a pause, shuffling sounds, and indistinct voices.

Ma'am, I asked if he was able to talk.

When I was talking to him, he was, the woman mumbled.

Where is the child now?

The woman gave an address in a run-down section of town, and the line went dead.

I TURNED NEXT to the first of the police reports filed by officers who'd responded to the call. They detailed how, as paramedics went to the child's lifeless body on the floor, Mrs. Dunn began to rinse food-crusted dishes, stopped in mid-task, and then wandered into the living room, where she began moving the furniture about without clear purpose.

When the coroner's assistant went into the house, along with several police officers and two homicide investigators, Mrs. Dunn seemed not to notice them, according to one officer, wandering from sink to living room to stairs and back. Then, according to the report, she'd filled a kettle with water and put it on to boil. She was, he said, very quiet and showed no emotion.

The investigator questioning Mrs. Dunn asked if she'd ever hit the child. Mrs. Dunn answered that she sometimes did, like when he snuck into the kitchen at night while she was sleeping, to eat Crisco. "I don't know why he needed to eat all the time because I fed him good . . . I let him eat right off my plate with me . . . I told him, 'Raymie you should be full by now.' I caught him cooking on my stove and I told him not to do that. He got burned. No matter what I beat Raymie with he kept doing these things. He was different from my other kids. If I told them that I would beat their butts for doing something wrong, and they still did it, it only took one beating for them not to do it again. Raymie, I had to beat over and over again. I never seen nobody's child like that."

She continued, "I had to whup him sometimes, because he were always trying to eat. Lots of times, really. He were eating too much. Day and night. He weren't supposed to be eating like that," she said. "His belly blowed all up. It weren't natural. My other kids never done like that. . . . My daddy used to whup me with a belt or a coat hanger, but I don't do like that. Raymie's too little for being hit with a belt. I just like tapped him a little with the board when he wouldn't mind. Just like I do my other children. But he hardheaded. He don't want to learn. I only hit him on his butt, or on his legs. I don't want to hurt him." Now I understood why the picture of the cutting board had been taken; she had used it to paddle the boy.

The police had regarded her statement as a confession, and only then was she given the Miranda warnings informing her of her right to refrain from answering questions and her right to have the assistance of an attorney. "I want the lawyer," she had said, but they continued to question her.

I FLIPPED THROUGH the materials Karen Hughes had sent over and found a second witness statement that the police had taken, this one from Dunn's ten-year-old daughter, Alice. The girl reported that she'd been upstairs sleeping and had heard a loud thump downstairs. So she'd crept down the stairs, she said, and found her mother, Dorothy, asleep on the couch and Raymie lying dazed on his back on the pantry floor, covered in a shower of sugar. A kitchen chair had been pulled up alongside the counter, and a burst bag of sugar lay on the floor beside him. The door to the high cupboard where her mother kept the sugar was hanging open. On the stove, a pan with a smattering of dry cornmeal, pepper, and sugar was beginning to smoke.

She said she woke her mother, Mrs. Dunn, who came in, grabbed the pan off the stove and turned off the burner, then scolded Raymie for going into the kitchen and turning on the stove. Finally, Mrs. Dunn made him a butter and sugar sandwich and sat down with him at the table while he ate it. Then she paddled him with the board and told him to go lie down on the couch. Alice said Raymie had staggered a bit and fallen and her mother had taken him to the couch and lain down beside him. Then Alice had gone back up to bed, where her older sister Tonette and her little brother, Scoot, were still sleeping. In the morning, Raymie was cold and there was "stuff coming out of his nose." Her mother put him on the heat vent to warm him up, and when he got too warm, she took him off.

I KNEW THE medical examiner's autopsy report would be crucial to understanding what had happened to the boy, so I rifled through the materials until I found it. The case had been assigned to Dr. Ernest Welch, a new deputy medical examiner who had recently graduated from a medical school in the Caribbean and had not yet completed his training. The boss got the powdered, rose-scented old ladies who died peacefully in their sleep and the tanned CEOs who dropped dead from coronaries on private tennis courts. But this guy, inexperienced and new to the team, got the bloated bodies fished out of the Erie Canal, the charred fire victims, and the toothless winos found by passersby in dumpsters once the smell of decomposition became unmistakable. And he got the mortal remains of Raymie, the dead child from an invisible part of town, a neighborhood nobody gives a damn about.

I pulled out the glossy eight-by-ten color photos the medical examiner had taken of the dead child, Raymie, lying on the pantry floor in his grandmother's house. He was on his back, arms and legs akimbo, in a toddler's thin blue onesie. Beside him was an empty bag of sugar and a rickety wooden kitchen chair pulled up alongside the cupboard and countertop. His eyes were milky white, like pearly opaque marbles. Something that looked like granulated sugar was scattered on the floor around him.

The other pictures were of the boy's naked body on the stainless steel table in the morgue, his skin ashy brown, as if lightly dusted with powder. There was a large swelling on his forehead. His arms and legs were stick-thin, but his belly was round and distended. He had bruises on his buttocks and thighs, some scabs on his knees and shins, and several old cigarette burns on his forearms. A scabby sore encircled one ankle, open and weeping in places.

The scabs on his knees and shins I could understand; he was an active three-year-old and probably ran into things all the time. The bruised butt and thighs had to be from spanking, probably with a wooden paddle, the way teachers used to paddle us in junior high school for talking or chewing gum. And the cigarette burns, while disturbing, weren't so unusual on kids in the city in my experience; many parents touched their kids with a lit cigarette to show them not to play with a hot stove. But I couldn't figure out the mark around his ankle. And then there was the head wound. How could his grandmother explain that? Had he climbed up on the kitchen counter and lost his balance, hitting his head on the counter, the chair, or the floor as he fell, as suggested in Alice's account? Or had Mrs. Dunn bashed him in the head with her wooden paddle?

Finally, I turned to the report: "The body is that of a three-and-a-half-year-old, well-formed African-American male," the report began.

It is emaciated, with little or no subcutaneous fat. The abdomen is distended. Hair is sparse and patchy, consistent with chronic malnutrition. There is a trace quantity of caked, dried vomitus around the nostrils and mouth.

A large hematoma is observable on the right forehead. A small laceration associated with it appears to have been cleaned. The degree of discoloration and swelling suggests that this injury occurred a few hours before death.

The skin shows evidence of multiple lesions of various types. There are several round, healed lesions, consistent with old, healed cigarette burns. There is new bruising on the buttocks and upper right thigh. There are numerous small bruises of indeterminate shape, faded and recent, on the shins and left knee. There is a lesion around the right ankle that appears to be a ligature mark, such as from a rope or cord tied around the ankle.

Next, Dr. Welch had made a broad Y incision, from each of the child's small nipples to the base of the breastbone and then straight down to the belly button, exposing the child's abdominal viscera. The internal organs appeared normal, according to the report, intact and undamaged—no tears, bleeding, or bruising. So the child had not been beaten about the torso or kicked or thrown.

Dr. Welch had cut open the stomach:

> In the stomach are several grams of what appears to be dry cornmeal, a quantity of black pepper, and several tablespoons of granulated sugar, all undigested.

Then he'd cut Raymie's skull open with a bone saw, popping it off as if taking the top off a jack-o'-lantern:

> The brain shows evidence of a small, fresh hematoma in the mid-occipital region, in the back of the skull, and a much larger hematoma in the front of the skull, from above the eye socket to mid-hairline level. There is significant accumulation of blood. The pressure on the brain tissue has caused it to liquefy. This appears to be the immediate cause of death: brain swelling and damage associated with blunt force trauma to the head, occurring several hours before death.

The last step was to order X-rays of Raymie's ribs, arms, and leg bones to look for evidence of old or new fractures that would point to a history of abuse. But these all came back negative: no old or new fractures.

The report concluded:

> Cause of Death: Brain damage from blunt force trauma to the head. Severe Child Abuse. Malnutrition. Homicide.

So he was assuming that the woman had repeatedly, intentionally beaten and burned the child and deprived him of food.

And then I saw an odd note, added to the end of the report: the medical examiner estimated that Raymie had been dead for three days before his body was found by the paramedics.

So far, I knew the following: Dorothy Dunn was oddly detached and emotionally flat, she was marginally coherent, the police had not informed her of her Miranda rights before questioning her, and when she'd finally asked for an attorney, they'd continued, illegally, to question her. Alice, who was only ten, swore her mother had been asleep when she'd heard a thud and found Raymie lying on the pantry floor, covered in sugar from that burst bag. Mrs. Dunn claimed, erroneously, that it had been her daughter Tonette who woke her. I saw that most of the bruises on the child were superficial and in places typical for an active three-year-old and that none of the cigarette burns were recent.

The medical examiner's report raised more questions for me than it answered. The child had obvious injuries and was significantly underweight. But if he had been abused, why were there no retinal hemorrhages, typical in abused children who are shaken? And why were there no old or new fractures, either, or broken teeth, so often found in cases of chronic abuse?

And why had the assistant examiner concluded that there was "Severe Child Abuse"? That smacked more of an emotional reaction than a scientific or medical finding. The cause should have been "blunt force trauma to the head," and the manner of death should have been "undetermined," given that there were no witnesses and that there were conflicting statements about what might have happened to Raymie. How could the medical examiner conclude that the main injuries were intentional and inflicted, rather than accidental? He seemed to have already decided that Dorothy Dunn was guilty of murder.

But if Dorothy Dunn had killed the child, I wondered, why had she called 911 instead of just hiding the body? No one would have missed him; hardly anyone would have known he was gone.

Most curious of all, what had she been doing with the child's body for those three days after his death?

CHAPTER 6

A PROSECUTOR WIELDS awesome power: the power to seek a prosecution or let something go. Legal scholar and commentator Jeffrey Toobin has observed, "Prosecutors decide whether to bring a case or drop charges against a defendant; charge a misdemeanor or a felony; demand a prison sentence or accept probation. Most cases are resolved through plea bargains, where prosecutors, not judges, negotiate whether and for how long a defendant goes to prison. And prosecutors make these judgments almost entirely outside public scrutiny."

This power is largely unchecked, but for the formality of obtaining a grand jury indictment, for which the prosecution needs to present only enough evidence to establish probable cause: that it is more probable than not that the crime was committed and that it was committed by the defendant. Any prosecutor worth his or her salt can get an indictment against a defendant with a minimum of fuss and bother. Author Tom Wolfe quotes Sol Wachtler, the New York State chief judge, as saying that a grand jury "would 'indict a ham sandwich,' if that's what you wanted."

A prosecutor represents the state and the people, and a good prosecutor charges a defendant only with the crime indicated by a fair view of the evidence, and no more. Legal ethics hold that the prosecutor must be a "minister of justice." This is not a calculation of win/loss statistics but a loftier goal. As early as 1935, the Supreme Court observed, "The U.S. attorney is the representative . . . of a sovereignty whose obligation to govern impartially is as compelling as its obligation to govern at all, and whose interest . . . is not that it shall win the case, but that justice shall be done."

But the vast majority of prosecutors are white, male, and from middle-class backgrounds, giving them a limited lens through which to see the world. They tend to be conservative, supporters of traditional law and order. They often respect authority and regard the police as their natural allies and clients. They frequently see themselves as a bulwark against the forces of evil; they can fall into the assumption, like King Louis XIV, that *"l'état c'est moi"*: I am the state. It is a heady drug. Many have a strong punitive streak; whatever the reality, they *believe* that stern punishment deters crime.

Prosecutors win office through popular election and are thus also subject to the vicissitudes of public opinion, which is, in turn, heavily influenced by media coverage. Most prosecutors believe that their electability and job security are determined by whether the public sees them as "tough on crime."

Prosecutors generally have no special knowledge of mental health issues and little faith in mental health testimony; they often shop around for an expert who will support their side of the case. (They're under no obligation to notify the court of conflicting opinions; neither is the defense attorney.) Respected prosecutor and author Gerald Nora, noting that prosecutors generally attempt to undermine proof of mental illness, has urged reform and a rapprochement between law and psychiatry. According to Nora, prosecutors "have a biased view of mental health issues and know virtually nothing about psychiatric issues." He laments "the criminal justice system's current regime of willful ignorance" and believes that "if we persist in prosecuting mentally ill defendants in willful ignorance of their medical problems, our system will stand as an asylum whose keepers are as deluded as the inmates."

But prosecutors' power also gives them some flexibility. In my community, an old woman confined to a nursing home due to advanced dementia believed that a ninety-four-year-old lady down the hall was having an affair with her husband (who had died years before). She dragged the poor old lady from bed in the middle of the night, breaking her leg and ultimately causing her death. This technically constitutes reckless homicide, or even murder in the second degree. But investigators found that our eighty-five-year-old demented perpetrator "was not an individual with a history of any kind of violent behavior" and concluded that she "does not have the level of capability to form criminal intent." The prosecutor decided not to bring criminal charges.

This seems a just result. The woman "knew" what she had done on one level: that is, she knew she had intentionally attacked the woman and dragged her from her bed. And she could have told you, in the abstract, that attacking people is wrong. But her dementia had robbed her of her moral reasoning, and even of her grasp of reality.

She was lucky: public opinion doesn't clamor for the prosecution of old white women, who are regarded with more sympathy and less fear than are young black men. That gave the prosecutor some room to maneuver, out of the public eye.

THE PROSECUTOR IN CHARGE of Dorothy Dunn's case was Denny Gallo. I knew of Gallo a little. He wasn't an especially physically imposing man, not a big man, but there was an intensity to him. He had deep-set eyes, so dark you couldn't discern the pupils. He was known in the legal community as a good prosecutor—not creative or flashy but solid. That is to say, he won more cases than he lost.

I don't know why Gallo discounted Alice's account of what happened the night of Raymie's death. Perhaps he'd had the same reaction I initially had: that Dunn was monstrous and evil and had to pay for what she'd done. Perhaps he was influenced by the medical examiner's conclusion that the cause of death was child abuse, rather than accident. Perhaps Gallo reasoned that even if the head injury had been caused by an accidental fall, Mrs. Dunn must have intentionally withheld the medical care that might have saved the boy because of some malice or callousness, not just ignorance and inadequacy.

Maybe he thought the head injury was just the last of many blows, Raymie's overall poor physical condition convincing him that Dorothy Dunn was an abuser and a monster who deserved punishment, whether she'd caused the terminal injury or not.

As Gallo read the police reports and the medical examiner's report, he undoubtedly saw the descriptions of the filth and squalor in Dorothy's house. He would have read the officer's observation that she seemed uninterested in the dead child on her kitchen floor, with no signs of grief or remorse. He would have seen her admission that she sometimes beat the child and noted possible evidence of "guilty knowledge"—knowledge that she'd done wrong—when she asked if she was going to prison.

He would have reviewed the medical examiner's report, detailing the child's multiple bruises and old cigarette-burn scars, his wasted, grossly underweight body, the weeping sore encircling one ankle, and the blow to the head, which had not been immediately fatal. With proper medical care, the boy might have survived.

And he may have calculated—I would have, in his place—that the case against Dorothy Dunn wouldn't be hard to win: he had a sympathetic victim in little Raymie and an unsympathetic defendant in the pouty, dead-eyed Dorothy Dunn. Jurors' natural impulse to punish someone when a child dies would work in his favor.

In any event, Gallo concluded that the initial charge of child endan-

germent against Dorothy Dunn was insufficient. He decided to seek a
grand jury indictment against her for the felony of murder in the second degree: intentionally causing a death "under circumstances evincing
depraved indifference to human life."

A grand jury is a strange animal. The twenty-three grand jurors,
ordinary citizens pulled from voter registration lists, are assembled for
terms of thirty days to approve indictments sought by the prosecutor.
They hear only the prosecution's case. There are no defense attorneys
present, no cross-examinations, no rebuttal witnesses. The grand jury is
to assume that all the state's offered evidence is true.

Many of the grand jurors convened to hear the prosecution's case
against Dorothy Dunn had already seen the television news coverage and
read the news headline in the *Democrat and Chronicle*, Rochester's local
paper:

GRANDMOTHER HELD FOR MURDER IN DEATH
OF YOUNG GRANDSON, FOUND BEATEN AND
STARVED

Under the caption were side-by-side pictures of a smiling Raymie in hap-
pier times and Dorothy's glowering mug shot.

I had presided over a special grand jury myself during my time as a
prosecutor, and I could picture the scene: the grand jurors would have
shuffled in, strangers to one another, a little self-conscious and ill at ease,
wanting to do the right thing but not sure what it was. Trials are like
Kabuki theater, with its highly stylized, ritualized movements and elab-
orate costumes, and you could think of the grand jury presentment as
Act One.

Gallo would have cut an imposing figure. He would have instructed
the jurors on their obligation to hear the evidence and vote on whether
there was probable cause to believe that Dorothy Dunn had caused the

death of her little grandson, Raymie, and then he might have told them where to find the restrooms and drinking fountain and where they could buy lunch when the hour came.

By the end of the day, Gallo had the indictment he wanted for murder in the second degree, a class A felony that carries a potential life sentence.

The stakes for Dorothy Dunn had just gone up.

CHAPTER 7

THE PROSECUTOR HAD TAKEN the position that Mrs. Dunn was a child abuser who battered and starved her grandson and finally struck him a fatal blow to the head or, at the very least, ignored his injury while he lay dying. Karen's only possible lines of defense were that the old injuries were put there by someone else, before Dorothy took over the boy's care; that she was too ignorant or mentally ill to realize he was severely malnourished; and that the head injury was the result of a fall, and she was either too ignorant to understand that he had a head injury or was too mentally ill to know what she was doing if she'd struck that fatal blow. Who in their right mind would sleep with a corpse for two days, after all, then call 911 and think that the child could be revived?

My job wasn't to convict the woman or to absolve her. It was, simply, to determine, if I could, from the psychological evidence, whether the woman had the intelligence and the relatively normal, intact psychological status to have known what she was doing, and that it was wrong, on the eve of Raymie's death. Was she capable of "reckless disregard," the mental state required for a conviction for murder in the second degree? Win or lose, innocent or guilty—that was for the law, not me, to decide.

FORENSIC PSYCHOLOGY, according the American Board of Forensic Psychology (ABFP), is "the application of the science and profession of psychology to questions and issues relating to law and the legal system." In taking on the Dunn case, I was assuming the role of forensic psychologist.

Clinical psychology—the use of psychological means and knowledge to identify and alleviate mental and emotional distress—is a delicate amalgam of art and science, intuition and learning. But forensic psychology—the application of psychological knowledge to the answering of psycho-legal questions—is quite another matter. It rests primarily on science; there is little room for art.

Forensic psychological assessment depends on logic, objectivity, and analytical thinking. It requires methodical and dispassionate investigation of an individual's temperament, personality, and circumstances, with such particularity that it can determine with some confidence which behaviors, past or future, are "in character" for that person and which are "out of character." What did they know, and when did they know it? What did they foresee and intend?

How is this possible? As former FBI director James Comey has noted, "Knowing and proving what is in someone's head is always a hard task." But this task is assisted by some basic principles. First, a person's behaviors are not random. Under normal circumstances, absent psychological illness, brain disease, or severe trauma, people are coherent, goal-directed, and relatively stable. They are determined by the confluence of intellect and temperament, personality and circumstance, things that can be measured using psychological tools and techniques.

Second, contemporary psychology has mapped the normal course of human development, from infancy to maturity. It has identified the basic personality structures. And it has discovered the core principles of human learning and behavior. To this are added psychiatry's contributions to the genetics, neurology, and biochemistry of brain and behavior.

Temperament is innate, determined genetically in the womb. But personality structure is acquired. It is the scaffolding on which we hang our behavior, emotions, and perceptions, our way of perceiving, interpreting, and reacting to the world around us. It helps set the parameters of our behaviors, just as our bony skeleton sets the parameters of our size, shape, and way of moving.

Psychological evaluation allows us to measure intellect and to map personality. A person's current emotional state is revealed: Are they happy? Sad? Afraid? Angry? Bitter? Hopeful? Armed with this three-dimensional picture, we can do a kind of psychological triangulation, a sort of orienteering of the mind, and make informed predictions about what a person is likely to have done in the past or is likely to do in the future.

The more psychological data available, obtained from multiple independent sources and going back over time, the more likely that the probability statements will be accurate. We can never make projections with absolute certainty, but we can make pretty sound probabilistic statements.

This is the premise behind criminal profiling. FBI profilers look at the characteristics of the crime and determine what character traits, personality, and intelligence are compatible with them. Say, for example, that you have a shy, cautious, anxious person, of normal intelligence but not very persistent. That person is not likely to spend months planning a complicated Brinks heist involving directly confronting people with guns and shooting at them. You'd look instead, if you were the detective on the case, for a highly intelligent person, patient and persistent, not needing immediate gratification, with a high tolerance for risk and not much regard for others or being bound by the rules of "ordinary" people.

This was what I was going to do with Dorothy Dunn: determine if she was currently competent to stand trial, within the strict legal definition, and gauge the goodness of fit between the behavior alleged—abusing and starving a child and withholding medical care while he died of a brain injury—and the defendant. Was it "in character" for her to intentionally inflict harm and suffering on the boy? And if not, what had happened? For there is one more piece of the puzzle that must be considered: a person can be thrown off their usual track by severe trauma, by brain injury, or by mental illness. That, too, was a question I had to answer in the case of Dorothy Dunn. Had some significant mental illness made her be "not herself"?

But ultimately, there were, for the law, only two questions: Had she struck the fatal blow? And if so, had she been legally insane on the night Raymie died? That is, had she known what she was doing and that it was wrong?

Most psychologists and psychiatrists eschew taking on cases embroiled in court. Some feel unqualified, not knowing the law or not excelling in analytic reasoning, and many just don't want the aggravation, stress, and risk involved. Going deep into the nub of a person's innermost thoughts and motivations is not merely a dispassionate intellectual exercise; you must be willing to get down in the mud and wallow. And when you're that psychologically intimate with a person and are playing a role in whether they'll be free or incarcerated, or have or lose custody of their children, feelings can run high.

I've had parents upend the furniture in my office in a rage, threaten to kill me as we've stood outside the courtroom awaiting trial, and even follow me home in the shadows at night. One aggrieved father picked up a heavy wooden captain's chair from the defense table and hurled it at the judge's head during a custody hearing, narrowly missing me and breaking the bailiff's arm. Another father left court on the day I testified, went to his ex-wife's home, and stabbed her fifty-seven times before the ink on the court order granting her custody of their children was dry. If I'm ever shot and killed at work, it won't be by a patient; it'll be by an enraged parent after I've testified in a child abuse or custody case. Recently, well-known forensic psychiatrist Steven Pitt was shot dead by a disgruntled parent after a custody trial. A friend of mine who does custody evaluations always carries a loaded pistol in his briefcase, but all I carry is a small Swiss Army knife and an attitude.

Despite the risk and the stress, I'm strangely drawn to the intellectual challenge of finding out what makes a person "tick," perhaps the same way a rock climber is drawn to attempt an ascent that's never been conquered before; it's like solving an intricate, three-dimensional puzzle. And perhaps we all try in one way or another to gain some mastery over the traumas in our lives, and this was my way. Perhaps I think that if I get to know the monster in the closet, the monster in my own will seem less scary.

In exchange for our testimony in court, we mental health experts are often treated with hostility and even contempt by attorneys hoping to use our testimony merely to further their clients' ends. Writer Rachel Aviv notes, "It is not uncommon for law-enforcement officials, even judges, to suspend common sense in the presence of a scientific expert, whose superior training lends his personal opinions the weight of truth." But this does not square with my experience; more common is the misbelief that psychiatry is really no more than common sense and is, therefore, the purview of any reasonably intelligent and educated person.

Journalists, lawyers, professors, and pundits of all types expound about psychological issues as self-proclaimed experts. Take, for example, the case of Anders Breivik, who set off a bomb that killed eight people in Oslo in 2011 and then went to Utoya Island and shot sixty-nine more. This national tragedy for Norway engendered much soul-searching, prompting novelist Karl Ove Knausgaard, citing work by war correspondent Asne Seierstad, to grapple with the question of what led Breivik to commit the murders. He offers opinions, as Seierstad does in her book *One of Us*, about Breivik's supposed state of mind, character, and motivations, asserting, "He is a person filled to the brim with himself. And that is perhaps the most painful thing of all, the realization that this whole gruesome massacre, all those extinguished lives, was the result of a frustrated young man's need for self-representation." Knausgaard goes on to postulate about the psychological factors that drove this crime: "We know that he grew up with . . . a mother who, without being aware of it, neglected him in ways that destroyed him so completely that, really, he had no chance."

Yet Knausgaard has no mental health training or experience and never met, let alone evaluated, Mr. Breivik. Nor was he privy to the voluminous material about the murderer's earlier life and mental health treatment. Nor is Asne Seierstad a person with mental health training. They are such good and intelligent writers that their words convey authority and a sense of truth, but what they offer is really only speculation and philosophical musing.

On the witness stand, mental health experts are often restricted to yes or no answers to highly complex questions that cannot be reduced to black or white without resulting in massive distortion. They watch helplessly as their testimony is intentionally misrepresented by prosecutors or defense attorneys or both. When I testify, I spend half my energy just trying to prevent the misuse and distortion of the psychological evidence. And cross-examination brings on a dry mouth and racing heart as I struggle to defend the conclusions that most fully and reliably represent the psychological data. Rarely are the most important questions asked, and there is little chance to share the most crucial psychological factors in a case.

In the adversarial arena of a trial, one attorney is likely to perceive mental health testimony as just a convenient tool to be used to further her objective, while the other sees it as no more than an inconvenient obstacle to be overcome. Forensic psychology (again, according to the ABFP) is supposed to be "the application of scientific principles and practices to the adversary process where scientists with specialized knowledge play a role." But in my experience, this is too rosy a picture. All too often, forensic psychology is subverted by the application of the adversarial process to obscure and obfuscate crucial psychological factors. Whether this is intentional or not on the part of the attorneys, I cannot say. Perhaps they are genuinely skeptical about the reliability of mental health evidence, or, perhaps, they just want to win.

The forensic cases make me feel the greatest sense of physical and moral jeopardy, as the questions asked—about competency, sanity, motivation, dangerousness, intent—hold the keys to legal guilt or innocence, freedom or punishment. Guilt and criminal responsibility ultimately rest upon a defendant's intention and state of mind, and this is the province of forensic psychiatry. As one forensic psychiatrist observed, "The psychiatrist is the only expert witness who is asked to form opinions as to man's responsibility and man's punishability." I agree with psychiatrist Alan Stone, who said, "to choose a career in forensic psychiatry is to choose to increase the risks in a life of moral adventure."

CHAPTER 8

To be guilty of a crime, committing a bad act is generally not enough; one must have also had an evil intent. If there is no guilty intent—*mens rea*, in legal parlance—a defendant is not guilty. As the Roman statesman Cicero said, "Crimes are not to be measured by the issue of events but from the bad intentions of men." That's why forensic psychologists and psychiatrists find ourselves playing a role in criminal trials; we are called upon to offer evidence and opinions about a defendant's state of mind when the criminal act was committed, what he or she knew and understood in that moment. Karen Hughes would try to convince the jury that there was reasonable doubt that Dorothy Dunn had caused her grandson's fatal head injury. Failing that, she would rely on my evaluation to tell her, and the jury, whether her client had a "guilty mind."

This idea that a person isn't legally responsible if they don't have an evil intent goes back at least as far as the ancient Babylonians. According to the Code of Hammurabi, "A man who killed another in a quarrel must swear he did not do so intentionally, and was then only fined according to the rank of the deceased," instead of being sentenced to death. If an assault was unintentional, the penalty was just to pay the doctor's fees. Reparations were called for, but not retribution. The insanity defense has its roots here: if a person is too mentally ill or intellectually limited to know and understand what they are doing, to be responsible for their actions, they shouldn't be held liable.

In the fourth century B.C.E., the Greek philosopher Aristotle reasoned that "that which is done in ignorance, or though not in ignorance is not in the actor's power, or is done under compulsion, is involuntary," and blame attaches only to voluntary acts. This has come down to us as the legal maxim that a person is morally and legally responsible for an act only if, "with knowledge of the circumstances and the absence of external compulsion, he deliberately chooses to commit a forbidden act." Punishment is thought appropriate only if a person had a *mens rea*—a "guilty mind."

Rome's Justinian Code, in the sixth century, held that children and the insane were *non compos mentis* (of unsound or uncontrolled mind) and that "such persons were regarded as having no will of their own . . . because they lack entirely the understanding (*intellectus*) and judgment (*judicium*), or the capacity to comprehend the effect of their actions." The insane and children, because they did not have *mens rea*—a guilty mind—were exempted from punishment: "the one is excused by the innocence of his intentions, the other by the fact of his misfortune: *furiosus solo furore punitur*"—a madman is punished by his madness alone.

This idea of *mens rea*—guilt being dependent upon whether or not the accused had an intent to do wrong, a guilty state of mind—is a foundational part of Western law and ethics. William Blackstone, the foremost English jurist of the eighteenth century, tells us, "To make a complete crime . . . there must be both a will and an act" and "All of the several pleas and excuses which protect the committer of a forbidden act from punishment . . . may be reduced to this single consideration, the want [absence] or defect of *will*." This was echoed by Lord Henry de Bracton: "We must consider with what mind or with what intent a thing is done. . . . A crime is not committed unless the intent to injure intervene."

To illustrate: if I intentionally push a brick off a second-story windowsill onto a passerby below, meaning to kill the poor fellow, and succeed, I am guilty of murder. But if I accidentally dislodge that same brick, not intending to hurt anyone, though it strikes and kills that same passerby, I am not guilty of murder, because I had no intent to injure. The act and its consequences for the poor pedestrian are the same, but the intent, my state of mind, are different, and that makes all the difference in criminal law.

However, the issue of guilt became increasingly complicated after Saint Augustine. Augustine believed that men are rational beings with free will, free to choose either good or evil and thus morally and legally responsible for their choices. This leads to a kind of religious morality test: a man is guilty if, having free will and reason, he *chooses* to do something wrong. Now we are in murkier territory; the court is asked to distinguish between good and evil *people*, rather than to assess their motivation or intent, in the Augustinian weltanschauung.

If the act was evil, then they *chose* evil and are, de facto, evil and deserving of punishment. With this moral tilt, the emphasis of the law began to shift. The judgment of the court became an affirmation of society's condemnation of sinners, doers of evil. But today we know that things aren't quite so simple. "Free will" is a kind of chimera. What we do is determined by many factors, including those over which we have no direct control. Our genetics, our brain chemistry, our intellectual endowment, our learning and life experiences—all of these affect how we respond to choices. We do make choices, but they are hardly as free as philosophers during the Age of Enlightenment (sometimes called the Age of Reason) conceived. Some neuroscientists even go so far as to say that there is no "will" at all; all of our choices are predetermined, set by our biology.

We are not born with an innate moral sense, altruism, and empathy, only with the capacity to develop these qualities if taught and supported by our environment. William Golding, in his novel *Lord of the Flies*, explores this chillingly; the power of his story about what boys do when left to their own devices comes from our recognition of the truth of it. Cormac McCarthy's *The Road* shows us how thin and fragile the veneer of "civilized" behavior can be.

I had a thirteen-year-old client once who was the new kid at a tough city school. She was alone, and was singled out for bullying and harassment by the class's alpha female—call her Shaniqua—and her clique of five or six other girls. My client—call her Monique—was scared. She was being threatened. Her mother, who'd grown up in an urban jungle of guns and gangs with the idea of every man for himself, advised her to take a knife to school for protection. Monique followed her mother's advice.

The next morning, as she got off the bus at school, she was surrounded by the hostile pack of girls, taunting and threatening her. Shaniqua stepped forward and shoved Monique, hard, and Monique pulled the knife out of her backpack and stabbed blindly at the girl, meaning to ward her off and convey the message that she wasn't helpless and could fight back. Unfortunately, she struck the girl in the neck, puncturing her carotid artery and causing her to bleed to death before the teachers even knew there was an altercation.

New York State had recently passed laws allowing children as young as thirteen to be tried as adults for serious offenses, like murder. Monique, who didn't know a carotid artery from a rutabaga, was charged with murder and convicted. The result of her act—stabbing—was evil: Shaniqua's death. But what had her intent been? Only nonlethal self-defense and a warning. She'd had no murderous intent.

So how does what we know about mental illness, behavior, and the brain fit contemporary legal concepts and definitions of guilt? How guilty is an intellectually limited person, or one who is mentally ill, or one suffering from a significant dementia, like Alzheimer's disease? How about someone who falls into all three categories? Should he or she be held to the same standard, suffer the same punishment, as one who is well? Law and order demand that we convict the guilty, while justice demands that we acquit the innocent. But it is often hard to tell where justice lies when mental health and legal issues collide.

CHAPTER 9

THE MAIN QUESTIONS in the case were whether Dorothy Dunn had abused and fatally injured Raymie, whether she was currently competent to stand trial, and whether she had been sane and responsible on the night of Raymie's death. *My* job was to provide an answer to the two crucial questions about the defendant's mental state: First, was she *currently* coherent and sane enough to help her attorney prepare her defense? That is, was she competent to stand trial? Second, what had been her state of mind on the day the boy suffered the fatal blow? At the time of the crime (if indeed a crime had been committed), had she acted intentionally and knowingly, or had she been in the grips of a mental disorder that prevented her from understanding what she was doing or that it was wrong? In other words, had she been legally insane at the time and, therefore, not guilty?

A person can have been insane at the time of the crime but be competent by the time of trial, just as they can be sane enough to be guilty but too incompetent thereafter to be tried. These are entirely separate questions. If Mrs. Dunn was not competent, she couldn't be tried unless and until she became competent. If I concluded that she wasn't, an evaluation by a second expert would be arranged, and if we both agreed, most likely the judge would accept our conclusion and refuse to move the case to trial. The prosecutor could drop the charges or keep the defendant in a locked psychiatric facility until she became competent, for up to two-thirds of the maximum term of imprisonment for the offense with which she was charged. In other words, he could lock Mrs. Dunn away for as long as eighteen years without trial, conviction, or finding of guilt.

To gain insight into her state of mind, I didn't need to examine the particulars of the case so much as the nature of her intentions and understanding. So I wouldn't interrogate her, in the sense that a detective does, but would, rather, interview her, forge a relationship with her, look at her from all sides, like a glass held up to the light, to examine the shadows and imperfections within.

So, was Dorothy Dunn competent? What was the current state of her mind? Though this sounds like a straightforward matter, it is anything but. People have a misconception about law. It's not about abstract ideals, like truth and justice or right and wrong. It's about words, formulaic definitions, handed down through the ages and susceptible to the whims of fad and fate, judicial wisdom and caprice, especially where the words of the law are ambiguous and uncertain in their interpretation. In law, words very often don't retain their common meanings but are transmogrified into something denatured and rigid. They are stitched together over time, case by case, to make phrases with very particular meanings that take on a life of their own, much like Frankenstein's monster.

To be sure, laws have their *origin* in ideas and intents, but words are only approximations of the ideas they are meant to convey; there is always an inexactness, a degree of error, between the concept—the thing that was meant—and the words. In law, this error is referred to as the tension between the *spirit* and the *letter* of the law, the gap between the intent of a statute and its specific words and phrases. The gap between the two tends to be magnified over time.

This is what being a lawyer or a judge is about. The language of a statute or of a previous judicial decision may not be completely clear or may not clearly cover the situation a judge has before her. So interpretations and inferences must be made, and these gradually, over time, alter the shape of the law and the meaning of its words. This is what conservatives sometimes call "judges legislating from the bench" or "judges making law." But some degree of interpretation is necessary, because each case that comes to court is slightly novel, slightly distinctive, and requires that the judge and the lawyers specifically fit the law to it, by interpreting and shaping the words of the law or of previous court decisions to the uniqueness of the case.

These judicial interpretations—definitions of the words of statutes—become precedent, binding on the judges who follow. As the language is interpreted and applied, parts are lost or added, and the law gets distorted and strays from its original intent and purpose.

The ambient political and social climate, the culture in which the court is embedded, also plays a role. For example, the list of what people considered a "cruel and unusual" punishment in 1787, when our Constitution was drafted, would not be the same in the Middle Ages or today. In 1305, the Scottish patriot William Wallace, taken prisoner by King Edward I, was drawn—dragged behind a horse—then hanged and cut down alive, disemboweled, beheaded, and finally, somewhat anticlimactically, quartered—a punishment harsh even for that day. Most executed prisoners were merely hanged or beheaded, their severed heads displayed on spikes.

In the American West of the 1800s, executions by hanging or firing squad were common, not considered cruel or unusual, though both are generally regarded as such today; we find electrocution or fatal IV injections to be more acceptable. (Interestingly, Utah reintroduced death by firing squad in 2004.) There is no absolute standard for cruel *or* unusual. As Chief Justice Oliver Wendell Holmes once observed, "The life of the law has not been logic; it has been experience."

Added to that complication, if a judge isn't very bright (and I've had the dubious pleasure of knowing some who are neither bright nor sober when they take the bench, particularly after lunch) or has a strong personal bias, it may, and probably will, affect his or her decisions. Among law students, this is referred to as "the breakfast theory of jurisprudence," the notion that a judge's rulings may depend on who he had breakfast with and whether his digestion was satisfactory.

It also happens that a judge may think she is correctly understanding and applying the reasoning of previous judgments but may be missing the essential point in some crucial way. And if the attorneys arguing the case are particularly good or bad, or are mismatched, or if the facts of the case are particularly eccentric or egregious, or if the prevailing social or political climate is creating pressure, this can also color individual judicial rulings and lead to the making of very bad law.

So what is "competency to stand trial"?

The U.S. Supreme Court set the basic standard for competency to stand trial in *Dusky v. United States* in 1960. As a forensic psychologist, I have no power to change a law, only to know it and give an opinion about where a particular defendant may fit into it. So my evaluation must always take the existing legal standard as the starting point. The Supreme Court held that a defendant is competent to stand trial if she has "sufficient present ability to consult with her lawyer with a reasonable degree of rational understanding." The premise, or underlying principle or concept, is that if a person cannot rationally consult with her attorney, it interferes with her prospects for the fair trial guaranteed by the Constitution's Sixth Amendment.

But what does the law hold to be "sufficient" ability and what is "a reasonable" degree of "rational understanding"? Judges in New York, as in most other states, have focused more on whether a defendant "knows" he is being tried and has an attorney to assist him, and less on whether the defendant has "a reasonable degree of rational understanding" of his circumstances. To "know" is just to be aware of the fact in some basic way.

To illustrate: I was once asked to give an opinion on whether a young man in a criminal trespass case was competent to stand trial. Everyone agreed that the young man was psychotic—he had a paranoid delusion that all the people in town were space aliens communicating in code about him via their license plates. He believed that the only safe place for him was jail, so he had broken into a warehouse in order to set off the alarm, so he could be arrested and taken there. After all, you can't just waltz up to a jail and request lodging.

Now, you may think that because he was clearly crazy, having psychotic delusions, he was not competent to stand trial. But he "knew" who and where he was, and he clearly understood that he was being charged with a crime and had an attorney to defend him. He also knew that he had illegally entered the warehouse. However, his psychotic delusion, his mental illness, precluded him from being able to *want* a defense; he wanted to plead guilty, so that he could stay safely in jail, away from the aliens. I offered the opinion that he was not competent to stand trial because he lacked a reasonable, rational understanding of his situation and was unable to rationally assist in his own defense. But two independent opinions are required as to competency, and the second psychologist opined that he *was* competent, since he had a basic *factual* understanding of his legal circumstances.

Nothing is simple when it comes to the intersection of the law and mental health. This is one of the complex dilemmas for mental health experts: are you to merely describe a defendant's functioning, in terms the law recognizes, or are you to give an opinion about how the defendant meets a particular legal standard, the ultimate legal question? The court tells us that we are only to do the former, to work within the legal standard. But the answer to the question is elusive, ethically as well as practically. At least the case above is an example of two experts independently applying their individual skills and judgment. I once did a competency evaluation where the second appointed expert called me, before preparing his report, and suggested that I share my opinion with him, so he could just agree with it. I reported this ethical breach to the governing body for psychologists but never heard any follow-up, and the practitioner involved is still frequently used by the local courts.

When both mental health evaluators believe a defendant is not competent, judges accept their opinion nearly 80 percent of the time. But when the experts are not in accord, defendants are generally ruled competent. So it went with my young man: the judge ruled that he was competent, he pled guilty, and he was sentenced to three years in prison, where, being slight and attractive, he was most likely sexually assaulted by the earthlings confined there and was most certainly not treated for his psychosis.

THE QUESTION I had to answer in Dorothy Dunn's case was whether she had a basic "rational and factual understanding" of the charges against her. If she "knew" she was being charged with causing the boy's death, that Karen was her attorney, and that she was entitled to a defense and a presumption of innocence, then she was competent in the eyes of New York and the Supreme Court.

I didn't know her well enough yet to have an answer to that question, but I would before I was through.

CHAPTER 10

I T WAS TIME FOR ME to meet Dorothy Dunn.

I hate jails, with their caged, restless inmates and the mingled smells of sweat, boredom, and fear. And yet five or six times a year I find myself in one, sitting with someone who has battered his wife or beaten her child or torched a house. They might be legally insane or hopelessly stupid. They might be simply evil and predatory. They might even be innocent. I never know until I meet them. In meeting Mrs. Dunn, what would I find? Was she a sociopath, devoid of remorse or empathy, a malignant and evil being? Had she hurt the child on purpose and enjoyed it? Did she hate the boy? Or was she mentally ill, and, if so, did she meet the legal definitions of incompetency to stand trial or insanity?

I dressed carefully, choosing clothing that wouldn't provoke the male prisoners whose cells I had to pass, eschewing jewelry that would set off the metal detectors. I even remembered, for once, to take the Swiss Army knife off my keychain so it wouldn't get confiscated at security; I was tired of losing my knives.

Dodging the commuter traffic, I crossed over the silted brown waters of the Genesee River and pulled into the jail parking lot, trying to steer clear of the broken-beer-bottle glass scattered about like sequins off a cheap ball gown. I stepped out of the car into a biting wind and hurried up the broad cement steps to the jail's entrance. My cheeks and forehead stung with the cold.

The county jail sits on prime real estate right along the riverfront. It is a monolithic sandstone structure with 1960s architectural charm—which is to say, none at all. Small, barred windows dot its surface like unseeing eyes. As to the charm of its interior, it was described by a city historian as "grey steel cages, 5 by 8 in size and equipped with a bunk, a wash basin and a toilet, arranged in tiers or blocks, each with thirteen cells."

Entering the visitors' lobby, a cinder-block room with metal benches bolted to the floor, I looked around for Karen Hughes, who had arranged to meet me and make the initial introduction. She had suggested that her client might be more receptive to meeting me for the first time if she were present. "Not that I've gained her trust, either," she had added.

The cramped lobby was crowded with women with small children in tow. The children played on the filthy cement floor, amid the benches and cement-block walls, as if this place were as familiar to them as their own living rooms. They chased one another, tripping over purses and diaper bags, brandishing sticky suckers like swords. Babies fretted and wailed, and the women rummaged in bottomless purses to pull out crackers, diapers, bottles, or teething rings. The women spoke to the children gruffly, occasionally swatting a child's diaper-padded bottom or jerking a child up by the arm, setting off a new round of wails, and making me wince.

"Over here," I heard.

I turned and saw Karen, smaller and younger than I'd imagined, with soft brown eyes and short, curly hair that made her look perpetually startled. I knew it was her because she wore a tailored navy suit, particularly lawyerlike, carried a scuffed briefcase, and wore no-nonsense shoes that wouldn't kill her feet after hours of standing on the marble floors at the courthouse.

I threaded my way over to her through the crowd.

Behind a thick bulletproof glass partition running from countertop to ceiling (like the ones in every Taco Bell and Burger King in Detroit in the years I lived there), a deputy appeared and began barking out names through a small metal vent. Some inmates were on punishment for the day and could have no visitors. As their names were called out, their women gathered up their diaper bags, purses, and children, muttering in frustration, and trudged out the door, back into the dreary November drizzle. Most of them were facing a cold walk to the bus stop and a long wait in the freezing rain. The others milled around, jostling one another as if gathering to board steerage on the *Titanic*.

Karen cut to the head of the line, braving the glares of those behind her, and told the sergeant she had an appointment to see Dorothy Dunn. With a jerk of his stubby thumb, he directed us over to a heavy metal door at the far side of the room. As we headed over toward it, I spied a water fountain on the wall. I was looking forward to wetting my lips until I got close to it. Long defunct, it hung from the wall like a urinal, its enamel stained rusty brown.

The door swung open and a khaki-clad deputy appeared. "McLoughlin" his name tag read. He had a smooth, pink face with full cheeks and the beginnings of a sizable gut bulging over his belt.

"Follow me," he said, trotting off through a labyrinth of corridors, keys and handcuffs jangling against his hip with each step.

It was like falling down the rabbit hole into a kind of malevolent Wonderland. We twisted this way and that, deeper into the catacombs of the building, and every hall and door looked the same. I knew I would never be able to find my way out of this maze on my own. Finally we passed a cramped holding area, a wire cell like a giant rat cage, filled with half a dozen men.

It is an odd feeling to walk past people in cages.

The men leered and made suggestive noises. I felt the hair go up on the back of my neck, like when you are being stalked by wolves in the forest. But I knew better than to give any evidence of being intimidated and feigned an air of indifferent disregard.

"Yo, mama," one man called out. "I got something for you. You wanna see my *thing*?"

He punctuated this with a grab at his crotch; this was greeted by a chorus of hoots and laughter from the other men. The deputy gave the bars a menacing thwack with his stick and glared at the men. I had seen zookeepers do the same thing to the big cats at feeding time to move them away from the bars. The men backed away a step.

An elevator took us up into the belly of the building, and after traversing another series of locked doors and echoing corridors, we arrived at the women's unit. It was indistinguishable from the others but for the presence of burly female guards. The men's wards, the women's wards— it didn't matter: they both reminded me of the cattle feedlots I'd seen out in Greeley, Colorado, as a kid, animals crowded together, milling around aimlessly, waiting to be shipped off to the slaughterhouses at the Chicago stockyards.

The sickening smell of prison food rose up through the ventilation system as if from some great gaseous bowel, the smell of years of sauerkraut and Brussels sprouts, of old grease, burnt coffee, and runny eggs on blackened toast. It turned my stomach. It got into my hair and stuck to my clothes; it invaded my nostrils and lodged there. It insinuated itself into my pores and burrowed into some reptilian crevasse in my brain; I felt like I would never be free of that smell again.

Two dozen women inmates, mostly young and black or Hispanic, were gathered in the large common room. In the center of the room were a few flimsy tables and chairs. A blaring television dominated the ward. One of the younger women was braiding a pale Caucasian's thin hair into a pattern of tight plaits. Another woman, with mottled skin and coarse features, was playing solitaire, cackling loudly to herself in a hoarse rasp between drags on a cigarette.

But most of the women were gathered around the television, jeering and hooting along with the talk show audience. The show featured lurid topics of the "my mother stole my boyfriend" variety, inciting the guests to acts of mock violence against each other. The sound track was punctuated by frequent loud beeps censoring out profanities and by the screaming of the guests and the audience. The volume was at full blast and the inmates ate it up, applauding each sudden, violent eruption, laughing and jabbing at each other.

"Look at that bitch," I heard one woman say. "She *ugly!*"

"She look like your mama," another chimed in, cackling.

One woman sat off by herself, mumbling and chewing on the ends of her hair, glancing up nervously from time to time.

The wardens seemed happy for anything that kept the women occupied; it broke the monotony of prison for them, too, I guess. But it brought to mind the research showing that you increase people's antisocial behaviors by showing them those behaviors while they are in a group that applauds them. I wondered if the taxpayers were aware that the jail was socializing inmates to applaud sociopathy and violence. It was like a psychological experiment gone mad: lock the women up for being violent and lacking self-control, then encourage them to applaud the same behaviors on television, then release them back into the community and see how they behave. I wondered if anybody had thought this through.

"Dorothy Dunn," McLoughlin called to the matron over his shoulder as he disappeared down another corridor, his booted footsteps echoing off the walls and receding into the distance.

We had arrived.

"Dorothy Dunn," the matron mumbled, more to herself than to us.

She pursed her lips and furrowed her brow. A big woman, thick and powerful, with skin the color of strong coffee, she could easily have played in the NFL, and I planned to stay on her good side. "She's an odd one," she said, looking down at her census sheet. "She's in segregation, on suicide watch."

The matron inclined her head slightly in the direction of a door I hadn't noticed before, so perfectly did it blend in with the wall, and stepped out of her booth and walked over with a few quick strides. Jabbing the door once, hard, with her stick, she peered through the eye slit and located the person inside, wanting to make sure, I guess, before opening the door, that the woman wasn't poised in ambush.

"Dunn! You got visitors!" she said, as she unlocked the door and swung it open.

The room inside was a five-by-eight cell, harshly lit, empty except for a concrete shelf with a thin, bare mattress and a metal toilet. Mrs. Dunn was sitting on the toilet, hugging her stomach and moaning softly with her prison trousers down around her ankles.

"I got to go," she groaned. "I got to go real bad."

The smell was overpowering; I could taste it in the back of my throat. I was embarrassed for the woman, and for myself, the unwitting witness to her exposure and misery. Of course, my job was to unmask her entirely, to reveal her character and person in all their nakedness. Still, I was sorry for the indignity of her situation. The matron was unmoved.

"Come on, Dorothy, you can't sit there all day," she said.

Mrs. Dunn struggled slowly to her feet, pulling the baggy pants up around her waist. Her short, frizzled hair was Brillo-pad gray and stood out all over like an uncombed fright wig. She smelled of sweat, urine, and unwashed clothing. Her two front teeth were missing, and the others were stained and yellowed.

The matron gestured Karen and me toward the cell with an expectant, impatient look. So much for my resolution not to rile her.

"We can't meet in here," I said. "There must be somewhere else, with a table and some chairs. Somewhere private."

She gave me a "Who do you think you are?" look and mumbled something under her breath. But she waved the prisoner out of her cell and led us to another locked door. Dorothy followed wordlessly, with a slow, shuffling gait, head down, eyes on the floor.

She belched loudly and moaned.

"Sorry," she said, to no one in particular.

Because of the suicide precautions, she had on only prison-issue pants, socks, and a shirt. Not even a bra—people can hang themselves with a bra if they are really determined—and of course no shoes or shoe-laces. She had no comb, no toothbrush, no writing implements: the "no pointy objects" rule.

The matron threw open the door and jerked her head at the tiny room beyond.

"You can use this, I guess," she said.

We filed in, Karen, Dorothy Dunn, and I. The atmosphere in the room was close and hot, the air stale. The fluorescent light fixture emitted a persistent high-pitched whine and flickered intermittently. There was another loud burp from Dorothy, followed by a burst of flatulence, as the matron closed the door to the airless compartment.

My nostrils flared, and I exhaled slowly.

"Sorry," Dorothy said.

She burped again, the low, rumbling seismic wave seeming to start in her toes, roll through her intestines, and escape in one gaseous emission from her throat. She held her head in her hands, moaning.

"Dorothy," Karen said, breathing shallowly, "I'm your attorney, you remember? This is the doctor I told you about. She wants to ask you some questions about yourself and Raymie and the other children. You remember I told you not to discuss your case with anyone, not to answer any questions about what happened with Raymie? But it's okay to talk with the doctor. Try to answer all of her questions. Just her or me, though. Still don't talk to anyone else. Okay?"

"Umhm," said Dorothy, staring down at the tabletop. She showed no signs of recognizing Karen or having any curiosity about her circumstances or our purpose in meeting with her.

Karen looked at me with a hopeful, expectant air.

"Mrs. Dunn," I began, "I'm sorry we have to bother you now; I can see you're not feeling very well."

"Yes, m'm."

"Would you like me to call you Dorothy or Mrs. Dunn?"

"Dorothy be okay," she said softly, without looking at me.

I told her why I was there and explained about confidentiality. She had a dull, glazed look in her eyes. I was pretty sure she didn't understand what I was telling her.

"Is it all right if I ask you some questions?" I asked her. The flickering lights, close quarters, and stale air were making me sweat.

"'S all right, I guess," said Dorothy, her bloated bowels still gurgling audibly. "'Scuse me. I ain't been feeling too good lately. My guts is in a knot or something."

It was clear that Mrs. Dunn was not very bright and had minimal education. Her hygiene was poor, and she seemed to have no interest in how she appeared. She spoke very slowly and hardly broke a whisper; she made no eye contact, her desultory gaze resting on the gray metal tabletop between us. She looked depressed, and I wondered if she might also be experiencing some derangement of her basic sense of reality. There was something oddly fuzzy and disconnected about her manner.

"That's all right, Dorothy," I said. "Don't worry about it."

"Yes, ma'am, I'll be awright," she said. Then: "Do you know, is my children okay?"

I didn't know what to make of this last question, and, like everything else about this case so far, I had no answer for it.

CHAPTER 11

W HEN I FIRST STARTED practicing law as a defense attorney for Legal Aid in Detroit in 1974, the days of the gentleman lawyer, with his polite quest for truth or justice, were mostly gone. The prevailing legal ethic was that a defendant is entitled to the best possible representation afforded by the law, regardless of right or wrong, guilt or innocence, and the state is entitled to vigorous prosecutions of anything that smacks of crime. After all, it is the job of the jury, not the lawyer, to determine guilt or innocence. This made us all mercenaries, hired troops, pullers of legal levers rather than seekers of truth.

There were a couple of hard-and-fast rules: Don't intentionally lie to the judge, though it's okay to create false impressions, tell half-truths, and intentionally mislead. Don't let your client testify to what you know to be a lie—we were always careful to tell our clients that we did not want to know whether they committed the crime or not, so that we were not in the position of offering what we knew to be perjured testimony. But almost everything else was fair game. You could treat a witness you knew to be as pure as a virgin like a liar and blackguard on the stand.

You could impugn a witness's ethics, competence, and character when you knew there was no basis for it. You could encourage the court or jury to believe what was a lie by omission, by distortion, and by shameless mischaracterization.

The prosecution played by the same rules, but with more resources and greater leverage. Police officers, who were often pivotal witnesses in the prosecution's case, clearly lied at times to ensure what they thought was justice (i.e., a conviction). I have heard partners in a squad car give the same testimony word for word, like a carefully rehearsed script. Prosecutors could afford special investigators, forensic testing, and expert witnesses to buttress their cases.

As defense attorneys, we justified various marginally legal shenanigans by reasoning that our impoverished, usually black clients were at a huge disadvantage, with insufficient money for investigative services, expert witnesses, or appeals, going up against the behemoth of state resources and fighting inherent racial bias in the court. It was David versus Goliath to us. We rationalized that a certain amount of trickery was needed to achieve a fairer balance of power.

The playing field was anything but level. Occasionally the police exercised their own brand of "street justice": if a kid was arrested but got off on some technicality, once out on the street again, he was fair game for rogue officers intent on holding him accountable. More than once, we had clients shot by police officers who claimed the "suspect" was reaching for a gun. No guns were found, and the dead kids were usually young black men whom the police regarded as punks with a bad attitude. This was in Detroit in the 1970s, but the same thing happens in New York or Chicago, Milwaukee or Ferguson today. The police usually knew who the bad cops were, the ones who took the law into their own hands and became judge, jury, and executioner. But they would never betray one of their own. They would never cross the blue line of their law enforcement brethren.

I represented all manner of defendants, from innocent kids who had no idea what was going on or how they'd ended up in the system to a stone-cold murderer whose specialty was robbing and killing elderly citizens as they left the bank with their monthly Social Security checks. I was not a very good defense attorney, in the end; while I could mount a vigorous defense regarding unreliable evidence, false witnesses, or coerced confessions, I couldn't bring myself to intentionally create a false impression to mislead a judge or jury. I couldn't try to tear down a witness I knew was giving truthful testimony, even if it hurt my client. Especially if I knew my client was guilty. That kind of trickery was beyond my emotional scope.

We thought we knew the difference between right and wrong, good and evil, but in truth, the lines were more than a little blurred: When does one wrong justify another? When do the ends justify the means, if ever? And who gets to decide? Ultimately, no one trusted the system very much; we knew that it could not be counted on to work as it should.

Twenty-five years later, this was the world in which Dorothy Dunn found herself. Her fate would depend on the ritual combat in the courtroom, the clash of the forces of good and evil, and the psychiatric evidence of her own goodness or evil.

CHAPTER 12

So was Dorothy Dunn good or evil? What had been her intent in her handling of little Raymie? "There is no present without the past," Nobel laureate Orhan Pamuk tells us. Childhood is the crucible in which we are psychologically formed, where character is built and memories reside, so you must start at the beginning if you wish to truly understand a person. To get to know Dorothy, her motives and intent, what she "knew" and understood and what she did not, I had to find out who Dorothy Dunn was before Raymie died, before anyone was looking. Would the signs point to murder or to madness? Did she have a mental disease or defect? Or was she the kind of person who would cause a child's death "with depraved indifference," as required for murder in the second degree? And if not, what *had* she done and what had been her state of mind?

One can't simply walk up to a defendant in a criminal case, ask them what was in their mind at the time, and rely on their answer. They are likely to lie, to deny, and to dissemble, and the guiltier they are, the more probable is this response. So I began the evaluation by reviewing the reams of documents Karen Hughes had amassed on her client's past history: school records, work records, medical records, police records (there were no previous police reports, as Dorothy had never been charged with anything before), and much, much more—over a thousand pages about Dorothy Dunn's past, going back to her earliest years. These were independent, objective records, their content not controlled by the defendant. I needed full command of this background research before I went to interview her again. It would give me an independent source of data. It would also provide an invaluable touchstone against which to compare what the woman would choose to tell me herself. Would her account be consistent with what the records showed, or would she try to lie to make herself look good and hide uncomfortable truths?

I got myself a cup of tea, small comfort for the task ahead, asked my secretary to fend off calls, and settled in for a long siege: forensic psychiatric evaluations are a precise, painstaking process when done well. Then I began to read, looking for early indications of her character, for patterns, for secrets and lies. Was she a person devoid of conscience and empathy, a predatory opportunist who used and discarded people, eliminating them without remorse if they got in her way? Was she a psychopath who killed without regret, as one might swat a fly? Had she hated this child and wanted him to suffer and die? What did she know, and what did she understand, of life?

From the looks of her, I had estimated Dorothy's age to be near sixty, but when I checked her birthdate, I was shocked to realize that she was only forty-nine. Life had not been kind; she had some hard miles on her.

This is what the records told me about Dorothy Dunn:

She had been born in Rochester, off Joseph Avenue, in 1948. The rows of tightly spaced, small clapboard homes there had already seen better days. Her mother had a history of significant mental illness—psychosis, hallucinations, delusions—and multiple psychiatric hospitalizations; she was the self-appointed reverend of her own church and placed religious tracts with dramatic renderings of hellfire strategically throughout the house as reminders to her husband and daughter. Psychosis has a partly genetic basis; children of a psychotic parent have an increased risk of developing psychosis themselves, especially under stress.

Dorothy's father had been one of the many black men who fled the economic stagnation of the South and migrated north to find a job after the war. He was a bitter man, by all accounts, an alcoholic who worked at night, slept in the morning, and drank in the afternoon. According to records in the file, Dorothy's father had repeatedly beaten Dorothy when she was a child—with coat hangers, wood switches, doubled-up electric cords, and the buckle of his belt. He had pushed burning cigarettes into her bare skin and once broke the wooden handle of a shovel over her back. Another time, he had flung a boiling kettle at her. Child Protective Services (CPS) had advised her father to desist, which he did not, and offered Dorothy no more assistance.

Dorothy's school records showed that she didn't know her numbers or her colors when she began first grade, didn't know her ABC's, and couldn't tell her left from her right or tie her shoes. She was frequently absent, and when she was present, she was often dirty and tired and fell asleep at her desk. I suspect that her parents kept her home when there were visible signs of abuse, as well as when her mother's psychosis bloomed, rendering her unable to get Dorothy off to school.

Grade cards and teachers' notes revealed that Dorothy was a slow learner and might have been classified as mentally retarded in those days, had anyone thought to test her for it. She did not master even the most basic reading or math and could not understand simple abstractions. She was a "trial and error" learner, one who couldn't generalize principles from one situation to another.

She took to sitting in the very back of the room, hidden among the damp-smelling wool coats hung on pegs along the rear wall. One teacher wrote of Dorothy: "Tries hard but lacks the tools for learning.

Becomes very confused and disoriented." Another wrote: "Cooperative but withdrawn." Was this, I wondered, an early indication of depression or impending psychosis?

Dorothy fell further behind each year. She never passed a subject after fourth grade; by high school, she could read at only a halting third-grade level. She continued to miss almost as many days of school as she attended, and a teacher's note described her social and academic skills as "on a par with those of a potted plant." Neither of her parents ever stepped through the school doors, and she was never offered any special education services or counseling. She dropped out of school before her sixteenth birthday, when her mother threw her out of the house.

Dorothy turned up at the Salvation Army shelter a few days later, not knowing where else to go. The director told the girl that the rules allowed her to stay at the shelter for only thirty days, and suggested she use that time to find a job and a more permanent place to live. But Dorothy seemed to have no idea how to go about any of it, the director told me, and by the end of the thirty days, she still had neither. The director granted her an extension at the shelter. One of the other women helped her fix her hair in fat cornrows ending with tight little tails at the nape of her thick neck. They showed her how to say "Hello" and give her name and make eye contact during job interviews. Then they sent her out again, like the dove leaving the ark to search for dry land after the flood.

This time she got a job on an assembly line and found a place to live: a roach-infested, lead-paint-contaminated second-floor walk-up with creaky stairs and a front door that wouldn't lock. But her supervisor at work said she "couldn't handle it"—the stress of all those parts going by so fast on the conveyor belt was too much for her. He said she thought and moved so slowly that she couldn't keep up with the pace and panicked and froze when she got behind. He let her go after less than three weeks. The only other jobs she held—briefly—were as a nurse's aide, emptying bedpans and changing soiled sheets.

I HEADED BACK to the jail to meet with Dorothy again, to compare what I knew of her so far from the independent records with what she would tell me herself. I expected her to lie and offer excuses, as defendants often do, and I expected to catch her at it by following where her early footsteps led. Her lies would shed light on how intelligent she was, how cunning and manipulative.

She didn't seem to remember me when I came to her this second time. It had been three weeks now since the boy's death. I noticed that her cuticles were chewed bloody and raw, and she said she was having trouble sleeping for worrying about her children. She cleared her throat, spit phlegm into her hand and examined it for a moment, then wiped it on her pants. "They don't give us no Kleenexes in here, miss," she said apologetically when she noticed me watching her.

The television evening news, capturing Dorothy's arrest, had shown a shapeless, pouting woman with a misshapen wig askew on her head. But the Dorothy now sitting hunched across from me had been relieved of housedress and wig, and I realized the pout was not so much an expression as the result of a natural fullness in her cheeks. Raymie had had the same full face.

Interviewing a criminal defendant usually involves a slow seduction, a gradual building of trust and lowering of defenses. Defendants are generally wary. They suspect—or know—that what you say can either help them or hurt them in court. You must play them slowly, gently, like a fish you are trying to land; I've found that if you give someone enough room, they will almost always show you who they are in time.

But with Dorothy, none of this subtlety proved necessary. She was compliant and meek. She spoke softly, barely audible at times, even in our tiny chamber. Her words were muddled. Sometimes her answers were so slow in coming it seemed that she had fallen asleep. At other times she cried, tears streaming down her cheeks and nose, running unchecked into little puddles pooling on the table in front of her.

As we sat in the cramped interview room at the jail, breathing in the fetid air together, she didn't have much to offer. She was homely and shapeless, her flesh sagging beneath her prison shirt and pants. Speaking in a flat monotone, she told me that she had had a normal, happy childhood and that her parents had been good parents, strict but not abusive. "I very rarely got a whupping," she said. When I asked her about the beatings and scaldings documented in the child protective records, she shrugged and said that she had been a "bad" child and deserving of punishment. She offered no embellishment. If she was trying to make excuses for herself, she was doing a bad job of it.

She told me that she had been a poor student. But rather than making excuses for her academic failures or blaming others, she said that she'd been "slow" and "lazy" in school, a disappointment to her parents and her teachers. "I didn't have no good grades, miss," Dorothy concluded, and this was the truth. She seemed apologetic, and embarrassed, about her limitations.

She could generally remember where she had worked, though the names ran together and she could not recall the dates, the years, or even the sequence. She did know that she had been let go from several jobs because she couldn't keep up with the pace or handle the stress of learning new routines. Her last brief job, as an aide in a nursing home, had ended while she was taking care of her dying father at home. "I just couldn't handle it," she said. "I was going through a hurting thing, with my father sick." She sighed deeply and looked downcast as she related this. Her weariness with life was palpable.

Dorothy couldn't accurately recall the birth dates of any of her children, and she told me she had four children, not the five shown on the records. She left out her second child, a son named Dante, altogether, for reasons I did not yet understand.

Though her children all appeared to have had different biological fathers, she said that her one husband, Frank Dunn, was the father of all of them, as if marriage had somehow realigned their DNA and made them his. She couldn't remember the year of her marriage to Frank— "sometime in the eighties—eighty or eighty-seven—I forget," she said, or of the separation that followed.

She knew that her daughters Precious Love and Tonette were "slow" but couldn't say exactly what this meant. She couldn't remember the schools they had gone to or the grades they were in. She didn't seem to know that her youngest son, Scoot, was also intellectually limited, according to his preschool records. Only Alice, her third daughter, was free of any significant intellectual or psychiatric disability. She couldn't remember the year her father died, which was the same year Scoot had been born.

Dorothy had only a vague sense of her own medical history. She denied having ever been battered or mistreated by anyone, and when I reminded her that police records documented that she had been assaulted with a tire iron by one gentleman and had her front teeth knocked out by another, she looked puzzled for a moment. Then she said, "Oh, that's right, then. I forgot. . . . When he started trying to mistreat me. . . . He tried to mistreat me, that's when we started falling out. I didn't want to go for being mistreated. I got tired of calling the police, and tired of things being broken up in the house. . . . He'd try to get violent. . . . He'd try to get physical. He tried to hit my kids, so I knew he weren't no good. . . ."

CPS had placed Raymie in Dorothy's home because his mother, Dorothy's oldest daughter, Precious Love, was mentally retarded and severely mentally ill. She was also homeless and addicted to cocaine and alcohol. But Dorothy had no real understanding of Precious's mental illness, believing it was somehow caused by an injury Precious had suffered to her thumb. She told me that Precious had gone to the hospital—where, I knew, she'd spent a month on a locked psychiatric ward on antipsychotic medication—"for her finger." "I think it got bit by some man, but she didn't tell them what happened to her. . . . I don't know who knows," Dorothy said.

"Where is Precious now?" I asked.

"I don't know. . . . She's somewhere" was all she could say, wiping a tear from her cheek.

I rapped on the door to our cubicle, a signal to the matron that I was ready to be let out. After waiting a few minutes to make sure I knew who was boss, she came and unlocked it. I thanked her as obsequiously as I could, turned my back on Dorothy, and wound my way through the warren of hallways in this Wonderland and up the rabbit hole and returned to the real world, the world of the privileged, and the lucky.

CHAPTER 13

As I curled up in an armchair after dinner, sitting before a warm fire with a glass of cheap wine, I remembered the first time my father struck out at me. I was three years old, the same age as Raymie James when he died. My father had suddenly kicked me down a flight of stairs for reasons I could not fathom. And then he had laughed, making an odd, hollow sound. I was startled and confused, as if I'd run into some invisible wall full tilt. Why had this person I adored just purposefully hurt me? There was a strange look on his face, something I could recognize as akin to pleasure or satisfaction, and I knew instinctively not to confront him, not to cry or register hurt, not to do anything that would require him to acknowledge what he had done. I don't remember feeling anger then, just bewilderment.

As time passed and the episodes became more frequent, he invariably acted afterward as though nothing had happened at all. This created an odd warp in the fabric of my universe; he could take on the darkened, twisted visage of a madman, strike me and knock out a tooth one moment, then look at me blandly in the next. There was a clear message that neither of us was ever to acknowledge that he'd done anything wrong.

It is natural for children to protest when mistreated, but I had no one to whom to protest. No family nearby, no friends who came calling. My mother, who'd been terrorized by her own father's rages, faded into the woodwork when my father went off. Like Dorothy and her children, my family was surrounded by a high wall of secrecy; I was as isolated as Red Riding Hood in the forest. In my case, the isolation was a product of whiteness, wealth, and social status: these created a buffer zone into which strangers, teachers, and social service agencies were loath to intrude. For Dorothy and her children, the isolation was a product of extreme poverty and chronic mental illness: they passed below the radar, nearly invisible to all who saw them, and Dorothy's children were equally devoid of allies or outside help.

For years, I saw my father's abusive behavior and rages as something alien to him, something foreign over which neither of us had any control, like a lightning strike, mindless and unreasoning. By the time my brother Eric began drawing my father's fire, I was almost twelve and had learned to read my father's moods and currents as well as a good riverboat captain could read the Mississippi's buried snags and sandbars. I had come to look at my father as someone both terrifying and pitiful, an emotional cripple who struck out at the defenseless when my mother's behavior frustrated him to the limits of his tolerance. But something fundamental changed for me the day Eric almost died in the kitchen.

Where I had until then seen my father as a man not fully in control of his faculties or actions, when he forced Eric to sit at the table and eat his eggs I saw him as cruel and sadistic, a selfish man who would protect himself emotionally, twist reality, deny the abuse and his responsibility for the harm it caused, no matter the cost to anyone else. This was an unforgivable betrayal of his duty to his children.

He wasn't mentally ill or a psychopath. He didn't drink or use drugs.

I've searched his childhood for some reason, some excuse, and can find none; there was no abuse or significant trauma there. He just had a mean streak, and no one had ever held him accountable and made him control himself.

I became exquisitely sensitive to any form of abuse or abuse of power. I frequently got into trouble for sticking up for kids who were being bullied at school, whether by teachers or peers. A man in a grocery store threatened to kill me when he tried to strike his three-year-old son with a belt and I grabbed his hand and told him I was calling the police.

Even now, many years removed, I struggle to remain disengaged in the face of injustice and abuse of power. As a clinical psychologist working with parents, I have no trouble being empathic with those who are merely incompetent, or are repeating the lessons from their own childhood, or who have been abusive but acknowledge the wrongness of it and are committed to change. But I don't do well with parents who enjoy their child's vulnerability and pain, those who are doing wrong and know it. The sadistic ones. When they try to justify the harm they're doing, my anger sneaks up on both of us.

One patient's father, a surgeon who was looking for an excuse to attack his defiant fourteen-year-old daughter, said, "I'm going to provoke her until she takes a swing at me. You know I can do it. Then I'm going to beat the crap out of her and it'll be self-defense. How do you like that?" He was a slight man, inches shorter than me and not much of a physical specimen. I heard myself say, "I'm going to grab you by your ankles and dangle you headfirst out of my third-floor window until your head explodes. You know I can do it. How would you like *that*?" I do not recommend this as a therapeutic intervention. But, by God, he needed to get the message that he'd be held accountable for his behavior. After that, we began to finally make progress.

Another father, a powerful attorney in town, bragged to me that he had no behavior problems with his six-year-old daughter because whenever she failed to immediately obey him he grabbed her by the ear, twisted it, and pulled up until she cried out. "What do you think of *that?*" he said with a smirk. Again, my mouth and heart engaged before my head did. "I think you're a sadistic asshole and a bully, and if I ever hear of you doing it again I'll have CPS at your house in a flash," I said. Another unintentional loss of control. I knew that CPS would never even take such a call, because his abuse left no permanent marks.

This is the personal lens I bring to the evaluation of defendants charged with harming children. But incompetence in a parent is not intent, and mental illness is not malice, and I doubted, from what I'd seen so far, that Dorothy Dunn was a sadistic bully who'd tortured her grandson and enjoyed it. If she were, the anger at the core of me would have been burning red hot by now.

So far, I could see no signs that the woman had a predilection for violence, malice, or rage. Hers was not the demeanor of a charming, narcissistic sociopath, either, a predator devoid of empathy or conscience. There was no record that she'd ever abused her own children or her other grandchildren.

Nor did the records indicate that she was anything other than what she appeared to be—an intellectually limited woman with little education. I considered the possibility that she might be malingering, trying to make a case for insanity, but I'd seen no evidence of this so far. I had not yet found the monster I had expected to be there, the woman who'd allegedly beaten and starved and bludgeoned a child. But I planned to keep looking.

CHAPTER 14

Iᴦ Dᴏʀᴏᴛʜʏ Dᴜɴɴ *had* intentionally abused, starved, and killed her grandson, Raymie—and I was beginning to doubt it—had she been able at the time to know what she was doing and that it was wrong? If so, she was guilty. If not, then legally she was insane, and not guilty by reason of insanity.

The legal concept of insanity has been forged in "general ignorance as to the nature of insanity." The law has recognized from its earliest days that children, people with severe mental illness, and those with severe intellectual disability may lack the capacity to form an evil intent, to exercise moral judgment, or to control their behaviors. This carried forward from antiquity to England in the Middle Ages. In 1313, a group of English judges heard a case at the eyre of Kent, a kind of circuit court intermittently convened, involving a child under the age of seven. The justices, ruling that the child should not be convicted and executed, held that "men's freedom is restrained in children, in fools, and in the witless who do not have *reason* whereby they can choose good from evil. . . .

An infant under the age of seven years, though he be convicted of felony, shall go free of judgment, because he *knoweth* not of good or evil" (italics added).

But there is a murky ambiguity here, an intertwining of the concept of *reason* or *understanding* and that of mere *knowledge* of good and evil, right and wrong. The transition from focusing on the defendant's "reason" (i.e., understanding) to a focus on mere "knowledge" was gradual, entering into the law case by case. In 1591, during the reign of the first Queen Elizabeth, the English legal scholar William Lambarde summed it up: "If a madman or a natural fool, or a lunatic in the time of his lunacy, or a child that apparently hath no *knowledge of good or evil* do kill a man, this is no felonious act, nor anything forfeited by it . . . for they cannot be said to have any *understanding will.* But upon examination it fall out that they knew what they did, and this it was ill, then seemeth otherwise" (the italics are mine).

By the end of the sixteenth century, a simple test of "knowledge of good and evil" was being applied by most courts to the question of the culpability of mentally ill defendants in England, though a few were still paying lip service to the notion that a person's state of mind and ability to control his actions were part of the "insanity" equation. Judge Michael Dalton wrote, "If one that is '*non compos mentis*' [mad], or an ideot, kill a man, this is no felony; for they have not *knowledge of good and evill*, nor can have a felonious intent, *nor a will or minde to doe harm* . . . An Infant . . . may commit Homicide, and shall be hanged for it viz. if it may appeare . . . that he had knowledge of good and evill, and of the peril and danger of that offence" (the italics are mine).

This is where things stood as the American colonies were being established, with their laws modeled on English legal precedent and custom. The two concepts—rationally understanding versus merely knowing—were thoroughly enmeshed, a confusing mixture of the old legal theory that a person is not responsible for their acts if they lack an "understanding will" and the new sin-based theory that they are guilty if they had knowledge of right and wrong, good and evil.

But psychiatrically, these ideas are not at all the same thing. Many people with severe mental illness "know" the difference between right and wrong in the abstract but still lack an accurate perception of reality and lack an understanding of the moral implications of their acts. How moral is it to convict and punish a person who is delusional and can't perceive reality accurately, or who is manic and unable to control their behaviors, or severely demented, with the parts of their brain that are responsible for inhibition and social judgment rotted away?

My mother developed Parkinson's disease, with Lewy body dementia, late in her life, and I often saw her sneaking food to a dog under the kitchen table. She "knew" better than to feed a dog at the table, but she had lost her ability to inhibit her behaviors and exercise judgment. And, sadly, there actually was no dog; it was a hallucination, visible and real only to her. Should we hold her accountable and punish her or just pick the food up off the floor? Punishment would neither restore her judgment and impulse control nor banish the hallucinatory dog; it would serve no purpose at all.

We don't charge intoxicated drivers who cause a death with first-degree murder (premeditated and intentional), even though they intended to consume alcohol and intended to drive their car; we recognize that their reasoning, perception, and judgment were impaired and they couldn't foresee and didn't intend the specific consequences of their action. We call this manslaughter or negligent homicide in most cases.

Why do we have so much trouble dealing compassionately with defendants who are severely mentally ill and similarly impaired? People choose to drink and drive; they don't choose to be psychotic or manic or have dementia, yet we hold the mentally ill to a higher standard than the willfully irresponsible. Perhaps so many of us have been impaired by alcohol somewhere in the past that we can relate to that defendant. But we don't feel a similar spirit of forgiveness toward the mentally ill. Some-how, we still think they are at fault and blame them for our fear of them.

WHEN JARED LEE LOUGHNER was convicted in the attempted murder of Congresswoman Gabrielle Giffords and the killing and wounding of nineteen others, Arizona senator John McCain said blame should be put where it belongs, on "a wicked person who has no sense of justice or compassion . . . a disgrace to Arizona, this country and the human race, and they deserve and will receive the contempt of all decent people and the strongest punishment of the law." Syndicated columnist Cal Thomas praised McCain, saying, "That is moral clarity. It places blame where it should be."

It is oddly comforting to have someone to blame, to think that tragedy is not merely random chance. There can be a satisfying simplicity in responding to hurt with rage. By all accounts, Loughner's mental health had deteriorated precipitously in the preceding years, with evidence of psychosis, paranoia, and delusions. But then at whom are we to direct our anger? Moral clarity, even if misplaced, gives more satisfaction than moral ambiguity, and the more stressful the times, the greater the craving for simple answers and certainty about who is to blame.

Aristotle told us that a man is not guilty if his act is forced by external compulsion. But this is an issue of *internal* compulsion. As neurologist Oliver Sacks observed, "The schizophrenic's complaint is always 'influence' from the outside: he is passive, he is played upon, he cannot be himself." The influence is internal, not external, the result of some abnormality in the working of the brain.

Author Primo Levi wrestled with the issue of the relationship between free will, moral guilt, and external compulsion in the context of Auschwitz, where, to survive an hour or a day longer in a highly immoral environment, people sometimes did unethical things. He confesses to small acts of taking advantage of other prisoners—stealing a spoon, a pair of shoes, a morsel of food—knowing that it might mean not the difference between life and death (for they were all expected to die) but the difference of a few hours more or less before that inevitable end. His will to live, that primitive, primal instinct with which we are all armed, led him to do things he later despised himself for. His writings suggest that he felt guilty, but I think all but the most morally self-righteous and arrogant of us would forgive him even if he did not forgive himself.

So the question I had to answer was this: if Dorothy Dunn caused the fatal injury to Raymie, did she have a malicious intent, a guilty mind? Was she good or was she evil?

LAW TRAVELS A circuitous route over time, with cases decided largely based on the precedent set in the cases that came before it. Some judges try to understand the intent, or *spirit*, of the law and make rulings that advance that intent, but often judges only apply the *letter* of the law—that is, the narrow definitions of specific words, like *insanity* or *knowing*, that have come down from previous judges. To understand what constitutes legal insanity, we have to look back in time, to the early cases, to precedent. But we also have to understand how the crosscurrents of politics, personality, prejudice, anger and fear of the mentally ill have shaped that law in specific cases at historic moments.

Shakespeare intuitively grasped the nature of madness in a way that Queen Elizabeth's lawmakers did not. He understood that madness is not a simple matter of knowing or not knowing the difference between right and wrong. The brain plays tricks on us, making delusions more real than facts; we can't distinguish what is real and what isn't when overtaken by a psychotic state. He also understood the moral dimensions of the problem. His Macbeth, descending into madness, says,

Is this a dagger which I see before me,

The handle toward my hand? Come, let me clutch thee:

I have thee not, and yet I see thee still.

Art thou not, fatal vision, sensible

To feeling as to sight? Or art thou but

A dagger of the mind, a false creation,

Proceeding from the heat-oppressed brain?

I see thee yet, in form as palpable

As this which now I draw.

TWO HUNDRED YEARS LATER, the law still lacked Shakespeare's grasp of madness, and the courts were still grappling with the question of who should be absolved of criminal guilt because of mental illness. Jurist Edward Coke, known as a hard and arrogant man by his contemporaries, endorsed a definition of madmen and idiots as only those who *"wholly loseth their memory and understanding."* But this is not a condition that actually exists for most people with severe mental illness; perception of reality, judgment, and rational thought may be severely distorted but not wholly absent.

Coke's contemporary Matthew Hale took quite another view. He argued that "it is very difficult to define the invisible line that divides perfect and partial insanity, but it must rest on circumstances duly to be weighed and considered by the jury, lest on the one side there be a kind of inhumanity towards the defects of human nature, or, on the other side, too great an indulgence given to crimes." He suggested that anyone with the level of understanding of an eight-year-old child should be held accountable. His focus was not on mere *knowing*, but on *understanding*, in all its subtle complexity and fullness.

Children age seven or younger were presumed not to know the difference between right and wrong; those eight and older were presumed to.

This is how an eight-year-old English boy came to be hanged for setting a barn ablaze—he hid afterward, suggesting that he must have known it was wrong. In legal parlance, this is evidence of "consciousness of guilt." And this is how four twelve-year-old slave boys—Clem in 1787, Bill in 1791, Jesse Ward in 1809, and "Little Jim" Guild in 1828—and one Native American girl of the same age—Hannah Ocuish—were also hanged in the United States. (I could find no record of white children being executed in this country.)

But this model, using childhood as a reference point for insanity, is inappropriate. As nineteenth-century legal scholar James Stephen remarked, "Surely no two states of mind can be more unlike than that of a healthy boy of fourteen, and that of a man 'laboring under such melancholy distempers.' The one is healthy immaturity, the other diseased maturity, and between them there is no sort of resemblance." Most people afflicted with severe mental illness have some ability to identify right and wrong in the abstract. They can be severely delusional, out of touch with reality, hallucinating, but capable of relatively intact planning and executive functioning within the framework of their own altered reality.

Hale reduced the moral and legal complexities of mental illness to the simplistic legal question of whether the defendant "knows" right from wrong—that is, whether he is choosing "good" or "evil." This results in a definition of legal insanity so stripped and simplified that it no longer encompasses the real reason those who are "mad" should be exempt from retaliatory punishments: they lack reason and understanding. It also fails to address whether a defendant must know that something is morally wrong or merely legally wrong. Some courts have defined "guilty knowledge" as simply knowing something is legally wrong—that is, against the law, while others have held that a defendant lacks guilty knowledge (and, therefore, a guilty intent or state of mind) if he or she does not realize that an act is wrong in a moral sense.

In 1853, the foremost forensic psychiatrist in America, Dr. Isaac Ray,

pointed out that the "right and wrong" test (the premise that a defendant is not guilty by reason of insanity only if he or she does not know
right from wrong) was a "fallacious" test of insanity, inconsistent with all
psychiatric knowledge. He characterized the criminal law as clinging to
"crude and imperfect notions" of insanity, noting that "the insane mind
is not entirely deprived of [the] . . . power of moral discernment, but on
many subjects is perfectly rational and displays the exercise of a sound
and well balanced mind."

POTENT MYTHS ABOUT the insanity defense exist: the myth that insanity is easy to fake, that falsely claimed insanity is a convenient excuse, and
that it must be narrowly defined and stringently proven or the floodgates
will open and every criminal will claim insanity and be loosed upon
the hapless public. These myths persist, promulgated by presidents and
queens, social media, news stories, even Hollywood. (For example, the
powerful *Anatomy of a Murder*, directed by Otto Preminger in 1959.)

But they are not supported by evidence. Of 5,111 murder cases in
New York in the last decade, only 43 defendants entered a plea of not
responsible by reason of mental disease or defect, and only 6 were found
not guilty by reason of insanity. The standard is so difficult to meet that
few defendants who present an insanity defense win at trial, even when
they have long, documented histories of psychosis. In each of those six
cases, the defendant was then confined in a psychiatric hospital until no
longer deemed a danger to others. In contrast, a person who is convicted
serves a prison term, receives no mental health treatment, and is released
when the sentence is up, dangerous or not.

CHAPTER 15

I WENT BACK to the jail to see Dorothy again, to give her plenty of
time to reveal herself to me. She would talk, and I would listen, and
eventually she'd tell me who she was, whether she meant to or not. But
I dreaded the meeting; there was nothing much to recommend about
spending an afternoon with Mrs. Dunn. As we sat in the cramped interview room at the jail, sucking down the stale air together, I asked her to
tell me about her life after leaving her parents' home.

"Time passed, and I thought maybe I'd been eating too many of them
candy bars," she said, "because my clothes was getting tight like they
never was before. And then one day I started having a bad stomach. I
didn't know what to do. I didn't have no doctor. After a while, my neighbor lady saw I was poorly, and called for the ambulance to come. They
took me to the hospital, and the doctor come in and said, 'Oh, watch out!
This girl's about to have a baby.' And I did."

And that's how her first child, Precious Love, was born.

The nursing notes described Dorothy as "very loving with baby." The
nurses wrote that the "father," whom they presumed to be a man with

a diamond in his tooth whom Dorothy had known briefly, came to take mother and baby home, and that Dorothy seemed happy.

Perhaps she was happy because her mother was letting her move back in. But the invitation was short-lived, and Dorothy was soon out on her own again. She found a shabby place to rent, but once there, she had no car, no phone, and no medical insurance for the baby. She had no one to look after the baby if she had to go to the store for diapers or baby formula, and the man with the diamond tooth drifted away. "I don't know where he went to, really, miss," she told me. "He just stopped coming 'round." Dorothy visited the shelter to show the baby off.

"The ladies there was glad to see her," Dorothy said. "They said, 'Oh, ain't she sweet,' and 'Oh, how cute.' And they helped learn me how to take care of Precious, and I done it pretty good, I think."

But nobody thought to tell her how a woman gets pregnant.

PRECIOUS LOVE was a quiet baby.

"You could just set her down, and she'd stay right there," Dorothy said. "She weren't hardly no trouble. Not like other girls' babies. She didn't really crawl, and she didn't know but two or three words, but I liked it, 'cause I was the only one who could understand her good. It was like it was just the two of us. I got my GED [high school equivalency diploma], so's I could get a better job, and after 'bout two or five months, I got a job as a nurse's aide in a different place, I can't give the name right now, and I started in to work again. The work weren't too hard, just making beds and emptying bedpans and feeding the old people they had there. . . . That job didn't last too long, though."

One day, when Precious was almost five, Dorothy didn't feel well. A neighbor gave her a ride to the emergency room, where they told her the news: she was seven months pregnant.

Dorothy's second baby was a son she named Dante. She wasn't sure who Dante's father was, she said; she thought it might be a man she had met at the mini-market when she was buying diapers for Precious. He came by and gave Dorothy cigarettes when he wanted sex. Sometimes, she said, he'd slap her, hard, so she'd know she'd done wrong.

"But it weren't too bad," she said. "He didn't hit no harder than my daddy did, and I was a growed woman, not a little kid anymore. But then he was took off to jail on charges, by his dealing drugs. After that, I didn't see him no more."

After Dante's birth, the maternity nurses observed that Dorothy, who was twenty-seven at the time, "behaves younger than her stated age." Of her daily living skills and general level of coping, they wrote simply, "ineffective individual." But no social worker or visiting nurse ever came by afterward to see how things were going at home. No one thought to help her or her children. She was sent home alone with the baby to cope as best she could.

Precious was five years old by then, still in diapers and unable to speak intelligibly.

"The teachers said she was slow, but I didn't mind, because every baby don't got to be fast," Dorothy told me.

Dorothy left Dante home alone one day while she went to the market, and a neighbor called Child Protective Services.

"I told the lady"—the child protective worker, she meant—"I had left Dante home while I went to the grocery because he was sleeping. I didn't want to disturb him. Babies need they sleep. I couldn't see no harm in it. After all, a baby can't really get into nothing. But the lady told me I couldn't leave the kids alone no more. After that, she went away and left me alone." The child protective worker "indicated" the case for inadequate supervision, meaning that she found probable cause to conclude that Dorothy had left the children alone, but did nothing more to help the family.

Life changed after Dante was born; he was a difficult child.

"He weren't nothing like Precious. He started in to pinch me and kick me, scratch me and pull at my hair when he was mad. I learned to give him what he wanted right away. We was all afraid of him. The neighbor lady would watch Precious for me sometimes, because she was sweet. But I couldn't get nobody to stay with Dante, because he was hard."

She developed raw blisters on her legs that needed treatment but didn't know enough to go to the doctor.

"It's just a case of sometimes you feels good, and lots of times you just feels bad. Ain't nothing for it. Can't nobody expect to feel good all the time," she said.

Her medical record also noted "a large, old burn scar on the upper chest, and on the left shoulder. On the lower extremities she has several scars, punctuate and round. On the upper gluteals and thighs there are multiple areas of linear de-pigmentation."

The burn was a legacy of the scalding by her father, as were the round scars from being touched with burning cigarettes. The stripe marks on her hips and thighs were from being hit with switches, coat hangers, and electrical cords as a child. She didn't think of this as abuse; it was familiar discipline in her neighborhood. As I write this, celebrity athletes are standing up on television to justify the use of switches and belts and lit cigarettes on children as a necessary and normal form of discipline. Spare the rod and spoil the child, they recite. I don't know what it's necessary for, after twenty years as a child psychologist, other than to prepare the children for a life of bullying and being bullied, to inure them to physical pain and harshness, and to make them prone to using physical aggression themselves. You don't have to strike a child to get him to behave. But when I worked as a child advocate in Detroit and upstate New York, while Child Protective Services investigators tended to regard putting marks on white children as abuse, they were more casual in their response to those same marks on black children. I couldn't then, and still can't, understand why black children are not entitled to the same protection as white ones.

Dorothy was eight months into her next pregnancy before she realized there was another baby on the way. She had no car and no job, no money or phone, and no one to stay with Dante.

Her next daughter, Tonette, was born at home on the bathroom floor. According to the medical records, Dorothy wrapped the baby in an old nightgown, wiped the bloodied floor with a towel, and waddled over to the neighbor's to ask her to call for an ambulance. Precious Love was thirteen, classified as mentally retarded at school and already showing the unmistakable signs of the schizophrenia that later overtook her.

"Precious didn't cause no trouble," Dorothy told me. "But she didn't seem happy no more, not like when she was a baby. Seemed like she was going down, somehow, instead of up. The teachers said Precious weren't doing too good in school. They said I had to help her more and to read to her every night. 'Yes, ma'am, I'm going to do that,' I told her. But I was thinking, How'm I going to do that? I can't really read so good, neither. Sometimes Precious just be off in her own little world, they said. I don't know how she could be in any other world, besides her own world, you ask me. They said I should have other children over to the house to play with her, but it's kind of hard; I couldn't be having no strangers in my house, in that kind of neighborhood. Maybe they didn't know that. You never could tell about people."

Precious's Committee on Special Education records noted that Dorothy was "an engaged parent who clearly cares for her child but can't seem to cope with her needs." And "Mother is cooperative and tries to help Precious but doesn't know how."

DOROTHY HAD BEEN married to Tonette's presumed father, Frank Dunn, briefly. It was her only actual marriage. But he turned out to be a drinker, like her daddy was.

"We argued something awful when he come home drunk, which was most days," Dorothy told me. "I didn't want that around my kids.

Sometimes, he'd stick a lit cigarette on Tonette so she'd leave him alone. Tonette left him alone after that, mostly."

One day, according to police reports, Frank Dunn struck Dorothy on the knee with a lead pipe. Neighbors, hearing her screams, called the police. But Dorothy didn't want to press charges. All these years later, the police officer remembered her. "She was an odd one," he said. "Didn't really seem to understand what was going on. I felt sorry for her and her kids."

The blow crippled Dorothy; the knee never fully recovered. But Dorothy didn't leave her husband. Not for his drinking, or his gambling, or even for beating her and Dante. "Them's things men do and women put up with," she said. *He* left *her*, because she didn't want to have sex with him after Tonette's birth, didn't want to give him "a man's rights," as she said.

Precious Love dropped out of school, pregnant, at sixteen, much as Dorothy had. Dante, who was only twelve, had introduced her to alcohol and weed by then; it quieted down the voices in her head, she said. He was terrorizing Dorothy and his younger siblings, kicking them, punching holes in walls, and spitting on his mother, Dorothy said. She tried to discipline him by swatting him with her hand, but it hurt her more than him, so she resorted to swatting him with the working end of a broom. Child Protective Services came calling when the school reported educational neglect because Dorothy couldn't get him to attend school. The CPS worker laughed at her feeble disciplinary strategy and advised her to take a firmer hand, to discipline him more strongly, Dorothy maintained.

And he already had an impressive juvenile record. He'd just been picked up on a warrant for failing to appear in court on a delinquency charge of robbery. I'd guess Dante waylaid the mail and tossed the notice of appearance ticket before Dorothy could see it, but she wouldn't have been able to understand it anyway. His arrest took her by surprise, and she was even more surprised when Dante's court-appointed law guardian showed up in person at the house (I admire his commitment to his client) and strong-armed her into agreeing to let Dante come back home so the judge would release him.

"'If you don't do that, Ms. Dunn, the judge will lock him up with a lot of bad boys, dangerous boys,'" Dorothy recalled him saying. "'You don't want that, do you?'"

"No, sir" was all she said. But she was afraid of Dante and had no control over him at all. How could she have him at home and still protect the younger children? she asked.

On court day, Dorothy put on her only dress and took a bus downtown. She sat on the hard wooden bench, polished by forty years of backsides, ready to say "Yes, sir" when the judge asked her if she was willing to take her boy back home. Two big deputies led in a line of gray-sweatshirted teenagers chained together at the ankles with clinking metal shackles.

As Dante saw his mother, his lip curled into a sneer.

"Fuck you, bitch," he mouthed, and turned away.

When the judge called Dante's case, he asked, "Is Mrs. Dunn present in the courtroom?"

Dorothy stood up. "Yes, sir," she answered in a low voice.

"Are you the mother of Dante Franklin?"

"Yes, sir," she replied, quieter still.

"Ms. Dunn, the law guardian informs me that you're willing to have Dante return to your home, and that you will vouch for his behavior. Is that right?"

She leaned heavily on the back of the wooden bench in front of her to steady herself.

"No, sir," she said in a barely audible whisper. She swayed slightly under the weight of her words. The judge peered at the law guardian over the top of his gold-rimmed half-glasses.

"All right, then. Defendant is remanded to the Children's Center," he said. "Children's Center" was the euphemistic term for the juvenile secure detention facility, which the law guardians referred to as the "kiddie jail."

"Fucking bitch!" Dante hollered after her as he was led out of the courtroom. His voice echoed off the polished walnut paneling and marble-tiled floors, bouncing off the ears of curious onlookers. "Fucking bitch!"

And that is how Dante was placed at a residential facility for youths for eighteen months and Dorothy stopped remembering him as her son.

Shortly after that, Dorothy gave birth to her daughter Alice. The telltale signs from her by now shapeless body had meant nothing to her, if she'd noticed them at all. She got to the hospital in an advanced stage of labor, thinking she had indigestion, and delivered in the emergency department before she could be transported up to the maternity ward.

At this point in the story, the jail matron rapped her bony knuckles on the door and glowered at me through the tiny eye slit. This was Dorothy's dinner bell. It was time for me to go.

CHAPTER 16

LEGAL SCHOLAR W. MIKELL TELLS US that "The fundamental question with respect to the insanity defense is always this: what kind and degree of insanity should excuse its victim from punishment for an act that, if done by a sane person, would bring upon him the sanction of the law?"

In 1639, Dorothy Talbye was executed in the Massachusetts Bay Colony. Governor Winthrop's diary tells us that Mistress Talbye "had been of good esteem for godliness but falling at difference with her husband, through melancholy or spiritual delusion, she sometimes attempted to kill him, and her children, and herself." She was excommunicated from the church and whipped, "whereupon she was reformed for a time, and carried herself more dutifully to her husband, etc.; but soon after she was so possessed with Satan, that he persuaded her (by his delusions, which she listened to as revelations from God) to break the neck of her own child, that she might free it from future misery." Her execution by hanging was ordered after she confessed to the crime when threatened with being pressed to death. Winthrop concludes with, "Mr. Peter, her late pastor, and Mr. Wilson, went with her to the place of execution, but could do no good with her." From this account, it very much sounds like Doro-thy Talbye suffered from severe postpartum psychosis, not demonic pos-session. In the words of Supreme Court justice Oliver Wendell Holmes, some two hundred years later, "see poor Dorothy Talbye, mad as Oph-elia." But in 1639, the treatment was death.

In 1724, an English commoner named Edward Arnold shot Lord Onslow for sending "devils and imps" that had "invaded his belly and his bosom such that he could not sleep."

Arnold's defense attorney argued that he was insane—delusional and incapable of normal reason—and, therefore, not guilty. He pointed out that previous cases had held that "guilt arises from the mind and the *wicked will and intention* of the man. If a man be deprived of his reason, and consequently of his intention, he cannot be guilty."

The prosecution and defense both agreed that the defendant suffered from insane delusions and that these were the cause of his act. The judge ruled that a man is not guilty by reason of insanity only if he was "totally deprived of his understanding and meaning, and doth not know what he is doing, no more than a brute, or a wild beast," noting that "such a one is never the subject of punishment." This became known as the "wild beast" test of insanity, and it required "absolute insanity"—that is, no ability whatever to reason or understand.

Arnold was convicted and sentenced to hang because he had *known* that he was shooting a man. (This was later commuted to a life sen-tence at the urging of Lord Onslow, who survived.) This is strictly a *cognitive* test, one that does not take into account the derangements in reality, understanding, or reasoning that can characterize severe men-tal illness.

By 1800, some progress had been made in understanding the nature of mental illness, particularly with regard to two concepts: that a psy-chotic delusion does not arise from bad character or an intentional choice to do evil, and that a person can be deranged and delusional on some subjects, depending on which brain area is affected, while remaining relatively intact and rational on others. My father, who recently had a massive stroke that destroyed much of the right side of his brain, can discuss contemporary events and modern astrophysics with perfect probity but cannot realize that his entire left side is paralyzed or even that he has a left side. He believes he is perfectly normal and keeps demanding that his bicycle be brought to him for a ride.

This brings us to the case of *Rex v. Hadfield* in 1800. James Hadfield had suffered serious head wounds from saber blows in His Majesty's service against the French and had come to believe that he, like Jesus Christ, had to be sacrificed in order to redeem mankind. Suicide being out of the question because it was a sin, Mr. Hadfield came up with a plan. He took a pistol to the theater at Drury Lane and attempted to assassinate King George III, who was in attendance, so that he would be executed and bring in the new millennium. He rose, said, "God bless your Royal Highness; I like you very well, you are a good fellow," and pulled the trigger. He missed (otherwise history might have been different) but was charged with attempted murder.

His defense attorney, Thomas Erskine, pled insanity on his behalf. Erskine acknowledged that Hadfield had planned and executed the crime and appeared coherent, but argued for further consideration:

> It is agreed by all jurists, and is established by the law of this and every other country, that it is the *Reason* of Man which makes him accountable for his actions; and that the deprivation of reason acquits him of crime. This principle is indisputable; yet so fearfully and wonderfully are we made, so infinitely subtle is the spiritual part of our being, so difficult it is to trace with accuracy the effect of diseased intellect upon human action, that I may appeal to all who hear me, whether there are any cases more difficult . . . as when insanity, or the effects and con-

sequences of insanity, become the subjects of legal consideration and judgment.

Erskine introduced testimony by three physicians—perhaps the first
case in which experts offered opinions as to a defendant's state of mind—
that Hadfield did indeed suffer from delusions that had resulted from his
head injury. Erskine then argued that you cannot define insanity as not
knowing the difference between right and wrong: Hadfield knew that
murder was generally wrong but, due to his delusion, believed that he
was doing a greater good for mankind. Erskine urged the court to recognize that entirely rational behavior can follow from an irrational idea, a
mad delusion.

A successful insanity defense at that time, however, required that if the
defendant be "lost to all sense, in consequence of the infirmity of disease,
that he is incapable of distinguishing between good and evil—that he is
incapable of forming a judgment upon the consequences of the act which
he is about to do, that then the mercy of our law says, he cannot be guilty
of a crime." And Hadfield had clearly carefully planned and executed his
strategy with full understanding that he would be hanged for murder if he
succeeded; this was his specific wish and intent, in fact. He surely had been
no "wild beast"; he knew, in one sense, what he was doing.

The defense attorney persisted, arguing that delusion was "the true
character of insanity" and reminded the court of Hale's commentary:
"the true rule is, to judge . . . whether there was that competent degree of
reason which enabled the person accused to judge whether he was doing
right or wrong."

The judge, convinced of Mr. Hadfield's clear psychosis, declared that
the verdict "was clearly an acquittal." In so doing, he explicitly rejected
the "wild beast" test, the requirement that a man must be "wholly" without reason, as well as the simple cognitive test, that a man is not insane
if he can distinguish between right and wrong, even if he is delusional as

to his own acts. But he also ruled that "the prisoner, for his own sake, and for the sake of society at large, must not be discharged."

Up until this time, defendants found not guilty due to insanity were generally released; there was no legal authority for holding a man who was not convicted. To fix this, Parliament quickly passed the Criminal Lunatics Act of 1800, legalizing the indefinite detention of insane defendants, and Hadfield spent the rest of his life in psychiatric confinement at Bedlam.

When William Blackstone, the noted English jurist, addressed the state of the insanity defense in 1803, he advised that the focus should be on a defendant's consciousness of guilt and the ability to discern between good and evil. He endorsed the execution of children as young as eight if they appeared to have some consciousness of guilt. As we have seen, in one case, a child ran and hid, proving, Blackstone reasoned, that he knew he had done wrong and was, therefore, guilty. He noted that "and as the sparing this boy merely on account of his tender years might be of dangerous consequence to the public, by propagating a notion that children might commit such atrocious crimes with impunity, it was unanimously agreed by all the judges that he was a proper subject of capital punishment." This was during the time of the "Bloody Code," when 220 offenses were punishable by death.

As to an "idiot" or "lunatic," Blackstone said, "the rule of law . . . is that *furiosus furore solum punitur* (a madman is punished by his madness alone). . . . Where there is a *defect of understanding* . . . there is no discernment, there is no choice; and where there is no choice, there can be no act of the will" and thus no blame (italics added). And so, Blackstone concluded, "In criminal cases, therefore, idiots and lunatics are not chargeable for their own acts, if committed when under these incapacities." He seems to say that a person who knows the difference between right and wrong is still not morally or legally culpable if their mental illness prevents them from exercising free will and choice.

But the bar was set very high; it favored a presumption that a person was of sound mind, possessed sufficient intelligence, and, if over age eight, knew right from wrong. It favored, in other words, an assumption of guilt. An absence of will must be absolute in a lunatic, and an absence of knowledge and reason absolute in an idiot; there must be *no* scintilla of discernment, *no* sliver of free choice, and *no* exercise of will. As Professor A. M. Kidd observed, "The chief criticism of Blackstone's exposition is that for a successful defense on this ground there is required 'absolute insanity,' as to which Erskine, counsel in Hadfield's case said, 'No such madman ever existed in the world.'"

The law proceeds unevenly, subject to the vicissitudes of public and political pressure, and bad facts often make bad law. Hadfield's case had little impact on future insanity cases. A scant twelve years later—the blink of an eye in terms of legal evolution—John Bellingham assassinated Sir Spencer Perceval, the prime minister in the House of Commons. He was not assigned an attorney until the night before his trial, and though clearly delusional, he was summarily hanged eight days later (under pressure from the Crown) because he was presumed to "know" the difference between good and evil and to have chosen evil. Thus did a bad case make bad law, its impact felt for years in the form of precedent.

Still, the general trajectory of the insanity defense over time has been to recognize that some people are not in control of their reasoning or behavior, because of mental illness, and are, therefore, not criminally culpable. In 1840, a man named Edward Oxford fired a pistol at Queen Victoria. Presented with evidence that Oxford had long been unstable and that the pistols had not even been loaded, the judge instructed the jury, "If some controlling disease was, in truth, the acting power within him, which he could not resist," then he was not criminally responsible. The jury found Oxford not guilty by reason of insanity, and he was committed to Bedlam for twenty-four years. (At that point, he was released on the condition that he emigrate to Australia and never return. He became a model citizen there.)

Queen Victoria, incensed at Oxford's escape from the hangman, wrote to Sir Robert Peel, "Punishment deters not only sane men but also eccentric men, whose supposed involuntary acts are really produced by a diseased brain capable of being acted upon by external influence. A knowledge that they would be protected by an acquittal on the grounds of insanity will encourage these men to commit desperate acts, while on the other hand certainty that they will not escape punishment will terrify them into a peaceful attitude toward others." But I've yet to either meet or hear of a person with insane delusions who is dissuaded from them or their commands by reason or the promise of punishment. It would be comforting to think that they can be deterred by such threats, but it simply isn't so. The wish is a vain wish, a sort of urban myth. As Lord Swinton, the judge in *Kinloch's Case*, rightly observed, "Punishment is intended for example; but a person insane can have no design; and to punish him can be no example." No amount of rational persuasion or threats of dire punishment will make mania or psychosis respond to reason.

CHAPTER 17

PRECIOUS'S FIRST BABY, and Dorothy's first grandchild, was Gloria. She had long, long eyelashes and beautiful round eyes. The pregnancy had been unintentional, the father only guessed at. "Precious didn't have no interest in that baby," Dorothy said. "She didn't even feed her." Precious started going out again, according to Dorothy, soon after the baby's birth. She'd come home days later, disheveled, smelling of liquor and stale smoke and sex. So Dorothy assumed care for the baby. "She weren't hardly no trouble," Dorothy told me. "I always liked babies."

Soon after Gloria's first birthday, Precious gave birth to a second daughter, Nikki, but again showed no interest in parenting, so Dorothy took over the care of that baby, too. She had no job, and because Gloria and Nikki were not officially placed with her, she had no medical cards for the children, no extra housing allowance or eligibility for subsidized housing that she knew of, and no benefits to help with the cost of the extra food. Nor did she have any respite or day care or friends to help out. She scraped by, as best she could.

Precious's new baby was thin and sickly, Dorothy recalled. "She just whimpered, but I could see there weren't nothing wrong, so I just let her lay in her crib mostly," Dorothy told me. "She come out pretty good in the end, so I guess I done all right. But Precious started bringing all kinds of boys and mens into the house. Precious was nearly always drunk or high. She started arguing with Tonette all the time. I told her, 'If you're not gonna take care of these babies, you got to at least get out the house and get a job,'" Dorothy said. One night, she told me, Precious Love struck Tonette across the face, hard. "That's it, Precious," Dorothy hollered. "I had enough now. You go find yourself another place to live."

So the next day, Precious left, taking her babies with her, and Dorothy didn't see them again for weeks. When Precious did finally show up at her door again, the children were in filthy, thin clothing on the cold fall day. Gloria reached out her arms to Dorothy's neck. "I took 'em in," Dorothy said. "What else could I do? Them children was in sorry shape. Somebody had to do something."

These were the words and actions of a person capable of empathy, I thought. This was a woman who gave of herself, what little there was, in an attempt at kindness. These were not the actions of a sociopath.

SHORTLY AFTER PRECIOUS left her two daughters on Dorothy's doorstep again, Dorothy got a call from her father's sister Bettina. It was a voice she had not heard for many years.

"Your daddy's poorly, Dorothy," Bettina said. "He's got no one to do for him. You've got to take him in." Dorothy had not seen or heard from her father in twenty years.

"All right" was all she said.

So he moved in, with his oxygen tank and his cigarettes and his booze, ravaged by emphysema and cirrhosis.

For sixteen months he sprawled on the threadbare couch in Dorothy's front room with a hacking cough, eyes crusted and rheumy, chain-smoking while a green cannula pumped oxygen in through his nose. For sixteen months Dorothy waited on him and cleaned up after him. A visiting nurse came by and threatened to take away his oxygen tank if he didn't stop smoking, afraid he'd blow up the house. He waited until she was almost to the street to light up again. The children—Tonette and Alice, Gloria and Precious's youngest, little Nikki—circled around him like moths to a flame, and he struck out at them with imprecations and spasms of his bony claw-like hands when he could, making them giggle and tease him the more. To them, it was a game of keep-away.

Dorothy began lying awake all night, listening for the crackling of flames. What if he fell asleep while smoking and set the couch ablaze? She'd had a fear of fire ever since she was a small child, perhaps ever since her father had touched his burning cigarettes to her skin and scalded her from a boiling pot on the stove. She felt she had to stay awake, to get herself and the children out if he set the house on fire. There was no smoke alarm—she didn't even know that such a thing existed—and the old wooden house was as dry as kindling and would have gone up like a torch. She knew that much, at least.

Dorothy's descent into a deep depression seems to have begun during this time; she couldn't sleep, and she had no energy for getting up. She experienced a kind of mental paralysis common with severe depression: she couldn't make decisions, couldn't concentrate, and had to struggle to answer the children when they tried to get her attention. She couldn't get them off to school, couldn't get food on the table. And the children began to act out. Tonette was becoming increasingly aggressive at school; concerned teachers were calling Dorothy, who had no answers. Everything was falling apart.

In the meantime, Dorothy continued to bring her father the whiskey and cigarettes he demanded, she nursed him, and she feared him. And when he finally died, having never said a kind word to her, Dorothy washed him off and laid him out, like she had learned at the nursing home. Then she asked a neighbor what she should do and, following her advice, called the ambulance. The medics listened to her father's still chest and felt for a pulse, then lifted his cold, leathery body into a black body bag and punctuated the whole affair with a decisive zip as they closed the bag and hauled him away.

Dorothy was seven months pregnant by then, probably by Mister, a bullying man who came around periodically to demand sex. I asked her how she had become pregnant. "Men takes what they wants, and then they leaves," she said with a shrug. If you're lucky, I thought. Sometimes they stay. By the time she realized she was pregnant and tried to get an abortion, it was too late.

She was tapped out, exhausted and depressed, unable to take on the demands of another baby. "All peoples got troubles," Dorothy told me as we sat together in her jail cell, five years and one death later. But in truth, she added, she had felt she wasn't up to it anymore. "I had to think on it a long time before I could figure what to do."

CHAPTER 18

WITH HER FATHER NEWLY DEAD, her beloved eldest daughter, Precious, drifting further into schizophrenia and drugs, her son Dante a dropout in trouble with the law, and Tonette emotionally disturbed and in trouble at school, Dorothy gave birth to her new son, Scoot, prematurely, at home on the toilet. "I thought I had to have a bowel movement, and my baby was born," she said. She scooped him up out of the toilet and dried him off on an old bath towel and then tried to figure out what to do. "I was feeling just plumb wore out, miss," she said. "That's why I did like I did with Scoot. It took me a while to sort it out, and figure on what I ought to do," she explained. "Babies need love, and I was all out of love. I wanted to do right by him. I prayed on it some, and then it come to me."

After three weeks of handling Scoot only enough to feed and change him, Dorothy called the Catholic Family Center and asked that Scoot be given to someone who could love him and look after him properly.

"I can't keep him, miss," Dorothy said to the social worker, a young woman named Alison Webb. "I want to give him to you so's you can find him someplace else. He'll be needing someone else to mother him. I never had no luck with boys."

Webb's intake note said:

[Dorothy] has five children. . . . She is interested in surrendering [Scoot] ASAP. Feels she can't parent him properly and wants a better life for him. Father in and out of the picture. . . . [Dorothy] appears very anxious to have her newborn son removed from her home. She does not appear to be bonded to the child. She describes herself as "slow."

Supervisor Calista Freed added:

Alison feels the baby is at risk of losing weight as [Dorothy] is low on formula and Alison fears [Dorothy] will either withhold feedings or water down the formula. Alison does not believe [Dorothy] would deliberately hurt the baby.

But Webb left the infant there. On the next home visit, the house was dark, with all the curtains drawn. Tonette and Alice, ages six and four, were watching television. Webb's note of the visit says:

[Dorothy] told worker she would like to surrender him for adoption because she cannot afford to provide for him. She said she tried to have an abortion but was too far along. She named "Mister," whose legal name and address she did not know, as the possible father. [Dorothy] said she has had a lot to deal with regarding her father's illness and death. She appears to be grieving over him. [Dorothy] told worker she "wants [Scoot] out of here as soon as possible." The house was again dark. [Dorothy] said the girls sometimes sleep on the floor in the living room where she sleeps on the couch.

Alison tracked down Mister, and when he failed to respond to her letters, she went to his home. He opened the door a crack, keeping one foot braced against it, and peered out at her suspiciously with one dark eye while she huddled on the porch. She asked if he was the father of the child, and with a furtive glance toward the kitchen, where Alison could hear pots banging, he said he didn't know, he might be. When asked if his wife knew, he grinned and said, "I ain't dead yet, am I?" "What do you mean?" Webb asked. "If my wife knew, I'd be dead," he scoffed. Asked if he had any objection to putting the child up for adoption, he said, "It don't matter one way or another to me."

Webb had been taught, and most likely believed, that the family unit was sacred and must be preserved. She was supported in this by the laws of New York, as in most states, which make the presumption that children are better off with their biological families. I have seen too many badly abused children in my career to feel certain of this anymore myself.

It was nearly five weeks after Dorothy's first plea to find a loving home for her son when Webb finally picked Scoot up and put him in a foster home. When Webb arrived, she found Dorothy disheveled and lethargic. The house was, as usual, darkened. Webb went to the bedroom and saw Scoot for the first time in weeks. He was lying unattended in his crib, listless, scrawny, and smelling foul; Dorothy had run out of diapers. Dorothy had also not consistently followed through with his needed medical care. She handed Scoot over to the woman without looking at him.

"Here, take him," she said. "He be better off somewheres else."

Webb's case notes said of Dorothy, "She wasn't angry, upset, shocked, sad—there was nothing in her face."

Most general social workers have very limited mental health training, but to me this sounded like the face of a person who was profoundly depressed or otherwise in the throes of mental illness.

So the social worker took the child and gave Dorothy a name and a phone number to call to sign up for a parenting class. She'd meant to also recommend counseling for her depression and to refer her to the Developmental Disabilities Services Office. But Dorothy had no phone and never called about the parenting class, and the other referrals were never made. Webb returned to Dorothy's home several more times over the next few weeks and finally concluded that although Dorothy had initially appeared to have no love for Scoot and no interest in him, she was more depressed and overwhelmed than neglectful and unfeeling. The house was a bit cleaner when she came for visits, and occasionally the curtains were open. Dorothy's hygiene had improved, and once she even offered Webb a cup of tea.

Webb decided to encourage Dorothy to take Scoot back. She scheduled appointments for Dorothy to visit with Scoot at the agency, but Dorothy missed almost all of them, a clue perhaps that she wasn't ready. But Webb was undaunted; she began bringing Scoot to Dorothy's home for visits. She noted that Dorothy was "very patient with him" when he screamed inconsolably at the sight of her. She also wrote:

> [Dorothy] does not understand the difference between foster care and adoption. She thought she could decide to bring [Scoot] home even after he has been adopted if she visits him. Worker asked if she loves [Scoot]. [Dorothy] would admit to no feelings regarding him. Worker took [Scoot] to [Dorothy's] house for a scheduled visit. [Dorothy] wasn't home.

But, a week later:

> [Dorothy] told worker she misses [Scoot]. She said she thinks she wants him to come home.

More missed visits; then:

> [Dorothy] told worker she wants her baby back. She said she
> was overwhelmed after he was born and needed some time.
> She feels badly about him being in foster care now.

So after less than two months of foster care, Webb returned Scoot to Dorothy and wrote a final note:

> [Dorothy] is doing fine. Her case will be closed. Worker gave
> her the name and number for the parenting group leader. [Dorothy] will call her.

But Dorothy's reality remained a stark one, and nothing had really changed. When the visiting nurse came to Dorothy's home to check on Scoot two weeks later, she found him home with only Tonette and Alice and called Child Protective Services to report inadequate supervision.

The CPS worker's notes said: "Mother appeared slightly upset. She stated how she's done everything possible to care for her children the best she can. Mother appears to care about the children but has questionable judgment and may be overwhelmed." She "indicated" the case, meaning she found probable cause to believe there was, in fact, inadequate supervision, and then closed it, as is the policy when a parent is "cooperative."

Scoot's father, Mister, still came sniffing around from time to time. He was a mean, abusive drunk. Dorothy was seen in the emergency room again that year, when Mister knocked out her front teeth in a fit of rage. When I asked her about it, a tear welled up and spilled over, tracing its course down her cheek.

"What are you thinking?" I asked.

"I thought maybe he done something to my girls," she whispered, her head hung deep in shame. "Some man thing. Then I found out he were giving Precious cocaine. That's when we argued."

She finally summoned the courage to drive him out. And after that, Dorothy swore off men for good.

"They never done me no good, anyhow," she said.

Soon after, Precious grabbed Tonette by the hair, shaking her as a dog shakes a rag, and Dorothy turned her out, too. "I didn't have no choice," she told me. "Not if she was going to keep hurting Tonette."

More and more, it seemed to Dorothy that there was just something wrong.

"It was like some dark thing had got in me," she said. "I just couldn't seem to think things out. I couldn't keep my mind on things."

And then Dante, who had been released from detention and had been holding the family hostage to his temper and bullying, went to prison for rape. Dorothy felt so guilty and ashamed about it that she could no longer bear thinking about him and stopped claiming him as her child.

"I guessed maybe it was my fault, like the lady from the Social Services said, because I didn't punish him enough when he were little."

Had someone from Social Services advised her to punish the boy more severely, I wondered? Not bloody likely.

CHAPTER 19

WHEN I SHOWED UP at the jail to see Dorothy Dunn this time, she seemed to remember me a little. Just generally, she appeared a little brighter. She even looked me in the eyes once or twice, and someone had braided her thick gray hair, imposing a semblance of order on it. Her speech was clearer and not quite as halting as in the past. It seemed that the regularity and predictability of jail life was steadying her a bit.

I asked her to continue her story, and, with frequent prompting and stops and starts, she related that over the next two years, Precious and her kids—by then there were three little girls and Raymie was two years old—moved in and out; sometimes Precious took the kids with her, out onto the streets, and sometimes she left them behind with Dorothy for weeks at a time.

Tonette was nine when Precious had her first psychiatric hospitalization. Dorothy took her to the emergency department "for her thumb," which was festering in a dirty gauze wrapping. Precious would let no one look at it or touch it, and would not take the antibiotics prescribed because she believed them to be poisoned.

"I knowed that thumb were giving her problems," Dorothy said. "It were bad. Real bad. If she just could of got that thumb took care of, things'd be all right again. Her mind just wasn't right about that thumb."

The admitting nurse wrote that twenty-three-year-old Precious was withdrawn and talking to herself, giggling oddly. She noted that Precious had "an unclear injury of the thumb, perhaps due to a human bite"; that Precious's mother, Dorothy, was suffering from depression; and that her grandmother Evelyn, Dorothy's mother, had a history of psychiatric problems. Dorothy's aunt Bettina, her father's seldom heard from sister, showed up and told the nurses that Precious's children had not been fed and the apartment she inhabited smelled of urine. Precious told the nurses that everything in her apartment "looked black" but could not explain what that meant.

After an examination, the admitting psychiatrist, whose greater familiarity was with white suburban housewives, wrote,

> The examiner's initial impression is that we are dealing with a person who is suffering from major deprivation of a sociocultural-sort, who has been educated only minimally, who has limited time to keep up-to-date with current events and this sort of thing. . . . [She] harbors no obvious signs of mental illness or psychosis on initial interview. Her presentation appears to represent evidence of the impoverishment, along with sociocultural and educational deprivation, so often seen in minority people within urban America.

Precious brightened a little in response to antipsychotic medication; he discontinued the medication, gave her a prescription for something to treat anxiety, and discharged her, concluding:

> The patient . . . apparently developed symptoms of what are colloquially called, "motherhood burn-out" and "cabin fever." . . .

> It was apparent that she had no serious mental illness. . . . The
> patient left the hospital in re-equilibrated state, grateful for care
> rendered to her, and without complaints.

All Precious needed, he said, was a little vacation and some outside
interests; he recommended that she look into a high school equivalency
course to keep her busy. Her thumb remained untreated. No one had
been able to persuade her to unwrap it, and she'd responded so violently
when they'd tried that the attempt had been abandoned.

"I didn't have no high hopes for her being better," Dorothy told me,
"because her thumb was still bad."

Dorothy took her home, but Precious disappeared again, then resur-
faced, some weeks later, agitated and incoherent. When her cigarette
brushed up against Raymie, making him cry out in pain, Dorothy threw
her out.

"I didn't want Precious putting marks on the boy," she said. "Raymie
were only two; he didn't understand. He kept going over to his mama,
looking for her attention. It seemed like the more Precious tried to get
Raymie to settle, the more he had to keep moving. Precious didn't have
no patience for him. And lately, seemed like she would get mean. I knew it
was her sickness coming on, because Precious's sweet, generally. But with
Raymie, you had to watch her. She would go off on that child sometimes,
so I kept an eye out. . . . Raymie could try just about anybody. He wasn't
bad, just busy, but I guess it got so's Precious couldn't take it no more."

CHAPTER 20

D OROTHY WAS NOW PROVIDING for Precious, Tonette, Alice, and Scoot, as well as Precious's three daughters and her son, Raymie. She still had no money, no phone, no car, no medical insurance cards for the kids, no clothing allowance, and, at times, no money for extra food, because the children were not officially placed with her. Dorothy had a neighbor help her call Social Services to see if she could get money for the children for food and doctors' bills. Given the desperateness of the situation—the intake worker thought it sounded like parental neglect— the call was rerouted to Child Protective Services.

The new caseworker who trotted out to investigate the situation— turnover in the agency is high, and the same person seldom comes twice—found Dorothy's home dark; the lights were not working. There was no phone. The refrigerator was essentially empty. He recorded that the home appeared unsafe, with multiple hazards, no smoke detector, and general squalor and poor repair. Dorothy herself seemed wholly dispirited and depleted.

"You can't handle it," he told Dorothy. "I'm taking Precious's girls to their father." Precious had named a putative father at some point, and the man, or his mother, had, at least for the moment, agreed to take the girls.

"Can't those girls stay with me?" Dorothy protested. "I always be the one taking care of them, and they knows me. They don't even hardly know they father. He don't have no interest. If he so interested, how come he never come by before, all this time? And what about Raymie?" Dorothy asked. "You ain't gonna take him, are you?"

"No," the CPS worker said. "He only wants the girls."

He led the girls out the door, into the back seat of his car, and out of Dorothy's life. They waved to her through the back window and she waved back with one hand, clutching Raymie's wiry wrist by the other, so he wouldn't rush headlong into the street. Two days later, when Precious returned and found her girls gone, she grabbed Raymie's wrist in her good hand and bolted out the door, dragging him like a limp rag doll behind her. For the next six months, Dorothy saw neither hide nor hair of Precious or her son Raymie, who turned three that March.

One night a patrolman spotted Precious Love sleeping on a park bench, a sodden, lumpy bundle by her side. He was taken aback by her odor, he told me. It was the smell of sweat, of unwashed sex, and of urine. He could see that she was in a bad way, he said. The lumpy bundle was Raymie, cold and dirty, wearing a cast-off old sweatshirt many sizes too big. He recalled that Precious had stared up at him blankly, seen his uniform, and then said, "I'm going to jail. . . . Am I going to jail?" It was an odd foreshadowing of Dorothy's own words later, as Raymie lay dead on her kitchen floor.

The patrolman took her and the child to the Salvation Army shelter, where they could stay for ten days. But as the tenth day drew near, and Precious had clearly made no plans for where to go with her child and was in no position to take care of herself, let alone a toddler, the director called Child Protective Services.

The same CPS worker arrived who had left Precious's girls with Dorothy on multiple occasions and finally removed them from her altogether.

"You remember me?" he asked Precious.

Precious's tuneless humming and rocking registered nothing.

"Listen to me for a minute," he said. "You can't just be out on the street with Raymie. Do you have an apartment? What about your mother? Can you stay with her until you get a place?"

No answer.

"Okay, then," he said. "I'm taking Raymie to your mother's house."

"No, not her," Precious said.

Dorothy had always been the only real backup plan for Precious's children. The CPS worker wasn't sure what else to do; other family resources were scarce. It occurred to him that perhaps Dorothy's mother would take Raymie in. He looked up her last known address in the file and headed for her house.

Evelyn, Dorothy's mother, answered the door with a look of suspicion and confusion. The worker introduced himself and said that Precious was in a bad way and Raymie needed a place to stay for a while.

"He be with my daughter Dorothy, usually," she said, raising an eyebrow.

"Yeah, I know," the caseworker answered. "But Precious'd be more comfortable right now if you took him. Just for a while. Till Precious gets squared away. Just until I can make another arrangement."

Evelyn peered at the scrawny ragamuffin squirming in the back seat of the car, struggling to free himself from his seat belt.

"Well," she began, but the man was already getting the boy, and in another minute the man was gone and the boy was running through the darkened house, heading for the kitchen.

"Hmm," she said, and turned and shut the door like a Christian turning the other cheek.

But the arrangement did not last; Evelyn could not keep up with the child, who was into everything and knew no rules. He wouldn't listen, wouldn't obey, wouldn't sleep, and, above all, wouldn't leave the refrigerator and stove alone.

Did she try to discipline him as she had disciplined Dorothy so long before? Did she put marks on him? It is impossible to know. But what we do know is that not even a week had gone by before Evelyn called the caseworker back and said Raymie had to go.

The CPS worker picked Raymie up late the next morning; actually, Evelyn more or less shoved the boy through a crack in her front door when the caseworker showed up, as if she were afraid he might try to come back in.

"Here he is," she said, and nothing more.

The worker took Raymie's hand and led him back to the car, belting him in tightly. Raymie was so squirmy that he seemed to have extra legs and arms, like an octopus. The caseworker drove to Dorothy's last known residence on Evergreen Street, an ironically named forlorn neighborhood of sagging, peeling houses and weedy yards.

Did he remember that he himself had decided that Dorothy was no longer functioning adequately only a few months before and had removed Precious's other children from her care? Did he ask himself how Dorothy, with her own three needy children, was going to manage if Evelyn could not?

These are questions to which there are no answers. But in any event, department policy said that placement with a family member is preferable to placement in a nonrelated foster home, and Dorothy was Raymie's grandmother, after all.

So now he found himself clutching Raymie's sticky hand, knocking on Dorothy's front door, its paint cracked by the succession of Rochester summers and winters, baking and freezing. Weeds and trash had overtaken the small strip of yard even more than before. The chain-link fence yawed and buckled. He climbed the rickety front steps, knocked on the door, and called out: "Mrs. Dunn? You in there? It's Child Protective. Open up. I've got to talk to you."

He heard a slow, heavy shuffle making its way to the door. The door opened a crack and Dorothy's familiar face, looking older and puffier than he remembered, appeared. She was disheveled and barely responsive. He wondered, he said, if she was drunk, but he smelled no alcohol on her breath. Later, he couldn't explain why he was willing to leave the child with Dorothy if he thought she might be drunk. Or why he had been content to leave Dorothy's own young children there without checking on their welfare.

"Hello?" she said in a low, gravelly voice. "Raymie," she said. She looked down at the boy, her face softening briefly; then she looked worried. "What is it?" she said. "Is Precious with you?"

"No," he said. "I don't know where she is just now. But I told her Raymie had to stay with you until she gets a place for herself."

"Precious's gonna come here, by and by?" Dorothy asked. "She say that?"

"I wouldn't hold my breath," he told her. "I brought Raymie by. He needs someone to look after him until Precious gets herself together."

Dorothy sighed and shook her head so slowly he wasn't sure it had actually happened. "I don't know as I can keep him just now," she said. "I haven't been feelin' too well, and my other kids is needing a lot."

"I was thinking about Scoot," Dorothy told me. "Sometimes, I'd imagine he was my Precious, come back as a child again, happy, like before. He weren't in school yet. He shoulda already started, but I couldn't get his shots on time and he didn't have no shoes, because I spent all the money on the girls so they'd have clothes for school. Scoot was only in kindygarden and it don't matter so much. I thought maybe Scoot and Raymie could get along. But Scoot was a real quiet child, and maybe Raymie would just beat on him."

The CPS worker thought a moment. He could see signs of chaos through the open front door: furniture cattywampus in the dim living room, clothes strewn about on the floor.

"You've got to take him," the worker said.

"I weren't too sure I could handle Raymie," Dorothy recalled dully as we sat in her cell, listening to the clanging of metal lunch trays out in the ward. "It looked to me like he weren't used to houses no more. He was going to be a handful for sure. I could see that. And I was thinking about Tonette. She'd slap Scoot, or hit him with a broom, and I'd have to make her stop. She was too rough with that boy. I wasn't sure Tonette would take too good to Raymie now, because Raymie would get into her stuff, and her so touchy. And really, I hadn't been good myself, lately, all tired and wore out like."

"I can't," she told the caseworker. "I just can't do it. That boy needs a lot, and I'm not doing so good lately. You need to find him somewheres else. Someplace better."

"Well, there's nobody else," she recalled the caseworker saying, finally. "He's your responsibility."

And with that, he headed out the door, leaving Raymie and Dorothy behind.

As Dorothy said in her police statement, "Raymie first stayed with my mother at her house on Sander Street but Raymie was too much for my mother, so he came to live with me."

The CPS caseworker never came back to check on Raymie, and Precious never came back, either. She'd been committed to a psychiatric hospital. She had shown up at her great-aunt Bettina's house, filthy and raving incoherently, and wouldn't bathe or change her clothes. Then she stopped eating, so Bettina loaded her into the car and hustled her into the emergency department. "She act like she don't even know me," she told the nurses.

The nurse saw that Precious had had a previous psychiatric admission and had a history of drug use. Then she saw the thumb. The infection had set into the bone. It had been festering for nearly two years by then and was gangrenous. But Precious had refused to give permission for it to be amputated, to lessen the pain. It sat propped up on the clean white sheet, shriveled and blackened, dead. The odor of rotting flesh was unmistakable. The nurse suppressed an urge to gag.

Precious opened her eyes and saw the nurse looking.

"It's getting better," Precious said, smiling a crooked grin.

CHAPTER 21

I SHOVED THE FILES back into my briefcase and took off my reading glasses. I needed a break, needed to clear my head, to get out of the squalor and hopelessness of Dorothy's world for a few hours. And unlike Dorothy, imprisoned first in poverty and ignorance and now in her tiny cell, I could.

An acquaintance was throwing a party, and it felt like it would be good to get out and be around regular people for a while, like Mole emerging from underground, up into the light of day. Fighting the rush-hour traffic on my way home, I pondered the desperateness of Dorothy's situation. What would I—what would any of us—have done in her situation to keep my family afloat?

I got home, patted the dogs, and let them out to chase squirrels in the backyard while I fixed their dinner. The squirrels were in no danger; they were crafty and quick. Jacob arrived, pecked me on the cheek, and poured himself a cold beer to chase away the workweek. We let the feeling of not being at work wash over us for a few minutes; then I wiggled out of my work clothes and into something more comfortable.

Driving over to the party, I sucked in the fresh air wafting through the car window, breathing deeply. It was a welcome change from the stale air of the jail. City air always felt thin and depleted to me, smelling of car fumes and asphalt rather than new-mown grass and flowers. We pulled up to our friend's home, a sparkling castle by comparison to the bedraggled house in which Dorothy and her children and grandchildren lived.

The guests were good people, people who voted and donated to charity, paid their taxes and volunteered for worthy causes, and regarded themselves as socially progressive. All had been born to the middle class and had risen above their parents' station in life. They all had college educations or beyond and good jobs. They believed in the American cultural myth of rags to riches. In their experience, people who worked hard and deserved it prospered, and the rest didn't. Believing that you get what you deserve in life comforted them and gave them a sense of order and predictability.

They had little awareness of the benefits of "white privilege" or the disadvantages of being black in America. It just didn't occur to them to doubt the validity of judging those in less fortunate circumstances. They never knew those people personally. Only people for whom the system worked could afford to live in their neighborhoods, shop at their stores, or attend their children's schools; they had little exposure to those for whom the system did not work. They never took an accounting of the misfortune of genetic roulette or catastrophic accident. And Dorothy would have agreed with them; she subscribed to those same middle-class mores. She just couldn't live them.

I felt disconnected and out of sorts. The reality of my day, in jail with Dorothy, seemed so distant from theirs that I was at a loss for how to convey it to them. It would be like Jane Austen showing up at a party with a long-denied bastard child. The isolation I'd felt as a child, suffering secret abuse, seemed to be continuing. That is one of the legacies of childhood trauma: having difficulty trusting and relating to others or reaching out for their help. It was one of the things that isolated Dorothy so completely.

I ate too much, then drank too much, and went home crabby. I couldn't bridge the gap between Dorothy's world and theirs, and the next morning, I knew, I would be reentering Dorothy's world, a place where they would never voluntarily go.

At home, even though it was late and I was tired, I slipped off my shoes and sat by myself in the living room. Jacob settled into the recliner in the family room, with the television murmuring in the background, and was soon snoring softly. I was thinking back to my days as a legal aid attorney for the juvenile defender's office in Detroit. Unemployment in the city had been almost 21 percent then because of an oil embargo. There were bumper stickers proclaiming, BURN JEWS, NOT OIL, which made my husband uneasy; during the Holocaust, his family had been nearly wiped out in Lithuania and the Ukraine by their neighbors. Most of the buildings damaged in the '67 riots remained standing, burnt-out skeletons, though a decade had passed, testament to the tense race relations in the city and how little we care about the neighborhoods in which some children grow up.

My job had been to represent children in abuse and neglect cases. I learned that there are people who will rape an eight-month-old, will forget to feed their six-month-old twins because of heroin abuse until they starve to death, and will swing a boy around a bathroom by his feet, bashing his head into the sink and tub and toilet, because he stutters when he says his father's name. The family is not always the best place for these children. Some parents can't be rehabilitated. Ordering them into therapy is as useful as watering a stone to make it grow.

And yet, foster care is not such a panacea, either. As many as 30 percent of the children I've encountered in foster care have experienced some kind of physical or sexual abuse in placement, whether by the foster parent or by another youth in the home. These kids are at high risk—they are often hard to like, with all the emotional and behavioral baggage they bring. They tend to draw fire, daring people to care about them. And more often than not, foster parents do not receive adequate training and support for dealing with the needs of these emotionally wounded children. They may have some idealistic fantasy that all the kids need is love and they will be grateful and gentled. But the reality can be more like a caged wild animal that tries to bite the hand that feeds it. And damaged children are at risk for growing into damaged adults.

As a society, as voters and taxpayers, we don't want to know about this. We say, "All men are created equal," which they manifestly are not. And without equality of birth, race, and gender, of intellectual endowment and basic good health, and of economic resources and social connection, there is no equal opportunity. But our cherished creed is that the deserving are rewarded and only the undeserving fail.

People who vote don't generally see or know children like Dorothy or Precious Love or Raymie firsthand; those kids live under the radar, in squalid homes in neighborhoods most of us choose to avoid. In these neighborhoods, kids can't be safely let out to play, and opportunism and predation, not hard work, are rewarded.

In one inner-city elementary school in Rochester, nearly 30 percent of the children still have toxic lead levels from contaminated housing, making it hard for them to concentrate or learn; the aging houses they live in are as dangerous to them as the streets. Some 55 percent of the children in the town live below the federal poverty level, defined in 2015 as a family of four living on an annual income of less than $12,000. Among cities of comparable size, it is the only one in the nation where more than half the children live in poverty. Many have parents with mental health or substance abuse problems. Many have been abused or exposed to domestic violence. Many have a parent in jail. These kids don't come to school ready to learn; they come tired, hungry, distracted, and traumatized, when they come at all. How does one count the wasted human potential or the social cost of so many youths unable to effectively enter the workforce or become the parents their children will need?

And yet, the needs can be overwhelming; it's easy to bury our heads in the sand and react not when the children need us but when one of these kids breaks out of the lethargy and apathy long enough to offend— to rob, or rape, or murder. Or to become an abuser. Then we react; then we talk about justice, and the wheels of criminal justice begin to grind. Then we hold them accountable to us.

So was Dorothy Dunn competent to stand trial? Did she understand the charges against her, and was she able to assist Karen Hughes in preparing her defense? The following day, I sat in my office, peering out into the January darkness, contemplating the issue. It was time to decide.

The decision weighed heavily on me: if I thought Dorothy Dunn was currently incompetent to stand trial, Karen would arrange for a second, independent, opinion, because judges usually accept that conclusion when two experts agree. This would mean that her case would not go to trial now. But if I was of the opinion that Mrs. Dunn was competent, then there would be no point in Karen obtaining a second opinion; in cases of a "split decision," the judge almost always rules that a defendant is competent and proceeds to trial.

It was late afternoon; the employees' parking lot was almost empty, and the halls of the hospital psychiatry department where I was an associate professor and director of the Child and Adolescent Forensic Psychiatry Program were quiet. Most of my colleagues were nestled snugly back in their homes. The weather had been dreary for months. I didn't want to be sitting here alone, wrestling with what to do about Dorothy Dunn. I wanted to be home as well, coddling a cup of tea, in my scruffy slippers in front of a warm fire, chatting with my husband and petting my dogs. But at least I finally had a few uninterrupted minutes to think.

I reached for the phone and dialed Karen Hughes's number. It was late, but I knew she'd still be in the office.

"Well, I have an opinion for you about competency," I said when she answered.

"Shoot," she said. I pictured her poised with her yellow legal pad on her knee, pencil in hand.

"She does understand that she is in jail, charged with Raymie's death," I said, "and she can give a reasonably coherent account of her activities, in general. She knows you're her lawyer, and she's able to speak with you. I'm not so sure she understands the presumption of innocence. Scratch that; I'm sure she doesn't understand that. But she's able at some basic level to assist you in preparing a defense to the charges, and she knows she'll be in jail for a very long time if the state proves its case against her."

"And so?"

"So she's legally competent to stand trial," I said.

CHAPTER 22

In New York City in 1816, almost two hundred years before Dorothy Dunn was to answer for Raymie's death, Richard Clark was charged with petit larceny, while the law of insanity in the United States was still in flux.

The judge advised the jury that "it is not every degree of madness or insanity which abridges the responsibility attached to the commission of a crime. In that species of madness, where the prisoner has lucid intervals, and when capable of distinguishing between good and evil, he perpetrates an offense, he is responsible. The principal subject of inquiry, therefore, . . . is whether the prisoner, at the time he committed this offense, had sufficient capacity to discern good from evil." These instructions acknowledged that a person could have specific psychotic delusions, intertwined with more rational, lucid thought, and that a person whose crime was the direct result of a delusion might be considered insane and not guilty. It also required more than mere "knowledge" from a defendant; it implied that a defendant must also be capable of some understanding and moral reasoning about an act.

But whether a jury accepts that someone is insane, rather than merely "bad," has always depended almost as much on who you are as on what you've done: Are you a person of means, from whom the behavior would not be expected? Or one of the unwashed masses, who are often assumed to be more bestial? Do the jurors personally identify with you or have an implicit negative bias toward you? Clark was a foreign immigrant "with a certain haughty demeanor," the judge pointed out, a man without status, means, or connections. He was convicted.

Contrast the outcome in Clark's case with that of Daniel Sickles, a defendant with considerable wealth and social standing, a United States congressman. He shot and killed U.S. district attorney Philip Barton Key (the son of Francis Scott Key of "The Star-Spangled Banner" fame) in broad daylight, in front of witnesses, practically on the White House lawn, and was charged with murder.

Key had been having a conspicuous affair with Sickles's wife. The jury was composed of educated, land-owning white men of the same social circle as both the victim and the defendant, and they may have identified with Sickles's outrage at being openly cuckolded. Sickles's defense attorney argued that he had been driven temporarily insane, due to his discovery of the affair. When it comes to the insanity defense, it pays to have social connections.

The all-male jury accepted this argument and acquitted Sickles, who later served as a major-general in the Civil War and received a Congressional Medal of Honor after losing a leg at Gettysburg.

ASSASSINATIONS TEND to raise the specter of insanity. The first recorded assassination attempt against a United States president occurred in 1835 and was again an occasion for ruling on a defendant's sanity. "Old Hickory," President Andrew Jackson, was walking through the Capitol rotunda when an unemployed house painter named Richard Lawrence fired a pistol at him. The pistol misfired, and the elderly, frail president lunged at Lawrence, trying to club him with his walking stick. Lawrence fired a second pistol, which also misfired. In the ensuing melee, Lawrence was subdued with the help of Davy Crockett, the congressman from Tennessee.

Lawrence was charged with attempted assassination. He informed the court and jury that he was Richard III, heir to the British throne and that Jackson had conspired against him by attempting to dismantle the national bank, keeping Lawrence from receiving his royal tribute. As he was king of England, he asserted, the United States belonged to him. He further informed the court that Jackson had killed his father (clearly untrue). He frequently interrupted the proceedings, loudly proclaiming that he was the king of England and Rome. It took the jury less than five minutes to acquit Lawrence by reason of insanity. "Hallucination of mind was evident," Senator Thomas Hart Benton later remarked, "and the wretched victim of a dreadful delusion was afterwards treated as insane." Lawrence spent the rest of his life in an asylum.

So here again is a case where the defendant was not absolutely deprived of reason, knew right from wrong in an abstract way, and planned the crime with some care. But he was clearly suffering from paranoid delusions and was, we would now say, psychotic. For Mr. Lawrence, this resulted in a verdict of not guilty by reason of insanity and confinement in a facility for the mentally ill.

Nearly forty years later, paranoid delusions also resulted in a not guilty by reason of insanity verdict for Dr. William Chester Minor, who shot George Merrett dead in Lambeth Marsh, a poor part of Victorian London, believing that the man (who had never met him) had been sexually abusing him in his sleep. Dr. Minor was an American, a surgeon, and a person of education and position; the evidence was clear that he had been suffering from a progressive derangement for some years. He was committed to Broadmoor, "until her Majesty's Pleasure be known," as a "certified criminal lunatic."

In his confinement, he became one of the principal contributors to the *Oxford English Dictionary*. But he never again became sane. Though he never caused significant harm to another person, some years after his murder of the hapless George Merrett, he cut off his own penis with a penknife. In legal parlance, *res ipsa loquitor:* the thing speaks for itself.

CHAPTER 23

DOROTHY DUNN DID NOT KNOW Daniel M'Naghten. But the rest of her life would be determined by his acts. The M'Naughten case is widely held to be the seminal one in the history of the development of today's insanity defense in the United States. It is the case from which most of our current law of criminal insanity flows.

M'Naghten was a Scottish woodcutter. In 1843, laboring under severe paranoid delusions that Tories were spying on him and would do him in, he tried to assassinate the prime minister of England, who was a Tory (and also a personal friend to the queen). In so doing, he mistakenly killed the minister's secretary and was tried for murder.

In the Edward Oxford case three years earlier, English courts had recognized that a person could be generally sane and reasonable on most subjects but still "partially insane" due to a paranoid delusion. (A paranoid delusion was defined as a false conception of reality that a person adheres to against all reason and evidence to the contrary, religious beliefs exempted.) This meant that a person could have knowledge of right and wrong, and even "know" what they had done, on some basic, factual level, but still be not guilty by reason of insanity if they had a delusion that kept them from understanding the true nature, the evil of their act; if they knew that the act was legally "wrong" but did not know that it was *morally* wrong, they would be not guilty by reason of insanity. This formulation appears to reflect the original ethical intent and purpose, reaching back into the earliest origins of written law in antiquity, of seeing severe mental illness as mitigating moral and, therefore, legal guilt.

The judge found that M'Naghten's delusional state—testified to by several medical experts—had deprived him of the ability to have any true understanding of his actions, and he instructed the jury to find M'Naghten not guilty by reason of insanity. M'Naghten joined Mr. Oxford (who had fired his unloaded pistol at the queen) at Bedlam and remained confined there under the Criminal Lunatics Act, clearly psychotic, for the rest of his life.

But Queen Victoria and the public were outraged that M'Naghten had escaped the gallows. "'Mad or not, the prisoner ought to have been hanged,' was the general sentiment," historian Alfred Taylor tells us. Under royal and public pressure, the House of Lords solicited advice about the insanity defense from a panel of judges. The judges advised that "jurors ought to be told . . . that every man is presumed to be sane, and to possess a sufficient degree of reason to be responsible for his crimes . . . and that to establish a defence on the ground of insanity, it must be clearly proved that . . . the party accused was labouring under *such a defect of reason, from disease of the mind, as to not know the nature and quality of the act he was doing; or, if he did know it, that he did not know what he was doing was wrong. . . . If the accused was conscious that the act was one that he ought not to do, and if the act was at the same time contrary to the law of the land, he is punishable*" (italics added). As to defendants suffering from psychotic delusions, they said, "notwithstanding the party accused did the act . . . under the influence of insane delusion . . . he is nevertheless punishable . . . if he knew at the time of committing such crime that he was acting contrary to the law."

And with the stroke of a pen and the blessing of the queen, the determination of insanity reverted once more to simply a question of whether the defendant *knew* (not understood) what he had done and had a general notion of right and wrong. Under what came to be called M'Naghten's rule, a person would be found legally insane only if he had no literal, factual awareness of his actions. It was no longer enough that he was not in contact with reality and did not "understand" his actions or their moral implications. Psychotic delusions were no excuse. Under this legal standard, Richard Lawrence, William Minor, Edward Oxford, and Daniel M'Naghten would all have been found guilty and hanged.

The M'Naghten test considers only the abstract ability to "know" right and wrong. It is a purely cognitive test. It does not consider the defects in judgment and reasoning or the dislocation of moral discernment that were part of the original formulation of insanity in antiquity, or that are the hallmark of psychosis. It confuses the issue of knowing, of basic intellect, with that of understanding, the ability to reason and comprehend. It obscures the difference between knowing that an act is legally wrong and knowing that it is morally wrong.

Long before we had any sophisticated knowledge of mental illness or the workings of the brain, thousands of years ago, we understood the essential injustice of holding a person guilty if their perception of reality and moral reasoning were fundamentally compromised. M'Naghten and Queen Victoria changed that. The Age of Enlightenment was drawing to a close.

In this gap between knowing and understanding, between legal and moral reasoning, and between law and justice, ambiguity and inconsistency reign and invite subjectivity and bias. Those hapless defendants who fall into the ill-defined gaps between the *intent*—the ethical rationale and purpose—of the insanity defense and this legal *definition* of insanity are disproportionately the disenfranchised of our society: the poor, the mentally ill, and people of color.

Take the case of Henry Rathbone, who was a wealthy familiar of President Lincoln's. He was acquitted as not guilty by reason of insanity after murdering his wife in a jealous rage, while just the previous year, the clearly delusional, friendless, and penniless Charles Guiteau had been hanged after shooting President Garfield.

Though Garfield's death was caused by infection from the doctors' unwashed hands, not by the bullet wound itself, Guiteau was charged with murder, and his trial became the first major insanity defense trial in the New World. Guiteau's mother had clearly been psychotic, ending her days in a lunatic asylum. His father had raging religious delusions. Guiteau himself had a long history of bizarre behaviors and ideas, culminating in his belief that the newly elected president, who had never met him, owed him an appointment as ambassador to France.

After shooting Garfield and being conveyed to prison to await trial, Guiteau wrote a quick note to General Sherman, of Civil War fame:

I have just shot the President. I shot him several times as I wished him to go as easily as possible. His death was a political necessity.

I am a lawyer, theologian, and politician. I am a Stalwart of the Stalwarts. I was with General Grant and the rest of our men in New York, during the canvass.

I am going to the jail. Please order out your troops, and take possession of the jail at once.

Sherman responded that he had never heard of the man.

At Guiteau's trial, the prosecution produced mental health experts, called "alienists" in that day, who testified that Guiteau's irrational behaviors were the result of vice, sin, and low character, not mental illness.

The defense attorney called his own alienists, who testified that Guiteau was, and had long been, out of his mind, insane. He argued to the jury in summation:

> As society has gained more knowledge of insanity it has come
> to recognize that persons so afflicted deserve sympathy and
> treatment, not punishment. This trend is part of becoming a
> civilized people.

The legal test of insanity applied by the court was whether the defendant had known—not comprehended, but merely been aware of in some basic way—what he was doing and that it was wrong, the old M'Naghten rule, but stripped of the psychologically elegant requirement of *understanding the nature and quality* of the act.

The prosecutor exhorted the jury in his closing argument:

> It is very hard to conceive of the individual with any degree of
> intelligence at all, incapable of comprehending that the head of
> a great constitutional republic is not to be shot down like a dog.

He reasoned that if a man has normal intelligence, he learned to tell right from wrong as a child, and therefore "knows" the difference. With intelligence thus confused with sanity, and knowing with understanding, the hopelessly deranged but satisfactorily intelligent Mr. Guiteau was found sane by the jury, convicted, and summarily hanged.

The premise is psychiatrically unsound. It implies that an intelligent or educated person can never be, legally, insane, and this is manifestly untrue. It misapprehends; "knowing" and "comprehending the nature of one's acts" are two entirely different faculties.

The tendency to believe that rich men who do heinous acts are insane rather than evil is not just a thing of the past; it continues today. In 1996,

John Eleuthère du Pont shot and killed Olympic wrestler Dave Schultz, in front of witnesses, and without any apparent provocation. One of the Forbes 400—the nation's richest people—du Pont was found mentally ill but not insane, and convicted of only third-degree murder (meaning there'd been no premeditation and no intent to kill).

But Dorothy Dunn had neither wealth nor position. She had no well-heeled connections and was, in fact, hardly able to connect with anyone at all; she had not a single friend. It was likely that if Dorothy went to trial, no one on the jury would look at her and think, "Oh, I can identify with her."

With the M'Naghten rule, we lost the original ethical principle that a person who doesn't comprehend the true nature of their acts should not be punished in the same way as sane but intentionally evil men. Lost, too, was any connection between legal insanity and psychiatric concepts of mental illness. Where the law talks in terms of "insanity," there is no corresponding psychiatric concept or disorder. And where psychiatry talks in terms of psychosis, with delusions and hallucinations, disorganized speech and behavior, and a gross impairment in perceiving reality, it has little bearing on legal insanity; there is no direct correspondence between the two.

This lack of congruity between real-life mental disorders and legal concepts of "knowing" and intentionality is poignantly illustrated in the case of James Holmes, who killed twelve and wounded seventy in the Century movie theater in Aurora, Colorado, in 2012. There was no question that Holmes had committed the murders. With his flaming orange hair and wild-eyed look, he was easy to identify. He offered to plead guilty in exchange for taking the death penalty off the table, but the prosecutor rejected the offer. The public defender representing Holmes pled not guilty by reason of insanity on Mr. Holmes's behalf, as there was a raft of evidence of his deteriorated and delusional state of mind. But he was an educated man; the prosecutor told the jury, "I'm going to ask you to reject that guy's claim that he didn't know right from wrong." He pointed out that Holmes was intelligent—he'd been a doctoral student in neuroscience—and argued, like the prosecutor in Guiteau's case 130 years before, that Holmes's detailed preparation proved he was sane.

Both defense and prosecution psychiatrists agreed that Holmes was certainly psychotic, suffering from extreme delusions, the culmination of several years of accelerating descent into schizophrenia and a loss of contact with reality. However, experts for the defense testified that Holmes was suffering from delusions and did not understand the true nature of his actions or that they were wrong; experts for the prosecution testified that he knew that he'd killed people and knew that killing is wrong, and he was therefore not legally insane.

The defense countered that both of Holmes's grandfathers and an aunt had been psychotic, that his first of many suicide attempts occurred when he was just eleven, and that his only previous legal violation was a single speeding ticket. While incarcerated awaiting trial, Holmes stripped naked and ran headlong into the cement wall of his cell.

Faced with this disagreement between experts, the jury convicted Holmes. Hearing the verdict, the mother of one of his victims said, "We are very happy that this animal, that this monster, will never see the light of day." The judge, in pronouncing twelve life sentences plus 3,318 years, said, "If there was ever a case that warranted a maximum sentence, this is the case. The defendant does not deserve any sympathy . . . Sheriff, get the defendant out of my courtroom." As forensic psychologist J. Reid Meloy notes, "The more horrendous the attack is, the more heinous the behavior, the less juries are willing to consider insanity."

Sir James Stephen, in a draft of a criminal code in 1871, wrote, "The inadequacy of this formula or test will be seen when it is remarked that it is based upon a conception of insanity that is a myth—a condition of mind that never exists." In the words of psychiatrist Gregory Zilboorg, if the language of M'Naghten was taken seriously, it would excuse very few people: "Except for totally deteriorated, drooling, hopeless psychotics of long standing, and congenital idiots—who seldom commit murder or have the opportunity to commit murder—the great majority and perhaps all murderers know what they are doing, the nature and quality of their act, and the consequences thereof, and they are therefore 'legally sane' regardless of the opinion of any psychiatrist."

But the M'Naghten rule had its staunch adherents. In 1852, Dr. William Wood addressed the responsibility of medical experts regarding the question of insanity: "Whilst we are tenderly alive to the frailties of our common nature, and feel it to be a Christian obligation to shield from man's vengeance one already withering under the chastening hand of God, we yet, as good citizens, have a solemn duty to perform towards society . . . when, as members of a learned and honourable profession, we are called upon to assist . . . in deciding whether or not the evidence adduced in defence of a criminal is sufficiently clear to justify the administrators of the law in departing from the course which is essentially necessary for the safety of society, and the protection of the lives and property of individuals." The criminal classes must be held at bay. And morality demands punishment for the wicked. If God afflicts a sinner with mental derangement and does not show mercy, why should we?

King Lear's words keep echoing in my mind: "O, let me not be mad, not mad, sweet heaven! / Keep me in temper; I would not be mad!"

CHAPTER 24

WHEN WE THINK OF monstrous, heinous crimes—those of Hitler or Pol Pot in Cambodia or Idi Amin in Uganda, for example—they often involve a perpetrator with a personality disorder, not one of the mental disorders with a more familiar name, like depression, psychosis, anxiety, or even bipolar disorder.

It is fair to say that we don't yet understand why some people develop a personality disorder, and we don't know how to treat these disorders effectively. They aren't acute; they're woven into the basic structure of one's psychological makeup. They don't strike suddenly in midlife; they are evident by adolescence. In this group of mental disorders—antisocial personality disorder, borderline personality disorder, narcissistic personality disorder—lies the greatest danger to others. These people aren't crazy or "insane"; they know what they are doing and that it is legally and morally wrong.

Those with antisocial personality disorder—psychopaths and sociopaths, in common parlance—disregard and violate the rights of others. They are aggressive, emotionally reactive, and lack remorse for hurting others. They are predators and opportunists who have no moral compass, no conscience, and no regard for right or wrong. Their motivation is to maximize personal gain and minimize personal pain. The effects of their acts on other people are immaterial to them, though some people with this personality type actually enjoy inflicting harm on others because it generates intense emotion.

History affords many examples. We learned about two of them from Truman Capote's book *In Cold Blood*. In 1959, Richard Hickock and Perry Smith met in jail. They both had long histories of petty crimes. A fellow inmate regaled them with tales of a Kansas farmer he used to work for, Herb Clutter, who supposedly kept a stash of money locked in a safe at home. Hickock and Smith decided that once they got out, they'd pay Mr. Clutter a visit.

They arrived at the Clutter farm in November, tied up Mr. Clutter, his wife, and his teenaged daughter and son, and tortured Mr. Clutter. Eventually, they realized that there was no safe. So they took what little he had, slit his throat, shot him, and shot and killed the three other members of his family. Then they fled the farm, wrote some bad checks, traveled to Mexico, stole a car, returned to Kansas, and were picked up six weeks after the crime and charged with murder, to which they confessed. Truman Capote quotes Smith as saying, "I didn't want to harm the man. I thought he was a very nice gentleman. Soft-spoken. I thought so right up to the moment I cut his throat."

A normal person, reading about this crime, says, "My God! They must be crazy! No one would commit such murders unless they were out of their mind." But Hickock and Smith weren't. They were perfectly sane and rational. They knew what they were doing. They knew it was wrong. They thought they could get away with it and that there would be a big payoff. They calculated that it was worth the risk.

They were convicted and ultimately hanged. Capote reports that Smith's last words, as he stood on the gallows and waited for the trapdoor to open, were "I think it's a helluva thing to take a life in this manner." That is what a sociopath looks like.

More recently, Steven Hayes and Joshua Komisarjevsky decided to rob the home of Dr. William Petit and his family in Cheshire, Connecticut, in 2007. They forced his wife, Jennifer Hawke-Petit, to withdraw a large sum of money from the bank, then took her home, bashed Dr. Petit in the head and left him bleeding and unconscious in the basement, and sexually assaulted Hawke-Petit and her eleven-year-old daughter, Michaela, whom they had tied to the bed, along with seventeen-year-old Hayley. Then they splashed gasoline on the women and set the house ablaze to cover their tracks. The women were still alive and died of smoke inhalation and burns, while Dr. Petit alone escaped.

Again, both men had extensive past histories of petty crimes, incarceration, and aggressive behavior. Both had been bullies and predators as far back as childhood. Hayes had drug problems and wanted money to support his habit. Their motive was robbery, and perhaps the adrenaline kick that comes with risk and aggression, and they murdered the Petits simply to reduce the chance of being found out. But they were found and convicted, and both were sentenced to death.

Sociopaths know right from wrong; they know what they are doing and that it is wrong. They just don't care—other people's lives have no value to them. They are not crazy; nor are they legally insane. They are, perhaps, the essence of what we think of as evil people.

Borderline personality disorder is another defect in the formation of character that can present a threat to others. Those with borderline personality (the term is misleading to laymen: it does *not* mean borderline crazy or borderline psychotic) have intense and unstable relationships, alternating between idealizing and then hating others. They often have suicidal and self-mutilating behaviors, intense and reactive moods, and attacks of rage directed at others. They are fully oriented to reality, can be very strategic, and have no confusion about right and wrong. But they have a strong urge to destroy anyone who rejects or disappoints them.

I think of Susan Smith, who shoved her car into a lake with her two young sons strapped into their car seats in the back, drowning them, because the man she was infatuated with wasn't interested in a woman with kids. Who can believe that a mother would willfully drown her own sons? She must be crazy, you may say. No: not necessarily. She may simply be monstrous and evil. She knew what she was doing, knew that it was wrong, but did it because she did not weigh others' lives on the same scale as her own and wanted what she wanted. Rage, disregard for others, and intensity are hallmarks of borderline personality disorder.

And then there is narcissistic personality disorder, another character malformation that can pose a danger to others, sometimes on a grand scale. This is a pervasive pattern of grandiosity and need for admiration, a lack of empathy, and the belief that one is too special to have to follow the rules made for others. People with narcissistic personality disorder are interpersonally exploitive and particularly sensitive to being criticized or rejected by others. "If I can't have you, no one can" is a frequent refrain heard from narcissists who murder their intimate partner or commit murder-suicides.

But narcissism can take on a much grander form. In 1978 in Guyana, Jim Jones led the Peoples Temple, where he ruled absolutely and told his followers that he was God and with his full faculties, but drunk with power, he led his followers to the slaughter as a shepherd leads his sheep. When the outside world intervened and threatened to hold him accountable and expose him, he ordered more than nine hundred of his followers to take their lives, and those of their young children, by drinking Kool-Aid laced with cyanide. He had named the place where this happened Jonestown, after himself, naturally.

In 1999, students Dylan Klebold and Eric Harris entered Columbine High School in Colorado on an April morning. Harris was armed with a 12-gauge pump-action shotgun and a 9mm carbine and thirteen ten-round magazines of ammunition. Klebold had a semiautomatic handgun and a 12-gauge double-barreled sawed-off shotgun. They tried to set off a propane bomb in the cafeteria, then started shooting. By the time they were done, they had killed thirteen of their fellow students and injured twenty-four others. As the police closed in, they both committed suicide.

Harris had a long history of breaking into vans and stealing computers. He could be charming; he'd once convinced a probation officer to discharge him early from a diversionary and anger-management program. But in his private journal, he wrote, "Isnt America supposed to be the land of the free? how come, if im free, I cant deprive a stupid fucking dumbshit from his possessions. If he leaves them sitting in the front seat of his fucking van out in plain sight and in the middle of fucking nowhere on a Frifuckingday night. NATURAL SELECTION. fucker should be shot." Predatory. Opportunistic. Specially exempt from rules. Lacking in remorse or empathy.

An earlier psychiatric evaluation of Harris, according to Dave Cullen, the author of *Columbine*, had reportedly concluded that he was a "cold-blooded, predatory psychopath," a charming liar with "a preposterously grand superiority complex, a revulsion for authority and an excruciating need for control," and lacked remorse or empathy. Robert Hare, a psychiatrist consulted by the FBI, has pointed out that "unlike psychotic individuals, psychopaths are rational and aware of what they are doing and why. Their behavior is the result of choice, freely exercised."

But psychotic delusions and mania with psychotic features *are* mental disorders, biochemically based, and sometimes result in violent acts directed at others. And there is another psychological manifestation that occasionally leads to violence against others in a person not ordinarily given to aggressive behavior. This is the phenomenon known legally as "extreme emotional disturbance." Unlike personality disorders, extreme emotional disturbance is an acute response triggered by specific over-whelming trauma. It is recognized as a defense in a few states.

Some years ago, I was involved in a case involving a two-year-old girl. While she and her mother were out of town on a car trip, she made statements to her mother that strongly suggested she had been molested by the next-door neighbor. The mother became nearly hysterical at this revelation because of her own history of having been raped as a young woman. She made a panicked call to her husband, who was at home in their kitchen. He was a mild-mannered man with an abhorrence of vio-lence, having been the helpless witness to a violent assault on his father as a child. He had a history of some depression but was otherwise a well-functioning person who held a good job and loved his young wife and child, whom he felt a strong protective impulse toward. He had no his-tory of criminal or violent behavior.

What happened next was horrific: he grabbed a handful of kitchen knives, bolted across the shared driveway, and burst through the screen in the neighbor's ground-floor bedroom window. There, in front of the neighbor's elderly mother, he fatally stabbed the neighbor, thirteen times. He then returned to his house and, hands and forearms splattered with blood, called 911 and asked for an ambulance.

Initially charged with first-degree murder—intentional and premed-itated homicide—he was evaluated before trial by a psychiatrist hired by the state. The psychiatrist concluded that the father had acted under "extreme emotional disturbance" and was not able at the time to control his actions. In Connecticut, this lack of rationality and self-control mat-ters; he was allowed to plead guilty to the lesser offense of first-degree manslaughter and sentenced to twelve years in prison.

In New York, a murder that occurs in the presence of "extreme emotional disturbance for which there [is] a reasonable explanation or excuse" is called murder in the second degree. But this applies only when some severe, acute, and specific emotionally traumatic event is the precipitating trigger for the murder. No such event had been identified in Dorothy's case. In any event, there was substantial question of whether she had even caused the fatal injury to Raymie.

So far, I could see no signs that Dorothy had a personality disorder. She had no previous predilection for violence or malice. She'd never aggressed against anyone, even when provoked. She'd never been suspended from school for bad behavior, never had a delinquency or assault charge or any other criminal charge against her. She had no documented drug or alcohol problem. There was no evidence that she'd ever abused any of her five children or her other grandchildren. In fact, she had consistently come to their rescue, including Raymie's. And, given my own history, I was like a tuning fork that vibrated at a special frequency in the presence of someone's anger or sadism, especially the subterranean kind, but I wasn't picking up anything.

Dorothy was dull-witted and largely ineffective, but I could detect no anger or malice in her, even against those who had clearly wronged her. She was no psychopath. *I* was more given to rage than she was, and I'd never hurt anyone and didn't plan to. Of course, I had never been under as much stress as she had, and I had never been utterly without other resources. She had no history of mania, and she reported no significant trauma in Raymie's last hours that could have triggered extreme emotional disturbance. As for psychotic delusion, if she had one, it was that Raymie could somehow magically be restored to life.

So perhaps she was just a malicious, unfeeling person who struck Raymie in anger. Perhaps she had intentionally physically abused him. Or perhaps she had been experiencing psychotic features in his last hours—a break with reality—related to post-traumatic stress disorder, exhaustion, and severe depression, in which case she might not have known what she was doing at all, or that it was wrong. This was the question I had to find the answer to. Who was she, and what was she capable of?

CHAPTER 25

I HAD MINED ALL OF Dorothy Dunn's history, followed all of her outward movements over the four decades of her life. But documents and interviews and observation tell an incomplete story; even a skilled interviewer can be fooled by a more skillful liar. And although Dorothy did not seem to be able to do anything, including lying, skillfully, I needed to plumb one more source of information about her before coming to any conclusions. This source was psychological testing; it would provide another window to her soul, and a view of herself that even she was not privy to.

Psychological testing has been a critical part of the armamentarium of a psychologist for a hundred years. It allows insights into a person's intelligence, moods, and psychological functioning—mental operations "sunk wholly below the level of consciousness"—that would not otherwise be possible. With it, I can measure a person's intellect and ability to learn and reason. I can probe their unconscious or intentionally hidden mind: sniff out their stress and anger, their sadness or bravura, their capacity for empathy and for self-control, their fantasies and preoccupations. I can see whether they are grounded in the common reality most of us share or have drifted away from those anchors we call reason and reality, to unfamiliar shores. I can discover whether they mean to be telling the truth or are trying to hide behind lies.

Part science and part art, the interpretation of psychological testing is like collecting bits of glass and putting them together until all have been used and they make a coherent mosaic, a portrait, in this case, because people are not random assortments of behaviors; there are orderly and recognizable patterns to the way personalities form. There are characteristics that occur together, and those that do not. In doing a psychological assessment, you are always looking for a "best fit" solution to a very complex three-dimensional puzzle. The picture that emerges will be the one that incorporates the greatest amount of reliable data, without violating it, disregarding it, or distorting it according to some preconceived notion of the person.

In skillful hands, psychological testing can be as useful in illuminating a person's psychological landscape as an MRI, CAT scan, or ultrasound are for revealing physiological structures. It is particularly useful when the person being evaluated wishes to create a false impression of him- or herself, as is frequently the case with criminal defendants.

This was what I was now going to subject Dorothy Dunn to, and in the end, I would see clearly what lay beneath her sullen pout. Dorothy's responses would allow me to know her even in ways she did not know herself. And it would give me more clues about whether she was simply feigning mental illness, as one must always consider in a criminal case, or was, truly, in a state of almost psychotic confusion and depression. With Dorothy, as limited as she was intellectually, there was little chance that she could "throw" the results and fake mental illness without my being able to catch her at it.

When you are a forensic psychologist who also sees patients, your world is split. When you're working with your patients, the relationship is based on trust and respect, undergirded with compassion and honesty. The assumption is that your patient is a valuable person with a future worth working for and that you share the common goal of relieving their distress and restoring their functioning. You are empathic and nonjudgmental.

But in forensic work, all this is changed. The relationship is based on skepticism, distrust, and, often, dishonesty: Is this person trying to look mentally ill as a dodge? And am I, the psychologist, feigning sympathy and acceptance in order to surmount the accused person's distrust and deception and trick her into being vulnerable and showing her hand? Of course I am; it is an adversarial role and empathy has little place in it, except as a tool to get access to the defendant's true state of mind and personality.

My goal is to root out any artifice or malingering and explain to the court what is really going on in a person's head. I poke and probe at every flaw and sore point to test out what is real. I am empathic enough to lull a person into a sense of trust, and dispassionate enough to pounce on any signs of dissimulation. It is at once one of the most honest and one of the most dishonest of undertakings. It is a lonely business. And the more lonely and isolated the defendant is, the better it works. Dorothy Dunn was almost totally isolated.

BACK TO THE JAIL I WENT. Dorothy's expression was as flat as ever. I explained to her that I had some things I would like her to try, and she acquiesced, as always.

We began with the intelligence testing. I wanted to know how bright she was. What was her capacity for problem-solving? What was her knowledge of the world? Was she able to understand abstractions and to generalize what she knew from one situation to a novel one? In other words, what intellectual tools did she have at her disposal in dealing with life?

The IQ testing is devoid of overt emotional content and is usually a safe place to start. But it proved stressful for Dorothy. She often apologized and looked embarrassed. She seemed to have a vague sense of her deficiencies but could do nothing about them.

"Where does the sun rise?" I asked.

"In the sky." She smiled shyly, seeming pleased that the question hadn't stumped her.

"In what direction must you go to get to Mexico?" I asked.

"Oh, I haven't traveled in so long. . . . I never went there. I think it's by Chicago."

I knew that Dorothy had, in fact, never traveled anywhere at all.

"How are air and water alike?" I asked.

"Water is outside, and air is outside, too," Dorothy said.

"Why do we need child labor laws?" I asked.

She looked perplexed, then brightened. "To keep people doing the right thing. If it wasn't, a lot of things might happen."

"What kind of things could happen, Dorothy?"

She squirmed in her chair.

"I don't know. You never can tell about people." She looked plaintively at me. "I wasn't no good student in school, miss," she said.

"It's all right, Dorothy. Nobody knows all of them."

I felt a little like I was slowly pulling the legs off an insect under a magnifying glass. Dorothy was clearly functioning in the intellectually disabled range. She had the general knowledge and skills of a dull eight-year-old and was capable of only the most basic problem-solving and personal care. Her thoughts had an unmistakably odd quality, as well.

We moved on. I pulled out a series of pictures and told her to make up a story to go with each picture. Her responses would tell me how she understood and interpreted relationships, whether her perceptions of reality were normal, and what her overall mood was.

Normal people—those without significant mental illness—tell stories related somehow to the picture, stories with some coherent plot or theme and organized thoughts. But Dorothy's stories were fragmented, bizarre, and incomprehensible, like images from a broken kaleidoscope. They had no appreciable relationship to the images on the cards. Her stories were dark, and all of her characters were sad, depressed, hopeless, and helpless—a mark of severe depression. Most people go through the exercise without any appreciable stress or emotional upheaval. But Dorothy got more and more upset and agitated as we proceeded. Her emotional anchors were not holding. By the time we reached the last card, sweat had beaded on her lip; she licked at it absently. When I showed her the last image, a black-robed figure sketched against an abstract background, she quickly pushed the card away, trembling. She seemed to lose herself in the image, like Alice tumbling headlong through the looking glass. I put it in front of her again, and she wrinkled her brow and pursed her lips.

"What is that?" she said, her eyes wide. She picked it up and stared at it, then put it down on the table again. "I wouldn't want to be in this one, or know nothing about this. It looks like a graveyard, at night. . . . I hardly ever be out at night. I try to do everything I have to during the day, when I can see, so nobody come out of the bushes and . . . I be out sometime if I'm sitting on the porch or taking my garbage out, that's it . . ." She stared down at the table, rubbing her face in her hands, her lips moving wordlessly.

"Dorothy . . . ?" I said.

She did not answer; her eyes looked vacant. I reached over and put my hand on her forearm gently.

"Dorothy?"

She startled, then spoke, her voice flat and hollow.

"I'm sorry, miss," she said. "I'm kinda tired."

"Let's stand up for a minute and stretch," I suggested. I stood and hunched my shoulders up to my ears, feeling the welcome stretch after two hours of sitting. Dorothy stood, too, but seemed uncertain what to do, shifting her weight from one foot to the other, looking down at the worn linoleum floor, with its pattern of gray on gray.

"Is there more we have to do?" she asked.

"No more of those pictures," I said. "We're going to do something different." The matrons don't appreciate it if I leave them a prisoner distraught or incoherent, with them having to pick up the pieces and settle someone down. And I needed to know whether Dorothy could steady herself.

She sat down heavily, giving another deep sigh.

I switched to the least stressful task I could.

"Dorothy, can you draw a picture of a person for me, please?" I said, pushing some blank pages and a pencil across the table to her. The pencil was a violation of her suicide precautions; I hoped the matron wouldn't catch us.

She took the pencil in her fist, using the awkward grip of a child. Her tongue worked in and out as she labored at the drawing. A stick figure emerged, with a big head, exaggerated eyes and ears, and arms with little hand buds and spiky, long fingers. It was a picture like those drawn by four-year-olds, those who are mentally deficient, and the psychotic. She set the pencil down, rubbing her face with her hands.

"Tell me something about this person," I said.

"I don't know nothin' about this person," she said, looking befuddled. Her voice had taken on a strained tone; her brows were knit. "I never met him."

I felt the hair on the back of my neck go up. Had this faint squiggle of lines, this figment of her imagination, suddenly become *real* to Dorothy, someone you could meet? Someone independent of her imagination and her pencil? This crossed over into the netherworld between the real and the unreal, fact and delusion.

I had one last thing I had to do—the famous "inkblot" test. There was a risk to this; a vulnerable person can lose her bearings when doing a Rorschach. But it would give me crucial information: Was she able to see the world in conventional ways? Was she able to keep herself together and her thoughts organized when confronted with a stressful task? What was her principal emotion—resentment, anger, fear, sadness? Was she able to keep her emotions firmly in check and not lose control of herself? Was her inner world a place of calm and order or more Hieronymus Bosch or Salvador Dalí?

I didn't want to stress her to the point that she broke down and became psychotic; the matron of the women's ward wouldn't be too happy about that. But after all, I had to determine which side of sanity she was on, and where she had been when Raymie died. How close to the edge was she right now? How much stress would it take to move her from sane to psychotic? I'd have to risk it.

I pulled out the first image and set it down on the table in front of her.

"What does this look like to you, Dorothy?" I asked.

She studied the image. She picked it up. She put it down.

"I don't got no idea about nothing like that," she said, pushing it away.

"Take your time," I said, putting it in front of her again. I felt like a doctor pressing on a broken bone to see how much it hurt.

There was a long pause. Dorothy burped.

"'Scuse me," she said. "I'm not feeling so good today."

"I know. Just do the best you can," I said.

"I be thinking about my children. They won't let me see my children. I ain't seen them since I been here. I don't know is they all right. I wanted to send them a letter, at least, but they won't give me no pen or pencil."

"I'm sorry, Dorothy. I know you miss them." I thought it was inhumane to allow her no contact and couldn't imagine how I would bear it myself.

I placed the card in front of her again, and she looked at it dully. "Tell me what it looks like to you," I prompted again.

"It might be two animals or something. I don't know about this part. This picture looks too weird. Maybe animals."

It looked nothing like animals.

"What makes it look like animals?" I asked.

"It could be a dog, with long ears, because everybody don't have their ears cut. . . . And a tail," she continued. "Now people take their dogs to the vet more than ever, you know, but . . ." Her mind wandered off. "I don't know," she finally said.

As I presented image after image, she fell apart completely, sitting slumped in her chair, chin on chest, as if in some trance, mumbling incoherently and trembling. She seemed unaware of my presence or even her own in our stark cubicle, with its glaring fluorescent lights that cast no shadows. Her responses and her demeanor were like those of the people I had worked with in a psychiatric facility for the severely mentally ill.

The evidence was clear: her thoughts were clouded and in disarray; her inner world as fractured and distorted as the shards of a broken mirror. It was a dark and scary place for her, and she was like a lost child, wandering. The only monsters here were in her head. I realized that the confused and dilapidated spaces in her home—its piled-up furniture, haphazardly boarded-up windows and darkened rooms, the rancid heaps of soiled clothing littering the floors, and the bare cupboards—were a reflection of the inner spaces of her mind. She was depressed, with psychotic features. And if she still looked this crazy now, after months of stability and adequate sleep in jail, what had her state of mind been when she was exhausted and alone, on the night Raymie James took his last ragged breaths?

CHAPTER 26

THE STORY OF DOROTHY and her children is also in many ways the story of Child Protective Services.

Child Protective Services was called when Dorothy was a child, after a teacher observed the marks her father had left on her. But CPS did nothing to protect Dorothy, time and again. The cigarette burns, extension-cord scars, welts, and, finally, burns from a scalding pot of water apparently went unremarked.

CPS was also called, years later, when Dorothy left her own infant home alone as she walked to the store to buy milk and diapers, and then when she did so again. But it did nothing to protect her children or offer her the assistance she and they so clearly needed. And it was called in again when Dante was terrorizing his mother and sisters as a young teen and skipping school to hang out and smoke weed. Dorothy contended that the caseworker had told her to beat the boy, to punish him more severely, but that seemed so unlikely as to be impossible, and Karen had not been able to get hold of those records as yet.

Child Protective Services was alerted to Precious Love and her children for the first time when Precious was eighteen years old, living out on the street with her first two babies. A caseworker talked with Precious briefly and gave the children a cursory glance. He heard that Dorothy was helping out with the children and wrote in the case log, "Precious is receiving emotional and logistical support from her mother, for her own care and the care of her children," and he closed the case.

But even during this brief encounter he should have seen that the children's situation was precarious. He described Precious as having "severe emotional reactions" and being reclusive. He alluded to the history of domestic violence from the parade of men who had been in Dorothy's home just long enough to plant seed, with about as much thought as taking a piss, before moving on. Dorothy was taking care of it, he would later testify, so there was no need for him to do anything. Like most CPS caseworkers, he was undertrained and underpaid, and his caseload was too large.

Precious and her children came to his attention again the next year, when he got another call about the homeless woman and her children. Again he noted that Dorothy was "providing support when she is able." And without further contact, without ever going out to revisit the children, he again closed her case. He had other, more pressing cases, he later testified.

It was shortly after that encounter that Precious gave birth to her son, Raymie. She was twenty-three years old, mentally disabled and addicted to drugs, and now she had four children, none of whose fathers assumed any responsibility for their offspring as they bounced from one bed to another, one woman to another, like rolling stones. Raymie's father wanted nothing to do with him.

Raymie was born under a bad star: premature, weighing barely five pounds, and addicted to cocaine, his scrawny body racked by spasms and convulsions. And yet, once he had put on some weight in the newborn nursery, he was discharged to his mother with no follow-up from Child

Protective Services. A visiting nurse, Kathleen Walker, happened to find Raymie and Precious at Dorothy's house when it was time for his four-week-old checkup and discovered that he had toxic lead levels. She told Precious to get treatment for him before it did permanent damage to his brain, but Raymie never got the needed treatment.

When he was six months old, Dorothy, having a dim recollection that babies need "shots," snuck Raymie to the doctor, unbeknownst to Precious. When the nurse removed his filthy clothes and soiled diaper, she gasped: he weighed barely more than a newborn. She told Dorothy to take him right to the hospital's emergency room, and Dorothy did, though she told me, "He didn't look no skinnier to me than my other babies had."

Raymie displayed a ravenous appetite in the hospital and began to look like a normal child, rather than the sunken, cadaverous creature Dorothy had brought in. It was clear that he had failed to gain weight only because Precious had not fed him. Dorothy came when she could to hold and feed him, and when he reached a safe weight, Dorothy brought Precious to the hospital to get him. She had combed Precious's hair, she told me, and dressed her up in clean clothes. Precious put out her arms when Dorothy told her to, and the nurses placed Raymie in them.

"Who's this?" Precious said.

I've seen this, a mother's failure to recognize her own child, three other times in all my work with abused children, and it is not a good sign. Those mothers were profoundly mentally ill. And yet Raymie was again discharged to his mother, with no plans for follow-up by Child Protective Services, visiting nurses, or anyone else but Dorothy.

When Raymie was eighteen months old, Dorothy once again got the chance to sneak him off to the pediatrician. Raymie's lead levels were very high, and he was receiving no treatment. The doctor's records indicate that Raymie was severely hyperactive, impulsive, and aggressive. The nurse called Child Protective Services to report the medical neglect, which was threatening to cause permanent brain damage. A new case-worker returned her call.

"Are there any signs that the mother is physically abusing them?" he asked.

"No, but the mother is mentally ill, and they're not getting medical care."

"Her mother looks after her and the kids," the caseworker replied.

There were no marks, no bruises, no fractures. These kids were just another few of the thousands of disadvantaged kids who could use help and, in the best of all possible worlds, would get it. But that wasn't the world they lived in.

"There's only so much I can do," he said. "It's not an emergency."

I THOUGHT OF THE beautiful child Danielle, whom I had lost so many years before in Detroit. Danielle and her mother lived with her mother's boyfriend, a petty thief and drug abuser. He lost his temper one day and threw Danielle across the room, breaking her leg. We determined that he was the abuser, not the mother, and that Danielle and her mother had a close, positive relationship. The mother didn't seem to pose any danger on her own, so we sent the guy to prison and let Danielle return home, on condition that the Department of Social Services regularly monitor the situation. We figured Mommy wasn't so good at picking men and could make the same mistake again.

I moved on to my other cases and thought no more about Danielle. Until six months later, that is, when I was reading the local section of the morning newspaper, the *Detroit Free Press*, and saw this headline: "MAN THROWS CHILD TO HER DEATH FROM 4TH STORY WINDOW." The article reported that a three-year-old girl named Danielle—*my* Danielle—had been thrown from a fourth-floor apartment window in a moment of rage by her mother's *new* boyfriend. No Social Services caseworker had been out to check on Danielle even once in those six months. I was profoundly saddened and felt partly responsible. Little has changed for the better; chronically under-resourced and overburdened, a Band-Aid on our social ills, CPS still fails to provide the needed ongoing monitoring of an at-risk child and family in far too many cases.

I thought, too, of Leilani Bernier, whose case had first brought me into the prosecutor's office. Leilani, at six weeks old, had been found by her pediatrician during a routine visit to have several broken bones in various states of healing, as well as retinal hemorrhages, probably from being shaken. The court determined that her parents had abused her and placed her in foster care.

But only two months later, unaccountably, the caseworker from Child Protective Services decided that it was now safe at home and returned the child to her parents. In less than a week, Leilani was dead of a skull fracture. A 2018 review of CPS showed that in only one case out of three did CPS investigators dig "deep enough into family histories and circumstances to analyze the likelihood of future maltreatment." And average turnover among protective workers nationally is two years—not nearly long enough to develop expertise. The county prosecutor hired me as a special assistant district attorney to investigate the county's handling of child abuse cases, to find out if anyone could or should be prosecuted for a gross dereliction of duty and common sense. Six months later, my special grand jury issued a two-hundred-page report detailing the failings in the system and making direct recommendations for change, including increased funding, increased staffing, increased training, and smaller caseloads.

But nothing has changed. Change takes money and steady commitment, and abused children have no advocacy group and do not vote. Three-year-old Brook Stagles was beaten to death in her home in the city in 2016 and died an agonizing death from ruptured intestines and sepsis. An investigation revealed that "no apparent action" had been taken in response to earlier calls to CPS from her grandparents reporting suspected abuse. The investigation also noted that reports of suspected abuse in Monroe County, New York, where Brook lived and died, rose by 32 percent between 2014 and 2017, with no increase in staffing levels, and that the county CPS unit had twenty-two unfilled positions on investigation teams and six on management teams. Some caseworkers have caseloads of more than fifty per month, instead of the recommended fifteen.

The investigation noted that "issues with Monroe County's agency oversight are not new: in 1979, in response to the 1977 beating death of three-month-old Leilani Bernier, an investigation by the District Attorney's Office into handling of child abuse cases here found child protective workers were underqualified, poorly trained and not properly supported by the Department of Social Services."

AFTER THE NURSE'S CALL, the CPS caseworker placed Raymie's case into the purgatory of "Inactive Status," having taken no action at all.

He was busy.

In fairness to the caseworker, he himself had never raised a child, never been destitute, mentally ill, or mentally retarded. He was three years out of social work school with a crushing caseload that showed no signs of abating, and he hadn't had a decent raise since he'd taken the job. He could have made more money as a bartender. Whatever early optimism and crusading spirit he may once have had was probably already worn down.

And when he was called for what would be the last time to protect Raymie, after Precious, raving and incoherent, had run out of time at the Salvation Army shelter, he dropped the child off with Dorothy, in spite of her protests that she wasn't up to it. He turned, went down the old porch steps, and never looked back. He never weighed the child or examined his body to see what condition he was in when he was deposited on Dorothy Dunn's porch.

"It was only a neglect call," he would testify. "I had no obligation."

And, contrary to all reason and sense, he was right. The law requires him to "investigate" reports of suspected neglect and abuse, but neither law nor departmental policy specifies that, as part of a neglect investigation, he ascertain the child's physical condition to determine if there are injuries or signs of abuse.

CHAPTER 27

K AREN HUGHES' FIRST HOPE had been to convince the court that her client was not competent to stand trial. Failing that, she had two options as a defense attorney: She could try to create reasonable doubt about whether Dorothy had caused the fatal head injury at all—perhaps it had happened in a fall, as Alice said, and then she would have to use the psychological evidence to show that Dorothy had not reacted with the depraved indifference that constitutes second-degree murder in failing to get him medical help: she was too impaired to understand the situation and that, rather than the depraved indifference, explained why she hadn't gotten him help after the injury. But if the jury believed that Dorothy had caused the injury by striking Raymie in the head, Karen hoped to argue that Mrs. Dunn had been legally insane at the time: that she had not realized what she was doing, and had not known that it was wrong. This second argument depended upon my coming to the conclusion that Dorothy met the legal definition of insanity on the night of Raymie's fatal injury and death. And then, if she was very lucky, Denny Gallo would accept my opinion and dismiss the charges or agree to accept a plea of guilty to some lesser offense, like endangering the welfare of a child. More likely, he would hire his own psychiatric expert to examine Dorothy and offer an opinion. The case would go to trial, and the jury would have to decide whether the defendant was sane, and therefore guilty, or insane, and not guilty. My dilemma in offering an opinion about insanity was going to be that the legal definition of insanity does not fit well with any psychiatric understanding of whether a person had an evil intent, knew what they were doing, and had the ability to control their actions.

The law regarding the insanity defense has often blown with the prevailing political winds rather than adhering to its original ethical and moral roots. Sometimes it has been briefly enlightened in unexpected ways, but often doubling back on itself, driven by anger and fear and almost always subject to the effects of privilege or poverty, politics, or position. As psychiatrist Phillip Resnick observed, "Lawyers have never been receptive to psychiatric attempts to modify the law" and "precedents were established without the benefit of any scientific help."

Prosecutors are theoretically answerable to some vaguely defined notions of justice and fairness. But they are also charged with "insuring the public safety by preventing the commission of offenses through the deterrent influence of the sentences authorized." They are elected by a public that wants long prison sentences when wronged. A prosecutor who wants to be reelected will want to be seen to vigorously prosecute those whom society condemns. This temptation is likely to be even greater when the aggrieved is a high public figure and the accused is someone of low estate. But sometimes events surprise us.

In 1912, just a few years before Dorothy's mother was born, Teddy Roosevelt, who was seeking a third term as president, failed to win the nomination of the Republican Party and formed a third party—the Bull Moose Party—and began actively campaigning for president. John Flammang Schrank did not approve. Schrank, who considered himself an astute student of history, felt that running for a third presidential term violated a basic tenet of American democracy. And then, too, the ghost of William McKinley had come to him in a dream and hinted that Mr. Roosevelt, who ascended to the presidency upon his demise, had been his true murderer.

Schrank began dogging Roosevelt and finally shot him during a campaign stop in Wisconsin. Mr. Roosevelt was wounded in the chest, though not gravely enough to cut short his campaign speech. Schrank was wrestled to the ground and arrested without protest. He freely admitted shooting Mr. Roosevelt with intent to kill. He was coherent and intelligent and had planned carefully. He was described by his jailers as quiet, well behaved, and generally cheerful in temperament, and he maintained that he was entirely sane.

But the district attorney, rather than rushing to trial, suggested that either Mr. Schrank should be tried for attempted murder or the judge should appoint a commission of alienists (psychiatrists in today's parlance) to examine him and determine whether he was competent to stand trial. The local newspaper screamed that the DA was a socialist.

The judge, in appointing five physicians, the court's own neutral experts, to examine Mr. Schrank, said,

> I have decided to take this method of procedure instead of a jury trial, because as a rule in trials by jury the case resolves itself into a battle of medical experts, and in my experience I have never witnessed a case where the testimony of experts on one side was not directly contradicted by the testimony of as many or more experts on the other side. Where men especially trained in mental and nervous disease disagree, how can it be expected that a jury of twelve laymen should agree? Such testimony has been very unsatisfactory to the jury and to the court. . . . Worse than that. It has been a scandal to the medical

profession, a source of travesty to judicial procedure and all too often a means of defeating the ends of justice.

All five experts agreed that Schrank was "suffering from insane delusions" and "unable to confer . . . intelligently with counsel or conduct his defense." The judge ruled that he was incompetent to stand trial, and Schrank was committed to a mental hospital until such time as he might become competent to stand trial, which he never did.

It is not entirely clear whether this result was in keeping with the strict letter of the law, but it seems a just result. In the words of the Roman playwright Terence, "Rigorous law is often rigorous injustice." Had Schrank been found competent to stand trial and tried, the prosecutor would doubtless have won a conviction because, in spite of Schrank's psychotic delusions and moral confusion, he "knew" what was legally right and what was wrong. The technical question in Dorothy's case would be whether she "knew" what she was doing and that it was wrong—if in fact she had done any wrong. But the real question was what would constitute a just result?

CHAPTER 28

Dorothy Dunn was charged with second-degree murder in New York State. Each state is free to make its own laws, subject only to the Constitution, as interpreted by the Supreme Court. Thus, people regarded as legally insane and not guilty in one state can be considered sane and guilty just across the road, in a neighboring state. But some judges are so admired for their sagacity that their legal reasoning and rulings, while not legally binding on other states, are highly influential. Judge David Bazelon, in the District of Columbia, was one of these judges, and that is how Monte Durham, a no-account thief with a long legal and psychiatric history, briefly became an unlikely hero in the history of the insanity defense in 1954. He was charged with housebreaking, and his defense attorney entered an insanity plea. The presiding judge ruled that the prevailing M'Naghten test of insanity was "an entirely obsolete and misleading conception of the nature of insanity."

He explained that when a criminal act is the product, or result, of a mental disease or defect "moral blame shall not attach, and hence there will not be criminal responsibility." This echoed the more enlightened reasoning of the Hadfield case 150 years earlier. Under this ruling, a person whose act arose directly out of an insane delusion and wouldn't have occurred but for that delusion would be not guilty by reason of insanity. This became known as the "product" test of insanity.

Many states, including New York, soon adopted this "test" of insanity and began looking at whether a defendant's wrongful act was the product of mental illness and would not have occurred but for that illness. Under this test, the question in Dorothy Dunn's case would be whether her maltreatment of little Raymie, and her failure to get him the needed medical care after his injury, was mainly the product of her mental illness, exhaustion, and intellectual deficits, rather than malice and abusive intent. If so, she would be not guilty by reason of insanity. But within a decade after the Durham case, most states abandoned this approach to legal insanity, feeling it was too liberal and too dependent on the opinions of experts.

The next attempt to reform the law was in 1964. The American Law Institute, recognizing that the M'Naghten rule neither satisfied the original philosophical and moral intent of the insanity defense nor reflected modern psychiatric understanding, drafted an updated definition of legal insanity: a defendant would be not guilty by reason of insanity if he "lacks substantial capacity to appreciate that his conduct is wrongful, or lacks substantial capacity to conform his conduct to the law."

This language harkened back to the idea that a person should be capable of understanding his actions, not just have some factual awareness of them, to be considered guilty. And it took into account two psychiatric realities: a person may have some literal knowledge of his actions without understanding that the act is wrong, and he can also, because of severe mental illness, be unable to control his behavior.

But courts continued to struggle to define what was meant by "mental disease or defect." Did it refer to *any* psychiatric symptom or condition or only certain ones? Was severe depression to be considered a mental disease or defect? And what about the additive effects of multiple mental illnesses, or of diminished intellect combined with mental illness, or of the impact of childhood abuse or trauma plus mental illness and/or cognitive disability? Nonetheless, the ALI definition of insanity was adopted by about half the states and was also the federal law when John Hinckley attempted to assassinate President Ronald Reagan in 1981.

When Hinckley, seeking to impress the actress Jodie Foster, with whom he was infatuated, shot President Reagan, all of this became moot. He declared that his act was "the greatest love offering in the history of the world." He said, "At one time Miss Foster was a star and I was the insignificant fan. Now everything is changed. I am Napoleon and she is Josephine. I am Romeo and she is Juliet."

Tried for attempted murder, Hinckley was found not guilty by reason of insanity by the jury because he was clearly psychotic and delusional and his attempted assassination was the direct product of his delusion. He was thus insane under the tests in Durham and the ALI.

Reagan, after recovering from his wound, proposed new restrictions on the insanity defense. In an act reminiscent of the House of Lords after the M'Naghten acquittal, Congress hurriedly passed the new Insanity Defense Reform Act, placing tight restrictions on the insanity defense. It was essentially a restatement of the old M'Naghten rule, rolling back the clock 140 years. Now, no matter how psychiatrically impaired, intellectually challenged, delusional, or psychotic defendants were, they would be sane and guilty as long as they "knew" in some purely factual way what they had done and that it was legally wrong. And the burden was no longer on the state to prove sanity; it was on the defendant to prove insanity. This is a substantial departure from the general principle of criminal law that the burden is on the state to prove every element of an offense, state of mind and intent being among the most crucial.

Reagan, never much of an intellectual and perhaps already showing signs of the dementia no one had yet acknowledged, quipped, "If you start thinking about even a lot of your friends, you have to say, 'Gee, if I had to prove they were sane, I would have a hard job.'" And under this new law, proving insanity by a "preponderance" of the evidence (51 percent) was no longer enough; now the evidence had to be "clear and convincing" (meaning highly and substantially more probable than not).

The federal Insanity Defense Reform Act of 1984 became the law in all federal courts. Four states abolished the insanity defense altogether (Idaho, Kansas, Montana, and Utah). Idaho's penal code now specifies that "mental condition shall not be a defense to any charge of criminal conduct." Several states adopted "guilty but mentally ill" laws, requiring that a person not guilty by reason of insanity under the former standard would now be found guilty and convicted, forced into psychiatric treatment, and then returned to prison to serve out the remainder of the regular criminal sentence. Half of the states, including New York, reverted to variations of the M'Naghten rule from nearly a century and a half before. Even this retrenchment was not enough for Vice President Dan Quayle, who echoed the sentiments of Queen Victoria, pronouncing that the insanity defense "pampered criminals and allowed them to kill with impunity."

Richard Lowell Nygaard, a former U.S. Court of Appeals judge and respected legal scholar, notes that the legal definition of insanity, "nebulous and often psychologically meaningless terms" results in "almost wholly arbitrary decision[s] as to who knows 'right' from 'wrong.'" And Bruce J. Winick, a scholar of therapeutic jurisprudence theory, has come to the conclusion that "the imprecision of legislative attempts to define mental illness . . . 'allow and mask arbitrariness and discrimination in the application of the law.'"

I'd argue that it not only invites but necessitates arbitrary discriminations on the part of jurors, who are not qualified to assess the relative merits and reliability of apparently conflicting expert opinions and can only look at a defendant and feel some empathic connection or not.

Unfortunately, it is hard to feel such a connection to a person who is a stranger to you, whose voice you will never hear if they don't testify, and who is mentally ill. This effect is magnified if the person is also racially, ethnically, or culturally distinct from you.

THIS WAS THE state of things as Jared Lee Loughner walked up to Senator Gabby Giffords and a cluster of her supporters in 2011 and began firing, killing six people and wounding nineteen others, including Gabby, who took a bullet to the head. The arresting sheriff remarked, "Based on what I've seen, he is psychotic, he has serious problems with reality, and I think he's delusional. Does he meet the legal test of guilty but insane? I don't know." He also remarked: "There's no doubt in my mind that the whole trial will be about did he know right from wrong."

The sheriff was right: Loughner was clearly psychotic and delusional—no one disagreed about that—but he just as clearly knew that he had shot people and that shooting people is, in a general sense, wrong; this left his attorneys with little to work with in terms of the insanity defense. They suggested that he plead guilty in exchange for a life sentence instead of the death penalty. This was sound advice, and he followed it.

And this is where things stood in New York on the day I was asked whether Dorothy Dunn had been legally insane at the time of her grandson's death. If she had abused and killed the child, as the police, medical examiner, and prosecution maintained, had she *known* what she was doing, and that it was wrong?

CHAPTER 29

A MONTH HAD PASSED since I'd last seen Dorothy Dunn. The trial date was fast approaching, and I had two weeks left to complete the evaluation. I was avoiding it, and her. The legal and moral morass of her guilt or innocence, her sanity or madness, was wearing on me. There would be no simple solution. But there was no time left for excuses.

I headed back to the jail. The bleak, wind-swept plaza abutting the jail was buffeted by icy crystals like shards of glass that stung my cheek and made my eyes water. A torn plastic bag skittered by. The trees were still bare, and patches of crusty snow, grayed and grimed, clung to the still-frozen earth. I checked in at the visitors' lobby, locked away all my belongings, save one pen and pad of paper, followed a guard through the rat maze of corridors, and found myself sitting once again across from Mrs. Dunn in our tiny room. She had been in jail for five months now, her three youngest children dispersed into separate foster homes. She had been allowed to neither see nor write to them.

I didn't think Dorothy had intentionally and wantonly inflicted pain or harm on Raymie, and I didn't think she'd caused the fatal injury. But

I knew she needn't have caused it to be guilty of murder in the second degree. The words of New York penal law echoed in my head: merely consciously disregarding the risk to Raymie's life in a way "that is a gross deviation from the standard of conduct that a reasonable person would observe in that situation" was sufficient to establish guilt. The question was, with her limitations, was it just to hold her to the standard of an average, reasonable person?

It was time to probe Dorothy about those last moments or hours of Raymie's death. What had been her state of mind on that last day?

"Tell me about when Raymie came to stay with you the last time," I said.

"I got him before school got out," Dorothy said, rubbing her forehead. "I can't remember just when." It had been in April, I knew. Dorothy's hands were shaking, and there was a tremor in her voice. "The man from Protectives brung Raymie over. He said I had to take him in, he was my responsibility and he don't got nobody else." Dorothy gave a soft, lowing moan, rocking on her chair. "I told him I couldn't take Raymie. I told him my other children needed me and Tonette weren't doing that good."

Tonette had been suspended from school multiple times that year for aggressive behavior, but no one had offered any special services or support.

Dorothy paused, wiping her nose and lip on her bare arm. "I knew Raymie needed a lot. I was afraid to take him. But that man, he told me there weren't no other way. He told me I had to take him, for Precious." She shook her head. "Tonette, she was mad about it. She'd try to pinch him or kick him, when she thought I wouldn't see. But I told her, 'Raymie needs somebody to love him and do for him.'" Her shoulders began to heave with silent sobs. "Oh, Lord," she said, "what we gonna do now?"

BY THE TIME school let out that June, after almost three months with Raymie, Dorothy had no longer had the strength to get up in the morning to get the younger children off to school. She was up most of the night, every night, with Raymie, who wouldn't stay in bed, and she was exhausted.

"Raymie, he just stayed up all night, eating," she said. "I was trying to full him up. At first, I thought maybe I ain't feeding him enough, because he was real small. He'd sneak into the kitchen and eat right out of pots cooking on the stove. Or he'd go down at night when we was all sleeping and take spoiled food out of the refrigerator and eat it and make himself sick. I didn't understand why he would still be hungry, because I thought I was feeding him enough. . . . I didn't want him in the kitchen because he took a pot hot off the stove, while it was cooking, and burned himself. . . . He didn't even cry, just sat there on the floor and ate the food. . . . I didn't even know he burned himself till later, when I bathed him." She shook her head. "My other boy did it when he was small, and I beat him and he stopped."

She thrust her tongue absently into the space where her two upper teeth should've been, a nervous gesture I'd seen her do before. Since she'd lost those teeth, she'd been self-conscious about her looks, she said. That was why she got the wig, to try to improve her looks, and why she had always kept her mouth shut, unsmiling, since. Dorothy paused and closed her eyes for a moment, and then began to cry.

"I'd try to stay up with that boy, and he out-stayed me up. Then he'd be up early again with us in the morning. He'd pick at the scab at night, when I couldn't watch him. I just couldn't stay up round the clock with that boy."

The medical examiner had documented the scabbed-over burn in the autopsy report, including it among the "horrific abuse" Dorothy had inflicted on Raymie. But her story was plausible to me. I didn't think she had given him that burn.

"Raymie would sneak into the kitchen at night and turn on the flame on the gas stove," Dorothy continued. "I was afraid he'd set fire to himself and the house and all of us in it. I'd try to tell him fire burns, but he didn't never listen. I'd touch him with my cigarette to show him, 'cause he didn't pay no attention to just talk. It were like he didn't understand nothing. He would just keep on doing it. I had to show him. That's how my people did me. I don't think it left a mark on him . . . not a bad mark. . . . He said, 'That hurt,' and I told him, 'Then leave the stove alone and stay out of the kitchen, so you don't get burned worse.' I thought it would teach him."

I heard raucous laughter, like the cawing of crows, and the clack of metal trays from the wardroom outside our cubicle and smelled lunch—something involving cooked cabbage—arriving on the unit.

"Dorothy, did you ever hit Raymie?" I asked.

"I'd try to talk to him first, try to make him understand," she said. "But sometimes I hit him. At first, I was hitting him with a belt, like my daddy done me. Just on his butt, with his clothes on. But I thought I wasn't hitting him hard enough, because he just kept on doing things. The Protectives told me you need to whup a child when he be's bad. By his being a boy, I thought he was tough. Raymie, he don't cry or nothing, he just keeps on doing it. So I started hitting him with a electric cord. But that put marks on him, so I stopped when I seen those. I never wanted to hurt him. I didn't never hit him when I was mad. I'd just walk away till I was calm. Then I'd hit him. That's how the Child Protectives said to do it. They told me if you're too easy on a child, they go the wrong way."

That was the second time she'd alleged that CPS workers had advised her to strike the boy. She seemed to be truthful on most subjects, even those that made her look bad, but this allegation was inherently unbelievable, and I didn't understand yet why she was making the claim.

Dorothy's tears made white salt trails down her cheeks. She told me how she became afraid to sleep at night, because that was when Raymie was wakeful and would roam the house. I thought of my elderly father: he was struggling then to care for my mother, who had advanced dementia. He didn't want to put her in a nursing home, where she would be disconsolate. But she needed twenty-four-hour supervision, and he was wearing thin, exhausted, and had begun losing his temper at her. I worried that he would abuse her. What would we call it then, if an eighty-seven-year-old man shoved his frail, demented wife during a momentary loss of control and she fell and was injured? What *should* we call it?

"I had to take care of my other babies," Dorothy said. "And I had to sleep. That boy didn't never sleep, seemed like. I got the idea of tying him up," she said, sighing. "I tied a rope around his ankle at night, and tied the other end to my wrist. That way, I knowed if he got up. I thought maybe I could sleep some if I had a sure way to wake up if he started going round the place."

I thought of the ligature marks the medical examiner had described around Raymie's ankle, raw in places and infected. Dorothy cried softly, dabbing at her eyes.

"If you didn't do it tight, he would just take it off, slip his foot right out of it, and go in the kitchen," she said. "But when I gave him a bath, after a few weeks, I saw his leg. I realized it was putting marks on him . . ."

When Dorothy noticed the mark, a deep red wound around his ankle that he had been picking at, she had stopped tying him, she said, but she soon became so exhausted that she began falling asleep, in spite of herself, during the day. This left Raymie free to wander unsupervised. So she once again resorted to tethering him during the day, tying the other end of the cord around a heavy heating grate in the floor, trying to keep him within the safety of the six-foot radius while she drifted off. She sighed again.

"He's a good boy, but he don't have no sense, really. You got to watch him all the time."

A chill went up the back of my neck: present tense. She was speaking of him in the present tense, as if he were still alive.

The fluorescent lights flickered and hummed.

Judges have ruled that depraved indifference "reflects a wicked, evil, or inhuman state of mind . . . as manifested by brutal, heinous, despicable acts . . . deficient in a moral sense." Or as the court held in *People v. Suarez*, "When the defendant intends neither to seriously injure, nor to kill, but nevertheless abandons a helpless and vulnerable victim in circumstances where the victim is highly likely to die, the defendant's utter callousness to the victim's plight—arising from a situation created by the defendant—properly establishes depraved indifference."

Raymie was surely a helpless and vulnerable victim. But was Dorothy Dunn, with her limited intelligence, profound exhaustion and depression, and fractured grasp of reality, utterly callous as to his plight? Was she deficient in a moral sense, and, therefore, guilty of second-degree murder?

CHAPTER 30

WHAT DO INTELLIGENCE or mental illness have to do with the capacity to have guilty intent (*mens rea*), moral comprehension of one's acts, or reckless disregard and depraved indifference?

We can't know exactly what people in the Dark and Middle Ages meant when they talked of "madness" or "lunacy." But it is likely that "lunacy" was mania, the manic end of the spectrum of bipolar disorder, in which a person's behavior is greatly accelerated. Though during a manic episode a person can be coherent and perform complex acts, he can also cross over into an agitated psychosis and be raving and incoherent, with hallucinations, delusions, and irrational thoughts and behaviors. I knew a churchgoing woman who ran down the street brandishing a butcher knife and singing hymns at the top of her lungs in a manic state, and a prim kindergarten teacher who raced naked through the streets in the middle of January one brutally cold Friday night.

In this state, people are unable to be self-aware, to monitor or curb their behavior, or to accurately perceive reality. Both of the women above, once restored to normalcy through creative pharmaceutical interventions, vaguely remembered what they had done but could give no reason for it or connect it to themselves.

The manic-depressive patient's sense of reality is significantly disturbed by the neurochemical abnormality of their brains, not by moral depravity, chastisement by God, or the intentions of the sufferer. The problem is a deficiency of lithium, without which the brain cannot function normally. Understanding, discernment, and reason are subverted, as are moral comprehension and impulse control.

If we are manic, we are not ourselves but don't know it. We can't perceive the alteration in ourselves, can't tell that anything is "off." People experiencing mania often feel wonderful, on top of the world. As neurologist Oliver Sacks observes about the particular tragedy of mania: "The paradox of an illness which can present as wellness—as a wonderful feeling of health and well-being, and only later reveal its malignant potentials—is one of the chimaeras, tricks, and ironies of nature."

Psychosis is another brain disorder, and it often has a genetic basis; people who develop a psychotic disorder often have a family history of psychosis. In Dorothy Dunn's case, both her mother and her daughter had had psychotic episodes, or "breaks." We call it a "psychotic break" because there is a break from reality; a person in a psychotic state is unable to perceive reality as the rest of us do.

Oliver Sacks relates his experience with a patient who had damage to her frontal lobes:

> "Yes, Father," she said to me on one occasion. "Yes, Sister," on another. "Yes, Doctor," on a third. She seemed to use the terms interchangeably. "What *am* I," I asked, stung, after a while. . . . "You realize the difference between a father, a sister, and a doctor?" "I *know* the difference, but it means nothing to me. Father, sister, doctor—what's the big deal?"

And thus it is for those who are psychotic. It is not *knowing* that is lost but perception, judgment, and the normal self. As Sacks says, "It is precisely the downfall of judgment which constitutes the essence of so many neuropsychological disorders."

The eruption of psychosis can be triggered by life stress and exhaustion in those with a genetic predisposition. We do not have any control over whether we become psychotic; if we have inherited the vulnerability and are subjected to enough stress, we will find ourselves there. As James Holmes's mother said in her testimony, trying to save her son from execution, "Schizophrenia chose him. He didn't choose it."

In some cases, such as postpartum psychosis, severe depression and delusional thinking seem to be caused by radical hormonal changes after pregnancy and birth. And the severity of the disorder tends to increase with each successive pregnancy, as in the case, for example, of Andrea Yates, who drowned her five children in the bathtub to save them, she said, from corruption and eternal damnation. She had a past history of depression, suicide attempts, and postpartum depression that worsened with each additional pregnancy. Echoes of Dorothy Talbye.

The human brain is remarkable, complex, and only partly understood. Though it can help us perceive and interpret the external reality around us, it can also create its own compelling "reality," independent of and indistinguishable from the external world others see and hear.

Wilder Penfield, an early researcher in seizure disorders, surgically opened patients' skulls while they were conscious and electrically stimulated discrete areas of their brains. This caused "intensely vivid hallucinations of tunes, people, scenes, which would be experienced, lived, as compellingly real." Temporal lobe seizures can cause hallucinations and "memories" of things that have never happened but that the individual having the seizure can't differentiate from real memories of actual events. In fact, unshakable "memories," resistant to debunking post-hypnotically, can also be created by hypnotic suggestion. (This is the principal reason that hypnotically evoked "memories" are no longer admissible in court.)

Psychosis has similar global effects on the brain. It can be accompanied by hallucinations—compelling voices that say disturbing things or command a person to do bad things. The sufferer can't distinguish between these hallucinations and reality. It can cause delusions—complex, irrational beliefs not based in reality. These delusions are generally unshakably real and convincing to the sufferer.

While some sufferers appear agitated and energized, others are blank and emotionless; this often looks to judges, prosecutors, and jurors like an "absence of remorse," but it is, in fact, a symptom of the illness: detachment from reality and normal emotion. Right and wrong are simply not an issue for one who is in the throes of psychosis. It is not a matter of choice; they are in an altered state. Quoting Sacks: "If a man has lost a leg or an eye, he knows he has lost a leg or an eye; but if he has lost a self—himself—he cannot know it, because he is no longer there to know it."

Perhaps the most daunting expression of mental illness from the forensic standpoint occurs when a person suffers an acute episode of extreme emotional disturbance in response to an immediate severe shock. Colloquially, we are familiar with this: a person is told of the sudden death of their child, for instance, and becomes hysterical, or collapses unresponsively, or begins tearing out her own hair or raking his own skin bloody with his fingernails. Ordinary methods of coping and self-control are utterly overwhelmed in that moment, as inaccessible as electricity when a fuse shorts out.

We know that this occurs, though we don't know exactly what the mechanism for it is, or when or to whom it will occur. When the emotional storm causes harm to someone else, the issue is a legal conundrum. I think there is general agreement in principle that people in that state should not be held fully morally or legally accountable for their actions. The uncertainty lies in knowing who was acting out of such a state and who is merely malingering and making excuses after the fact to avoid punishment.

Might such a scenario apply to Dorothy Dunn? Had the boy's fall and bloody head been such a trauma for her that she suffered an extreme emotional disturbance—on top of her already compromised mental and psychological state and exhaustion—that prevented her from responding to his injury in the way an average, reasonable person would have? This certainly seems possible, even likely, given her fraught condition approaching that night. But juries are wary of this defense, or any defense based on mental infirmity. When things go badly, we like to have someone answer for it.

The Association for Psychological Science tells us, "One survey revealed . . . that the average layperson believes that 26% of insanity acquittees are set free. Another survey indicated that 90% of the general population agreed with the statement 'The insanity plea is used too much. Too many people escape responsibilities for crimes by pleading insanity.'"

We tend to fear the unpredictable, the unexpected, and the not-understood. And we fear the mentally ill. Samuel Johnson observed, "If a madman were to come into this room with a stick in his hand, no doubt we should pity the state of his mind; but our primary consideration would be to take care of ourselves. We should knock him down first, and pity him afterwards." Still, we need to separate the issue of safeguarding ourselves from the issue of punishment and revenge. As the legal scholar William H. Parry said, "A law that punishes a man for an act that he is unable to prevent is abhorrent to every principle of right and justice. . . . The provision requiring the insane man to be confined, if acquitted because of his insanity, is sufficient protection to the interests of the community. . . . It is but just and right that we should provide for the benefit of the accused man a test of responsibility that will not leave the brand of a felon upon one whose act was the product of a diseased mind and not of a guilty intent."

CHAPTER 31

I LOOKED AT DOROTHY, sitting across the table from me in our cubbyhole, a yawning gulf between her world and mine.

"Tell me about what happened the day Raymie died," I said.

"I was asleep on the couch," she sighed. "I didn't even hear a noise. Then one of my kids told me Raymie was in the kitchen, laying down on the floor with the sugar on him."

Her voice was disembodied and distant; I'd often observed the same sort of response in trauma victims whose senses had numbed in response to some horror or shock and in people in a dissociative state.

"Who woke you?" I asked.

"Why you have to talk to her?" Dorothy asked, pleading. "She been through enough already. Raymie dying, and her mama in jail . . ."

"I'm sorry. I need to know," I said.

"Nah," Dorothy said, shaking her head. "Leave her be."

"Who was it?" I prodded, taking her soft hand in mine. She hesitated a moment.

"It were Alice," Dorothy answered in a low voice. "She said she was sleeping upstairs, and she heard a crash in the kitchen, so she come down to see what was it. She told me she found Raymie lying on the floor in the pantry, and he just looked up at her, blinking. An' he had pulled the bag of sugar off onto hisself. I had kept it up in the high cupboard, over his head, a five-pound bag, so's he couldn't get at it. And Alice said he had that bag broke open on him, and the sugar was spilled all out on him, and on the floor."

I pictured a crime scene, the shape of a child's small body outlined in white sugar instead of police chalk. Maybe reaching for some sweetness in life had done him in.

"Alice come and woke me. I got up and went in to where Raymie was. He was still laying there in the sugar. 'Raymie, what you doing in here?' I said to him. He just looked at me. I got him up to the table and gave him some bread. Ain't no sense sending him to bed hungry. He ate kind of slow; I thought maybe he was finally getting tired. When he finished, I put the sugar up again, so's the roaches couldn't get to it. . . . Oh, please don't mess with my children. They're going through enough. They didn't want me to keep the boy, but I said he needs somebody to keep him."

I thought about Raymie eating a butter and sugar sandwich in the middle of the night, while a slow, silent bleed from falling and striking his head was compressing his brain. I thought, too, about how sociopaths are incapable of empathy. Here was this woman, alone in her bare cell, looking at a long prison sentence, and worrying about not wanting to put her children through more. She was no sociopath.

"I started asking him why did he went to the kitchen," Dorothy said. "He didn't answer. He just kept looking at me. I had to teach him not to go in there on his own; I beat him with my little wooden paddle on the legs, and on the butt. If you too easy on a child, they goes the wrong way. You gots to discipline them, so's they turn out right. I'd walk away till I was calm, then I'd hit him. That's how they said to do it.

"He didn't cry or say nothing, just kept looking and wouldn't answer me. Then he kind of stumbled a step. So I thought he was tired; I told him to go lay down on the couch, where I could keep an eye on him. I said, 'Raymie, go lay down,' and then I lied down with him. He seemed all right. He looked like he was walking all right to me, but maybe a little crooked . . ." She rubbed her hand over her face. "Usually, if there was something wrong with Raymie, he would tell me, or he would tell my daughter. I had that much trust in him. He didn't say there were nothing wrong. He just lay down when I told him."

I had seen the police crime scene photos of Dorothy's home. The nearly empty old refrigerator, its dim light illuminating mostly empty shelves; what was there to eat in there for any of them? In the narrow pantry, the photos showed a rickety wooden kitchen chair pulled up against the counter. The cupboard above it, where Dorothy had stored the bag of sugar on the high shelf, was open. The shelves were nearly bare. Sugar was spilled on the counter, on the chair, and on the floor at the foot of the chair, where Dorothy and Alice said they had found Raymie lying on his back in a bed of sugar, blinking up at them.

"I woke up," she said. "I woke up kind of late. Let's see . . ." She slumped, worn down with the remembering. "I thought Raymie was still asleep. . . . Let me think what I did. . . . Always when I wake up, I look to see if he's there by me. It's the first thing I do. He was laying there by me on the couch, all right. I was cleaning up, talking to Tonette. It started getting late, and I went to check on Raymie. I looked at him. It's unusual for him to be asleep. Maybe he's tired. . . . I looked at him . . . I think maybe I made a cup of coffee . . . no . . ." Her voice trailed off, barely audible. I leaned forward, across the small table, straining to hear, to understand. "Maybe around eleven o'clock I touched him, and I thought something might had happened to him," she said softly.

"What did you think had happened to him?" I asked quietly.

"I don't know. Usually he would get up. But sometimes he would play-sleep. I just touched him, because I didn't know if something had happened to him. . . . I checked on him. He didn't move. . . . I didn't see him do nothing. I didn't see him moving. . . . I tried to feel if he was breathing. . . . I thought I felt him moving, but I don't know was it from him, or from me. After I saw it wasn't none from him, I got scared. I laid down." She was sobbing, silently, her words garbled in the flood of tears. "I just laid down."

She stopped. I could hear the television blaring in the room beyond the door. Out where the ordinary women—the shoplifters, the prostitutes, the lucky ones—were.

"During the day, I went to sleep," Dorothy said with a sigh. "I just couldn't face it. I thought I was in trouble. I didn't know what had happened to him, if he got up again during the night and got into something. We don't know what Raymie do or what he get into."

She sighed and shook her head.

"I thought they might could blame me, 'cause I didn't watch him good enough and he got into something that hurt him."

I hesitated a moment, looking deep into Dorothy's homely, toothless face.

"Dorothy," I finally said. "The doctor said Raymie had an injury on his forehead, a big, bloody mark where somebody hit him the night before he passed. They say you hit him in the head with the paddle. Did you hit him there?"

She looked up at me, stricken.

"Bloody mark? . . . Big bloody mark?" she gasped. "I sat up with him for a while, because I was drinking water. I don't remember no marks on him. . . . No fresh marks. . . . We went to sleep after a while. . . . They said I hit him in the head? I didn't hit that boy in the head. . . . I don't think I hit him in the head. . . . I should of got up and called the ambulance. I didn't think Raymie was dead. . . . People say he cold. . . ."

She drifted off, her gaze unfocused, muddled.

And then it hit me: I realized that up until now, Dorothy had thought she was in prison for failing to keep Raymie safe! She thought he'd gotten up in the night and eaten something bad that sickened him, when she should have been supervising him. That had seemed like reason enough to her. She hadn't even noticed his head injury, or maybe she had been so impaired, or so unhinged by it, that it had been stricken from her memory. She hadn't grasped that she was accused of beating his head in, starving him, torturing him, and killing him. She wasn't aware that she was accused of wishing him dead. She had not understood the charges against her, and probably never would.

"I woke up," Dorothy said. "I looked to see where was Raymie. I just sat there and waited to get myself completely woke. I think I'll wash the clothes . . . we ate hot dogs . . . I looked in the refrigerator to see did he mess with anything that could make him sick, because it weren't like him to still be asleep like that."

She stopped. I could feel the uneasy quivering of her mind, like a body shivering with the exhaustion of unending cold. Her awareness seemed to have dipped in and out, knowing he was dead, telling herself he was merely asleep. It was doing it even now, I thought.

"What did you do then?" I asked.

"I laid down after I ate my hot dog, because I been through a lot over there. There've been killings, people selling drugs. . . . I just don't like to be around anybody's death. I didn't want to think Raymie had passed in my house." She sighed, then went on: "I tried to figure out what might have happened to him. . . . After I laid down and they was watching TV, that must be when the heat cut on and Raymie was on the heat . . . I remember moving him onto the heat. My daughter said, 'Maybe he's cold.' Alice, she said it feels like he's too cold. After picking him up and he didn't wake up, I realized . . . I must've panicked . . . I didn't want to believe he was dead. . . . I don't know what happened to him. I put him over on the heat, to warm him up. I laid down. My son Scoot, he was nervous, crazy-like. I put Raymie back up on the sofa, so he wouldn't get too hot. Them grates is hot, they can burn you. I didn't want him to get burned. I went upstairs and I laid down on Scoot's bed. I had to get myself together to talk to my children without breaking, to be strong. Especially for my little boy . . . I wasn't ready for that yet. Then I told Alice, 'I'm in trouble,' because he was there in the house with me . . . to have a child die in your presence, and you don't know why."

But as rigor mortis passed and Raymie's body began to soften again, Dorothy felt hopeful for a time that it was going to pass.

"I thought maybe he was coming around again, after all," she said. "He might have just had some kind of spell, and might recover."

And so that morning, thirty-six hours or more after his death, she walked to the phone at the Public Market and called the only person she could think of, a coworker who had been kind to her during her brief stint as a health-care aide at the nursing home, to ask him what to do.

"Raymie's some kind of sick," she said. "He won't wake up. I don't know what do I need to do."

He told her to call the EMTs, and that was how she had come to make the call to 911. "Then I called the ambulance," she told me, "and put Raymie back in the pantry, where he was."

She could have buried him quietly in the backyard and no one would have been the wiser. No one would have asked after him. No one would have missed him. No one would have even known he was gone.

The paramedics arrived and found Raymie's lifeless and decomposing body and realized that the call had come far too late to save this child.

"He'll be all right, won't he? You can fix him, can't you?" Dorothy asked.

Now, sitting there with me in the jail, Dorothy seemed pensive.

"My concern was Raymie," she said. "One night, he got up and turned the stove on. He put dry cornmeal and pepper in a pan. He was trying to fry it up." Cornmeal and pepper, just what the medical examiner had found in his stomach. "It was smoking real bad when I got there, almost ready to fire. He could've burnt hisself up, by my sleeping and him doing that on his own. When I saw that, I was so afraid, I had to just go lie down. I couldn't stop shaking. . . . I can't see me hitting Raymie. . . . I never hit him on his head. . . . When I hit him, I tried to be so careful."

She paused, sighed, and wiped her nose on her sleeve.

"We had gotten attached to him," she said.

CHAPTER 32

A PERSON IS GUILTY OF MURDER in the second degree "when, under circumstances evincing a depraved indifference to human life, he or she recklessly engages in conduct which creates . . . the death of that person." Judges in New York have defined depraved indifference as "an utter disregard for the value of human life," so that the defendant "simply does not care whether or not grievous harm will result." Depraved indifference "reflects a wicked, evil, or inhuman state of mind . . . deficient in a moral sense." So what had been Dorothy Dunn's state of mind, her intent? Had she acted recklessly, with depraved indifference? Had she realized Raymie had a head injury and was in danger, or was she too intellectually and psychiatrically impaired to be capable of the ordinary perception and understanding of an average person?

THE EVALUATION WAS COMPLETE, and I had reached a conclusion. It was not what I had expected going in.

Fancy psychological theories abound, but when it comes right down to it, you find out who a person is by watching what they do. Upon first seeing Dorothy trundled out of her house on that Saturday morning months before, with Raymie's desiccating remains in a zippered black bag much too big for his small body, I thought I was looking at a woman who had struck out at a child in selfish rage or with indifferent cruelty and depraved indifference. Her pout conveyed sullen self-justification, her flat eyes the absence of feeling or remorse. The marks on the dead child's body seemed to have been caused by abuse, each one evidence of her depravity; his starvation, proof of months of disregard, callousness, and intentional malice. I'd hated the woman. I'd wanted her held accountable. I'd wanted to hurt her.

But now I had scoured Dorothy's whole history for any signs of aggressive behavior, of malice or depraved indifference toward others, and had found none. She had never assaulted anyone, even in self-defense, even those who sorely deserved it. She had no criminal history. She showed empathy and compassion for her children and grandchildren and had often come to their aid, especially Raymie's. After all, she had already saved him from starvation once before. She appeared to be a woman who just plodded along, accepting whatever life doled out to her in the moment, without expectations. She did not strike out or rage against it; she was passive, compliant, and uncomplaining, a woman without power, without a voice. She appeared to have cared about Raymie and was filled with remorse for the child's death. She was not the monster portrayed in the press.

It was clear that she was intellectually limited and had no knowledge of nutrition or normal child development. Her problem-solving abilities were deficient. Her understanding of when and how to use medical care was almost nonexistent. She learned only by trial and error, unable to grasp concepts or abstractions and apply them to new situations.

It was also clear that she had been in the grips of severe depres-

sion, going back to her time taking care of her father, before her son
Scoot was born, well before Raymie's death, and that the depression
had intensified under the added stress and chronic sleep deprivation that
came with Raymie, a wild child. She was sad, hopeless, and lethargic.
She couldn't cope with basic household and child-care tasks. She wasn't
functioning; she could barely pick up one foot and put it down in front
of the other.

And finally, it appeared that her genetic vulnerability to mental illness, under the added insult of depression and sleep deprivation, had
driven her to a psychotic breakdown, culminating at the time of Raymie's death: it doesn't take an expert to understand that a normal, sane
person doesn't sleep with a corpse for three days, put it on a heating vent
to warm it up, and then think it can be revived. But she was not a sociopath, devoid of conscience or empathy, with depraved indifference to her
children or grandchildren or even her malevolent dead father.

It is part of my job to be a skeptic, to consider all possible hypotheses equally, including guilt and deception. I had wanted to dislike this
woman, but the data were clear. This case was about the confluence of
poverty, ignorance, mental disability, and mental illness, not about evil.
As much as I hate child abuse and those who inflict it, I couldn't find a
way to hate Dorothy. She had loved Raymie, in her way.

Everyone had failed this family: Raymie's psychotic mother and his
faithless father; the hospital that more than once sent Raymie home to a
profoundly impaired mother and never called Child Protective Services
on his behalf; the school that knew Tonette was emotionally disturbed but
offered her no services; the psychiatrist who failed to diagnose Precious's
serious mental illness and sent her home to her children with a prescription for attending night school; the social worker who returned Scoot to
Dorothy when she tried to surrender him for adoption; even Child Protective Services, whose caseworker left Raymie with Dorothy when she said

she was too overwhelmed and depressed to meet his needs, then walked away and never looked back. The same undertrained and understaffed CPS that had left Dorothy to the mercies of her own abusive father when she was a child. Now the boy was dead and suddenly everyone was interested and concerned. But none of them, except Dorothy, had cared about him until he was gone. Would Karen Hughes and I also fail the family now?

CHAPTER 33

THANKS TO THE M'NAGHTEN RULE of the nineteenth century and the Insanity Defense Reform Act of 1984, the question I was being asked was not whether Dorothy was severely mentally ill or significantly intellectually impaired or both, which she clearly was. It was not even whether she'd had an evil intent. It was simply whether she "knew," in the most elemental way, what she was doing the night Raymie died and that it was wrong. I was up against what the American Psychiatric Association calls the "imperfect fit between the questions of ultimate concern to the law [the legal definition of insanity] and the information contained in clinical diagnosis." Richard Lowell Nygaard, a respected forensic practitioner and proponent of therapeutic jurisprudence (the view that legal sanctions should be used therapeutically, to correct and heal rather than to merely punish or extract revenge), has correctly observed that "law virtually has stood still" when it comes to the insanity defense. He notes that "with contemporary psychiatric and psychological data, the legitimate experts, who must testify about mental conditions, are unable to make accurate and scientific determinations fit into the rigid legal definitions the law imposes." He goes on to say that "our current process systematically eliminates what is psychiatrically sound and psychologically workable, leaving us with a test for responsibility that may have no relationship at all to whether the offender needs help, punishment, confinement, or a combination of all three." So, what could I swear to? Had she been, technically, "insane" at the time of Raymie's injury and death?

It would be so easy just to say that she was not insane; no one could find fault with it.

I picked up the phone and called Karen.

"It's time to talk," I said, and we arranged to meet in her office on Sunday morning, the only time she had free for the next week.

WE SAT TOGETHER in a conference room whose long wooden table was piled high with leaning stacks of law books. The office was cold, to save money on heating. I wrapped my fingers around my coffee cup to warm them.

The public defender's office is funded by state tax dollars and is at the mercy of the legislators who vote on state budgets and who, ultimately, serve at the pleasure of the voters. Defending alleged criminals is not popular with the public; the budget for hiring attorneys, conducting investigations, and obtaining examinations and witnesses—including expert witnesses—is paltry compared to the magnitude of the need. This means that the amount of time Karen could devote to preparing Dorothy's defense was also very limited; she had many other cases, with stakes equally high, demanding her time.

And yet Dorothy Dunn was lucky. Because Karen Hughes, after first meeting Dorothy, had thought there was something wrong with her client. It had occurred to her that Dorothy might have a psychiatric defense to the charges, and she'd resolved to obtain a psychological evaluation of her to explore that possibility. This was already an unusual occurrence; defense attorneys frequently do not perceive mental illness in defendants and do not even seek to ascertain a defendant's mental state or raise it at trial.

"What's the verdict?" Karen asked. She looked tired and preoccupied.

"Well," I said, "for what it's worth, I think Alice's story to the police was true. I don't think Dorothy inflicted the fatal head injury on Raymie; I think he hit his head when he fell off the counter. He was pulled off-balance by the heavy bag of sugar."

She raised an eyebrow and scribbled something on her yellow legal pad.

"And she's too intellectually limited to have realized he had a significant head injury and needed medical care," I added. "I'm certain she didn't know he was in any danger. Her failure to get him to a doctor was ignorance, not intentional malice or indifference."

"But what about the other injuries?" Karen asked.

"Some she clearly did—like the wound from the rope around his ankle, and some of the cigarette burns, maybe. But a lot were probably already there when he came to her. Precious used to stick cigarettes on him, and who knows what other people did to him when he was living out on the street; he was probably a hyper, irritating little kid because of his high lead levels, in utero drug exposure, and attention-deficit/hyperactivity disorder. Plus, he was living out on the streets without any real adult supervision. He would've been difficult to manage."

More frantic scribbling.

"And I don't think she had any idea he was starving," I said. "She took his big belly as a sign that he was eating too much, not too little. And he did actually gain weight while he was with her, as best I can tell."

"He did?"

"Yeah, he weighed six pounds more when he died, according to the medical examiner's report, than he had six months before CPS placed him at Dorothy's. I figure he must have lost some weight while out on the streets with Precious for those six months, so he must have gained at least six pounds since he came to Dorothy."

For the first time, I realized that Karen had not had an assistant in preparing the case. No one had read the entire messy case record but me. She hadn't had time.

Karen cut into my thoughts: "So you think she didn't know any of this because she's intellectually impaired?"

"That's part of it," I said. "But she was also severely depressed."

"We all get sad," she said.

"Not 'sad,'" I said. "She had a major clinical depression, complicated by exhaustion. And at the end, I think she became acutely psychotic. I really think she was too impaired by then to have even noticed his head injury; or maybe she *did* see it and it was a shock that sent her over the edge. She slept with a corpse for three days and then thought he could be revived, after all."

Karen stopped scribbling and looked up at me.

"But," she said, "if the jury decides that she *did* inflict the fatal head injury, are you prepared to swear that she was legally insane at the time of the blow? That's what it may all come down to."

That is, indeed, what it all came down to. Could I, in good conscience, swear that there was clear and convincing psychological evidence that Dorothy Dunn had not known what she was doing or that it was wrong? How could I swear that she *did* know it?

"I'm convinced that *if* she struck him, she didn't know what she was doing, didn't form any intent. It would be totally inconsistent with everything I know about her. The psychological evidence indicates that she didn't do it out of malice and didn't comprehend the situation; she was too out of it to know what she was doing that night or for the next several days. He died because of utter ignorance and incompetence, not depraved indifference or intent to cause his death."

"So, no depraved indifference? No guilty intent?" Karen said.

"No. I can't find any psychological evidence of it."

"So then she's not guilty of second-degree murder?" Karen said.

"She's not guilty of second-degree murder," I said.

"God," she sighed. "What am I going to do?"

Karen was a lawyer, not a psychologist. She had not studied psychology, beyond perhaps a basic college course, and, like most defense attorneys, had never before raised an insanity defense.

Karen didn't have the luxury of time; she couldn't make sure she knew each bit of evidence that led me to my opinion. I had reviewed a mountain of data, in painstaking detail, but she had seen only a molehill's worth. She had not reviewed all the data I had looked at, and she could not. Even if she had, she'd never be able to present it to a jury, in all its complexity and intricacy, the beautiful web that holds and molds human behavior, visible only to the trained eye of an experienced psychologist or psychiatrist.

It was all we could do to cover the basic concepts and terminology; they were foreign to her, as awkward and ill-fitting as a borrowed suit. But what she didn't know, she couldn't think to ask at trial. And what she didn't ask me, the jury would never hear. A witness can speak only to the questions asked. And a trial is an adversarial arena, more gladiatorial contest than enlightening seminar. It favors bright lines, not subtle shadings, a Manichaean model of black and white, right and wrong, good or evil. It is a weapon for hacking and maiming, not delicate dissection.

In cases involving a possible death penalty, defense attorneys must be "death penalty qualified"—that is, they must have special advanced training in defending death penalty cases. So much is at stake for defendants in these cases that we want to ensure competent legal counsel. But we have no such requirement for attorneys raising the insanity defense for mentally ill clients.

When the insanity defense *is* raised, we ask prosecutors without mental health expertise to decide whether to pursue a conviction against a defendant or instead to agree to a not guilty by reason of insanity plea with treatment and psychiatric detention. We ask jurors with no particular knowledge of mental illness to determine what mental health testimony to rely on when experts have differing opinions.

But this is not the only possible model that could be used. In the time of the tall sailing ships, cases involving claims of negligence in shipbuilding were recognized to be so technical that they were decided by a panel of three judges who were maritime experts, rather than by jurors, who generally had no special expertise in the intricacies of engineering and shipbuilding. We should consider having a defendant's sanity or lack thereof decided by a panel of judges with special training in psychology and psychiatry, as in the Roosevelt-era Schrank case, instead of expecting lay juries to understand and correctly weigh technical evidence about a person's intellectual functioning and mental health. If we had a more rational standard of legal insanity, one clearly related to psychiatric realities and grounded in the original ethical principle, we could have three independent evaluators examine a defendant and settle on the findings of the majority. This would be cheaper, quicker, and more just than our current system of two conflicting evaluations presented to a jury with no basis for evaluating the evaluators.

I spent the next two hours giving Karen a crash course in the mental health issues related to the case, pulling out a smattering of data here and there from the thick stack of documents about Dorothy—eleven pounds of it by that time—to illustrate the basic principles. But at the end she seemed confused, distracted, and overwhelmed. She had another big case starting Monday morning, she said, and it was hard to absorb so much technical psychological information piecemeal and in so short a time. She rubbed her eyes and pushed back from the conference table. I grew worried.

"I'll show your report to the prosecutor first thing tomorrow morning," she said, gathering up her notes. "Maybe he'll be willing to accept your finding and offer Dorothy a plea to a reduced charge—manslaughter, maybe."

"Maybe," I replied. But I didn't hold out too much hope.

I couldn't get to sleep that night, thinking about Dorothy and Raymie and the other children. I finally gave up on the idea of sleep altogether, slipped quietly out of bed, and padded into the cold, unlit kitchen. I stood alone, gazing out the window at the blackness beyond, for a long time.

The next morning, there was a phone message waiting from Karen. "I spoke to Gallo," it said. "He won't budge. We're on for trial."

Gallo would arrange a second psychiatric evaluation, by a person of his own choosing, and pursue a conviction.

Part of the fault lies with the mental health professions; we haven't established reliable enough standards for the training, expertise, and procedures required in conducting forensic evaluations. The quality and reliability varies too much from one practitioner to another. Many of us lack finely honed analytic skills. Some of us have a conflict of interest—we want an outcome that favors the side paying us, so they'll hire us again in the future. Some of us have strong personal biases or blind spots, though our training is designed to reduce this.

Some of us are too easily swayed by our wish to be liked and approved of and not made a fool of in court. Most of our professional lives as psychologists and psychiatrists are not subject to scrutiny and are answerable to the patient alone. It takes courage to testify in open court, before the media and the public, who may look askance at psychology, and to submit to questioning by attorneys whose fondest wish is to expose you as an idiot or a charlatan. It is hard to have our ethics and intelligence impugned, and not even be allowed to answer back. And it is essential, no matter how potentially painful, to ask whether our analysis stands up to the bright light of independent scrutiny.

For all that, there's something seductive about being considered an "expert": I've seen all kinds of expert witnesses—doctors, psychologists,

forensic analysts—give answers to questions for which they have insufficient evidence, just because they felt that they should somehow always
have an answer. It takes courage and mental clarity to say, "I don't know"
or "There isn't sufficient reliable data for me to form an opinion about
that" or "The data isn't reliable enough to support a conclusion." Every
time I take a forensic case, I begin with a disclaimer: I'll do my best to
answer your question, within the psychological evidence available. But
there's no guarantee that I'll be able to offer an opinion, in the end. If the
data isn't there, then my opinion won't be there, either. But no one wants
to disappoint the one who brought them to the party; there is a strong
psychological pull to say what the attorney who called you wants to hear.

And there's money to be made in the field. If you're not able to build a
robust clinical practice, you can always raise a few extra bucks by taking
on court evaluations. So the fields of forensic psychology and psychiatry,
which do not require any special certification beyond a general license,
do not always attract the ablest practitioners. Like any fields, ours have
their share of incompetents and charlatans. And judges, lawyers, and
jurors are not in the best position to spot them.

To me, there was little justice in the fact that Dorothy Dunn had
been born poor, to abusive parents, in a family saddled by mental illness. There was no justice to her intellectual deficits or the disadvantages
associated with race in the United States. There was nothing righteous
about her daughter Precious's schizophrenia or intellectual impairment
or about the victimization Dorothy had experienced from a succession of
men. Justice can sometimes seem like an arbitrary exercise, the province
of the privileged. But perhaps Gallo and I lived in worlds of very different
truths and justice and were both trying to do what we thought best.

PART II

The Trial

CHAPTER 34

DOROTHY DUNN'S TRIAL OPENED on a drizzly morning in April. The gallery was full of reporters and curious onlookers, gathered like a crowd drawn to an accident scene by the flashing lights and sirens. Deputies brought Dorothy over from the jail in shackles and directed her to take a seat next to Karen at the defense table, with a burly guard standing at her elbow. Her gray, grizzled hair had been wrestled into thick braids close upon her head by another inmate, and she was wearing a faded housedress Karen had found for her at Goodwill; Karen told me she had asked Dorothy's mother to bring some clothes for her to wear to court, but Evelyn had refused. "She done murdered my great-grandbaby," she told Karen. "She can rot naked in hell for all I care." Evelyn had also refused to meet with Karen or with me.

Denny Gallo and two assistants sat at a broad table on the right, surrounded by legal tomes and stacks of files about the case so numerous that they had to be wheeled in on a dolly. It made an impressive showing for the jury.

The judge was John Connell, who had a reputation for being intelligent and fair, but, like many judges, he was a former prosecutor; I wondered if he might have a more natural affinity for the prosecution than the defense. And I had other concerns: judges are only human, affected by their personal experiences, and some years before he had been stabbed in his chambers by a man wielding a knife. Had this sensitized Connell further against defendants? I also knew that he and his wife had adopted a baby boy from Peru four years ago and then his wife had unexpectedly died, leaving him with the four-year-old. Almost the same age as Raymie. Did this give Connell special empathy for Raymie or special anger toward Dorothy?

Trials are like duels: everyone follows the carefully prescribed, almost baroque rules, and the judge serves as the referee. But in this case, unlike a duel, the combatants did not have matched weapons. Gallo had the advantage in nearly every category: gender, age, experience, manpower, time, and financial resources. Every category but one: Karen and I believed in her client's innocence.

Gallo had already successfully used his peremptory challenges to reject more educated prospective jurors and those with any medical or psychiatric background. He had pushed for as many women on the jury as possible—there were eight women and four men; studies show that they are tougher, more unforgiving, especially of a woman who's had a child die in her care. Two of the jurors were black, and ten were white. All lived well above the poverty line. Only two had a college education or beyond, even though this case would involve complicated medical and psychiatric testimony.

The media portrayed the trial as a morality play: good versus evil, innocence versus sin. The front page of the local paper had already trumpeted,

---

TESTIMONY TODAY IN CHILD'S BEATING DEATH

---

though no beating had yet been proven. The article went on to say that the ambulance crew found the boy's "cold, stiff and battered body in the kitchen" and that the grandmother allegedly told homicide investigators that she beat her grandson "repeatedly with a wooden board because he ate too much."

At the start of the trial, Karen rose and requested a gag order, to keep the press from reporting on the case until it was over, so that negative publicity wouldn't generate public pressure against her client. Otherwise, the news reports would be like unsworn testimony that couldn't be subject to cross-examination; jurors would read them and likely think of them as "evidence," not just gossip and rumor.

"Your Honor," Gallo rejoined, half-rising from his seat, "the state opposes a gag order. After all, freedom of the press is one of our most cherished rights."

"Gag order denied," said the judge.

Karen objected to the ruling, then asked for the jurors to be sequestered, so they wouldn't see the media stories.

"I think the jurors are quite intelligent enough to differentiate between sworn testimony and media stories," Gallo said. "It would be an undue burden to sequester them."

"Request denied," ruled the judge. "No sequestration, no gag order."

"But Your Honor—" protested Karen.

"Sit down, counselor. You heard the ruling," the judge said. He turned toward the jury box. "The jurors are instructed to avoid media coverage of this case, in so far as is practical. The matter is to be decided solely based upon the evidence to be brought forth in this courtroom. Are the people ready?" he asked.

"We are," Gallo said.

"Then you may begin."

Gallo rose and strode to the jury box.

"Please the Court, Ms. Hughes, ladies and gentlemen of the jury. On the evening of September sixth, just into the early morning of September seventh, Raymie James, a three-year-old boy, closed his eyes for the last time. The last conscious moments that he spent were at the hands of a person who was yelling at him, beating him with a paddle, throwing him to the ground. His life was taken from him by the person who was responsible to protect him, who was responsible for his care. That person is in the courtroom this morning. That person is this defendant, Dorothy Dunn.

"Ladies and gentlemen, you're going to hear about the life of a little boy that was a living hell. He was beaten with a paddle, with the heel of a high-heeled shoe, with a belt. He had cigarettes put out on his chest. He was hit with kitchen implements. He was tied to objects in the house, the heating grate, the air conditioner. Tied so tightly that his ankle still showed an indentation from the rope. These acts didn't occur on one occasion and then stop. These acts occurred again and again. And all these injuries were inflicted by one person, and that person is the defendant.

"What was the history between Raymie James and Dorothy Dunn? Do those circumstances show an inhumanity, a callous disregard for the life of this little boy? You're going to hear from a number of witnesses, including Alice Dunn, the defendant's ten-year-old daughter, who was at home on the night of September 6th. She's going to tell you that she was in bed and heard a noise and found her nephew Raymie on the floor in the pantry. Raymie has sugar on him. Raymie's awake, he's alert, he's responsive, and he's made a mess. Alice will tell you that she goes to wake up her mother and that after cleaning up the mess and feeding a sugar sandwich to Raymie and then making him eat peppers, the defendant takes this little boy and begins to yell at him. Asking him how he could do this, why was he in the kitchen. And she gets a paddle and repeatedly beats Raymie James. And she'll describe to you that she sees her mother throw Raymie to the floor more than once, so that he's struck his head.

He's not able to walk properly and spits out water that the defendant gives him and then she sees the defendant lay Raymie in the front room by the air conditioner and Alice goes upstairs and goes to sleep.

"The ambulance personnel will tell you that when they get the call from 911 two days later they do an initial assessment on Raymie and he's cold, he's not breathing, there's no pulse. There's no indication of life whatsoever. You're going to hear a police technician who was standing near the defendant and overheard the defendant say, in a low voice, 'I am going to prison.' The technician said to her, 'What do you mean by that? Why do you say that?' The defendant then responded, 'I said, am I going to prison?' That is clear consciousness of guilt, that she was responsible for what's happened to her grandson. You'll hear the medical examiner testify that Raymie James died as a result of blows to the head. Blows that caused bleeding inside the skull, which caused pressure on the brain, and that pressure, those blows, are literally what killed this little boy.

"Ladies and gentlemen, at the beginning of the jury selection I talked to you about what kind of preconceived notions, what you might think when you first heard the allegations in this case. How could this happen to a little boy? You're going to hear how the defendant just didn't care about this little boy. He was taking food from her family. She never wanted him in the house. She just didn't care about him, ladies and gentlemen, it's that simple. You're going to find that this was a conscious, intentional act when she chose to beat this little boy and cause his death."

It was a performance worthy of Clarence Darrow. He shot a look at Karen and took his seat.

The judge looked at Karen. "Counselor?" he said. "Do you want to make an opening?"

"Yes," she said. She rose to make her opening statement, putting her hand on Dorothy's shoulder; it was important for the jurors to see that she was not personally repulsed by the woman, that she could stand to touch her.

"Ladies and gentlemen," she began, "everybody who looked at Raymie after he had died—the EMTs, the police, the medical examiner, child protective workers—everybody was horrified by the injuries they saw. Injuries which had nothing to do with the cause of Raymie's death, but they were so horrified by what they saw that they decided that Mrs. Dunn murdered Raymie."

"Objection," Gallo called out.

"Overruled," said the judge.

"Mrs. Dunn's daughter Alice is going to tell you that after she found Raymie on the floor of the pantry, where the sugar was kept on a high shelf, and she found him with sugar on him, that she had to go wake up her mom. It's a very important piece of evidence, ladies and gentlemen, that I want you all to focus on, because there was a fall. I suspect Dr. Welch is going to come in here and tell you that absolutely Raymie's injury was not caused by a fall, but it's ultimately up to you to decide, not Dr. Welch. And my suggestion is that he was horrified.

"Historical context, histories, are important. Raymie James did not end up at Mrs. Dunn's house because his mother, Precious Love, was strung out on drugs or alcohol. When he was still an infant, he and his three young sisters were discovered alone, unsupervised, in their mother's apartment. It was filthy, there was no food in the house. There were cockroaches everywhere. After that discovery, Precious was admitted to the hospital because she was found to be psychotic. Her girls were sent to their father, but Raymie had a different father, so Raymie went with Precious when she was released. She ended up in a shelter, and the Department of Social Services told her, You better find a place to live for you and Raymie or we're going to put Raymie in foster care.

"Mrs. Dunn had her three youngest kids living with her, but she cared enough for her child Precious Love and for her grandson, Raymie, to allow them to come live with her. And she did that because she's a caring person and she didn't want her daughter out on the street with her grandson and she wanted to give them a place to live and she didn't want to see her grandson go to foster care.

"Child Protective Services closed the case. But Precious didn't get better, she got worse. Eventually she and Raymie moved in with Mrs. Dunn's own mother. Sometimes Precious was out wandering on the street with Raymie. Mrs. Dunn took Raymie in again because she cared about him and she wanted to give him a place to stay and she wanted to make sure that he was cared for because he wasn't being cared for by Precious Love, who was eventually diagnosed as schizophrenic and involuntarily committed to the Rochester Psychiatric Center.

"What are the particular characteristics of Mrs. Dunn that created this situation where Raymie ultimately died? Mrs. Dunn does suffer from mental impairment. Coupled with that, she has a very limited IQ, and it affects her ability to function as you and I would function or to perceive what is appropriate under a circumstance or to perceive the danger in a situation. Place on top of that the many, many stressors in her life that were happening at that time, and it's going to start to make sense.

"At the time that Raymie died, things weren't right with Mrs. Dunn. She never was indifferent to Raymie. Some of the injuries that you will see on Raymie were the result of her trying to protect Raymie and her family. She became frustrated because she could not get him to behave, and she continually tried to discipline him and teach him to stay out of the kitchen, to stop playing with the stove, turning it on. To Mrs. Dunn, they were caring acts. She was never callous to Raymie, never indifferent to him. What happened here was not the result of Mrs. Dunn's evil mind, of a morally deficient intent. What happened here was not murder."

Karen sat down next to Dorothy. I looked over at Dorothy's blank, expressionless face and wondered what she was thinking. And, more importantly, what were the jurors thinking?

At the close of court that first day, Raymie's paternal grandmother, who had never before offered him so much as a crumb of bread or given

Dorothy ten minutes of respite—who had never, in fact, laid eyes on Raymie—was suddenly present, in her extravagant public grief, and available for interviews.

"She never done right by that child," she wailed to reporters, "and now he's gone. My poor baby."

How many of the jurors, I wondered, saw *that* on the evening news?

CHAPTER 35

THE PROSECUTOR'S CASE against Dorothy Dunn began in earnest on day two, with the 911 call she made. Gallo called the 911 operator to the stand. She testified that Dorothy was vague and emotionless on the phone and "resisted" giving information, "like she was trying to hide something." She went on to say that she repeatedly asked Dorothy about the child's condition and whether he was breathing, but Dorothy became "exasperated" and hung up on her. I wondered if the dispatcher would have drawn the same conclusions if the caller had sounded white and educated.

"Did she call and tell you the child needed help?" Karen asked on cross-exam.

"Well, yes."

"And give you the right address, so the ambulance could find him?" Karen asked.

"Yes. But he was already dead!" she blurted out, appearing eager for the jury to understand that she just *knew* that Dorothy was guilty.

"No more questions," Karen said.

The homicide investigator was called next; she testified that Dorothy spoke guardedly about Raymie's death. "It was like, 'I'll give you an answer when I'm good and ready,'" she said.

The jurors searched Dorothy's scowling face. It must have looked like she was capable of such an attitude.

"She didn't appear to have any remorse or feelings for the child," the investigator continued. "She was evasive. The more pointed our questions became, the more she avoided even making eye contact with us."

The jurors looked at Dorothy. She made no eye contact with them.

"Isn't it true, Officer," continued Gallo, "that Ms. Dunn showed an awareness that she had done wrong and would go to prison for it?"

This could imply consciousness of guilt.

"She said 'I'm going to prison,'" the officer replied. "I asked her, 'Why do you say that?' and she said, again, 'Am I going to prison?'"

"Thank you," Gallo said, with a smile. "No further questions."

Precious's words to the police officer that cold night in the park echoed in my head. "Am I going to jail?" she had asked, without having an idea in the world of who or where she was.

Karen rose for cross-examination.

"Did she make any attempt to hide the boy's body?" she asked.

"No, but—"

"No. And did she request a lawyer when you told her she was entitled to one?"

"Well, yes."

"And did you continue to question her, illegally, even after she invoked her constitutional right to remain silent and speak to a lawyer? Is that what you are referring to as her avoiding your questions?" (The judge had ruled Dorothy's statements from that morning inadmissible for that reason.)

"I . . ."

"No more questions," Karen said.

"But she said she beat him with a board," the officer blurted out, "and she must have known that she was doing wrong, because she knew she was going to jail!"

Karen immediately objected, and the judge agreed.

"The jury will disregard that last remark," he said. But of course they wouldn't, couldn't, even if they tried. You can't simply unhear something.

THE NEWSPAPER HEADLINES the next morning read, in bold type:

PROSECUTION PLAYS TAPE OF 911 CALL

Grandmother Hung Up as Operators Asked Her About the
Condition of the Child, Later Found Dead.

As [the 3-year-old's] cold, battered and burned body lay on a pantry floor, his grandmother called 911. . . . As the dispatcher repeatedly asked about the boy's condition—and whether he was breathing—[the grandmother] became exasperated and hung up, according to a tape of the call played yesterday in her trial for Second Degree Murder. . . . An ambulance crew found his malnourished body, covered with cuts, bruises and cigarette burns.

Thus did the journalist testify, on the pages of the morning paper, that Raymie was battered and burned, and that Dorothy was exasperated.

The judge had instructed the jurors to avoid news coverage, and perhaps they did, but it is difficult to do; it comes at you from all sides.

CHAPTER 36

THE WIND DROVE SLEET against the windshield as I headed to court for the third day of the trial. The wipers swiped fitfully at it, squeaking and leaving icy trails on the glass, and my fingers stung with the cold. April can be a cruel month in upstate New York; it can turn on you without warning, a meek sun shining on the tips of daffodils one moment and heavy snow burying those same tips the next.

Gallo was continuing his case against Dorothy with a taped deposition from the ambulance technician, who wasn't available in person because he was on a cruise. The jurors watched with rapt attention on the large-screen color television. I think something about television encourages suspending reason and critical judgment for a time, entering a land of a kind of virtual truth.

"Did you hear the defendant say anything?" Gallo had asked.

"She asked one time, 'You can fix this? He'll be all right?'" the witness replied.

"Did you respond to her?"

"No, sir. I didn't know what to say."

As the technician went on to describe Raymie's injuries, Dorothy wept silently, dabbing her eyes with the sleeve of her dress. But the jurors' view was blocked by the huge television set; I don't think they could see her. They remained stone-faced and silent.

The newspaper account that evening read:

> When the ambulance crew arrived . . . The child was obviously dead and had burn marks and scars on his chest and two fresh, recently cleaned cuts on his face . . .
>
> [The grandmother] rearranged furniture while an ambulance crew examined the cold, stiff and battered body of her three-year-old grandson . . . , an ambulance crewman testified. Moments later, after the crew noticed burn marks, scars and fresh wounds on the child, [the grandmother] inquired about him.
>
> [The grandmother], 41, allegedly told homicide investigators that she beat [the boy] repeatedly because he ate too much. In a pretrial hearing before the testimony, Assistant Public Defender . . . said [the boy]'s injuries may have been inflicted before he lived with [the grandmother]. But Assistant Prosecutor . . . said he expects two of [the grandmother's] children to testify she abused the boy for several months. He said they'll claim [she] burned him with cigarettes, beat him with a high-heel shoe, a board and a stick, and tied him to a heating grate.

GALLO'S STAR WITNESS for the day was Dr. Welch, the deputy medical examiner. "Deputy" was a code word for "junior," not fully fledged. He was a slender man, nice-looking, with erect posture and a direct gaze. Gallo asked about his credentials, and Welch poured forth an impressive-sounding litany of schools and degrees. But listening carefully between the lines, I realized that he'd been licensed to practice medicine for only

six months and had had only twenty days of experience at forensic medicine when he'd done Raymie's autopsy. I wondered whether the jurors
could identify the relevance of this bit of information: the man was no
expert yet in medico-legal examinations and opinions when it came to
unexpected deaths. He was a rookie as a medical examiner.

"The morning or early afternoon of September eighth, were you
asked to begin an investigation concerning a young boy identified as Raymie James?" Gallo asked.

"Yes, I was," Welch answered.

"And how did you begin that examination?"

"I looked at the body and had photographs taken. The body was
shipped over to the hospital for X-rays because there was a very strong
suspicion of child abuse."

This was an important step, I knew, because a majority of chronically
abused children have evidence of bone fractures. The X-rays would reveal
whether Raymie had had broken bones.

"Did those X-rays show anything?" Gallo asked.

"No, they did not. No old or new fractures."

Gallo then moved to display the gruesome color photographs of Raymie's dead body from the autopsy.

Karen had argued long and hard with the judge, out of the jury's presence, that the photos should be excluded. "Judge, these photos are going
to have a powerful emotional impact on the jury, all out of proportion to
any evidentiary value they might have. They should be excluded," she'd
said. But the judge had ruled against her. The photos could be admitted;
he would simply caution the jury not to react emotionally or give them
undue weight.

When the pictures went up, the jurors, who were not used to viewing
corpses of children, looked at them with horror. I saw a tear run down
Dorothy's cheek and she turned away, softly repeating Raymie's name to
herself.

"I caution you, ladies and gentlemen of the jury, to not react emotionally to these pictures," the judge instructed. "They are simply evidence,
like any other evidence, and are not accorded any greater weight due to
their possible emotional impact."

I thought of all the psychological research making it clear that such
instructions do not accomplish their goal; in fact, giving such an instruction actually makes the matter stick in the jurors' minds, underscores it
somehow. There are so many ways in which the law relies on eighteenth-
century notions of how people behave, in spite of all we have learned to
the contrary.

Gallo left the pictures up for a long time—long enough for the jurors
to gasp and look away, then force themselves, out of duty, to look again.
In that moment, I think, they could see Dorothy Dunn only as reflected
in Raymie's milky, death-clouded eyes.

"Can you describe your findings?" Gallo said.

"The child was wearing bed clothing which was far too small for his
age and size. The legs had been cut off to accommodate a fit. The clothing was filthy, and there was a strong stench of urine."

Anything else, Doctor?"

"Yes. The first observation was the presence of massive physical
abuse to almost every inch of the body, old injuries as well as fresh injuries. On the back of the head was a large, circular bump, approximately
a third to a half of an inch."

I wasn't sure why he'd called that "large"; a half-inch is smaller than
a dime.

He continued: "This little boy weighed twenty-eight pounds and
was thirty-seven inches long, and that's the tenth percentile in height
and weight. Now, this all goes into your brain, because you're filtering out information, filtering in information, trying to integrate your
findings."

I realized that he probably did not know that Precious Love was slight, as were all four of her children, that Raymie had been born prematurely and with low birth weight, and that he had then suffered failure to thrive until Dorothy whisked him away from Precious and took him to the hospital, where they fed him and he gained normally. He also probably did not know that Raymie might have gained as much as six pounds during his six-month stay with Dorothy. I wasn't even sure that Karen Hughes knew that, and there was no opportunity to tell her now.

Next he identified what he concluded were two old cigarette burns on Raymie's chest.

"How do you determine these to be old, healed cigarette burns?" Gallo asked.

"Well, if you wanted to get really analytical, you would take a section of this and on a black person, you will see in this case—since they are healed, you will see the epidermis has been reformed, but the number of melanocytes, those little cells that make pigment, are decreased in the basal layer of the epidermis, and simply put is this, the centers of these areas are hypopigmented, lighter in color and tinctorial quality than the surrounding tissue. They are then rimmed by an area of hyperpigmentation, slightly darker than the surrounding skin. Classically described as thermal injury, and when you look at the shape of them, they can be classically described as injury resulted from cigarette burns."

Epidermis, melanocytes, basal layer, tinctorial quality—I wondered if the jury was able to understand any of this technical jargon. Simply put, how were they to decipher this?

He went on to describe bruises and said some of the bruising was in the subcutaneous fat. "You have to have applied a devastating amount of force, a large, substantial amount of force, to have hemorrhage in the deep fat," he volunteered. He went on: "There was under the armpits a deep circumferential kind of ligature mark and our best estimation is that there was some kind of ligature used to affix the child to something. And there was another more marked imprint all the way around the left ankle, consistent with a ligature being tightly bound around the ankle of the deceased."

"A ligature?" Gallo asked.

"A rope, cord, string," said Welch.

"What else did you do to determine cause of death?" asked Gallo.

Welch began to describe sawing open Raymie's skull, finding accumulated blood on his brain, and ruling out an epidural hematoma, something that could be caused by a fall, and concluding that it was, instead, a subdural hematoma, because "epidural hematomas are very, very rare, especially in cases of suspected child abuse."

It sounded as though he had already decided it was a case of child abuse, before examining the most important data, which he then interpreted in light of what he had already decided. The cause of death, he said, was closed head trauma—being struck in the head with a wooden paddle with devastating force.

"Are there cases where children who are not being abused present with these types of injuries?" Gallo asked.

"No," Welch replied.

Now it was time for Karen Hughes's cross-examination of Dr. Welch. First, she had him acknowledge that "there are very normal, healthy people who are in the tenth percentile" for weight, that he knew nothing of Raymie's mother's stature and had never reviewed any of Raymie's medical records, showing his failure to gain weight normally while in his mother's care. Then she asked him about the faint marks under Raymie's armpits.

"Upon first investigation of this case, it was your opinion, wasn't it, Doctor, that those marks may have been caused by clothing that was too small or too tightly bound?"

"That was the other possibility," he said. "Tight clothing versus ligature."

Next, she got him to acknowledge that he couldn't date most of Raymie's injuries; they could have occurred at any time, even months before, while Raymie was out on the streets with his mother, before Dorothy had taken over his care. He also admitted that he couldn't tell with any certainty who had inflicted the injuries. Important point on paper, but pale and lifeless compared to the photos.

Finally, she turned to Welch's testimony about Raymie's fatal head injury. There was no question that it had caused Raymie's death. The question was whether it could have been caused by a fall from the kitchen counter, striking his head against the edge of the counter, the chair, the floor, or had to be the result of being struck with the paddle.

After his initial gross examination, Welch had sent it out to be examined by a pathologist with special expertise in brains.

"Is it fair to say, Doctor, that you did not feel sufficiently qualified to review that brain?" she asked.

"In difficult cases," he said, "we always ask for a neuropathology consultation."

"Well, you say 'we have always.' On September 8th you had worked for the medical examiner's office for only two months, correct?"

"Yes."

"And in fact, out of that two months, you worked ten days per month, right?"

"Yeah."

"So that would have been, approximately, a total of twenty days at that point, correct?"

"Yes."

"In fact, your initial impression was that there was a subarachnoid hemorrhage in the spinal cord—"

"Yes."

"And you were wrong?"

"Yes."

And furthermore, she established, the amount of bleeding had been

only minimal to moderate, according to the specialist, in direct contra-
diction of Welch's testimony.

"Is it fair to say that you were upset by what you saw on Raymie
James's body?" Hughes asked.

"Most decidedly," Welch said.

"In fact, this case continues to upset you, does it not?"

"Yes."

"In fact, you had tears in your eyes when you testified at the grand
jury, did you not?"

"Yes, I did," he said.

Karen sat down.

"Any redirect?" the judge asked Gallo.

"Yes, Your Honor," Gallo said, rising and walking toward the witness.

"Doctor, why is it that this particular case continues to upset you,
compared to all the other cases that you have seen?"

Dr. Welch looked directly at the jury. "Because," he said, "this is one
of the most horrific cases of child abuse I have ever seen."

"Thank you, Doctor," Gallo said with a faint smile as he returned to
his seat.

What he didn't tell the jurors was that, since he had been practicing
forensic medicine for less than three weeks at the time of Raymie's death,
this was, in fact, one of the first cases of potential child abuse he had ever
seen in his young career.

CHAPTER 37

O N THE MORNING OF the fourth day of the trial, Gallo called
Tonette and Alice to testify against their mother. He couldn't call
Precious Love, who remained in the state hospital for the chronically
mentally ill; I pictured her shuffling along the linoleum floor with the
other patients in a slow line of frayed terry-cloth robes and slippers, queu-
ing up for her morning dose of antipsychotic medication, and then sitting
in a stupor in the solarium until it was time for her next dose. And he
couldn't call Dante, who was back in prison on his second major felony;
perhaps he was afraid that the jurors might regard Dante as a somewhat
unreliable witness. He couldn't call Scoot, who at six years old was still
incapable of comprehensible speech and clearly mentally impaired.

But to what would the girls testify? It seemed a particularly cruel and
cynical move to call them. Tonette, by all accounts, had slept through the
main events surrounding Raymie's death, showing up only at the end,
and knew almost nothing firsthand. In addition, she was an intellectually compromised child whose understanding of events would likely be
skewed and unreliable.

The girls had been in foster homes ever since their mother's arrest, allowed no contact with her in all the months since she had been dragged out of the home in handcuffs in front of them. Memory is a funny thing, plastic and unreliable, even in adults. A clumsy therapist can create false memories in children, and trauma can twist memory, too, creating shadows and shimmers in its fabric, like the flickering of light through water. Added to this, each of the girls had been interviewed multiple times by prosecution staff in preparation for their testimony.

First to testify was thirteen-year-old Tonette, a big, lumbering girl like her mother, with a stolid, thick quality and cow eyes. She shambled slowly through the swinging gates and deposited herself with a thump in the witness chair, her expression as blank as Dorothy's. Gallo's careful questions called for only simple yes or no responses. There was little opportunity for the jury to see how limited her understanding was. Their back-and-forth reminded me of a ventriloquist and his dummy.

"Did your mother abuse Raymie?" Gallo asked.

"Yeah," Tonette testified. She replied the same way when asked if her mother hit Raymie and tied him by the ankle and burned him with cigarettes. And "Yeah," she punished him for going into the kitchen. "She don't want him to eat nothin'." And: "She hit him with high-heeled shoes, too," she said. "The pointy end." As she said it, she glared at her mother.

But Tonette was an unhappy, angry, and confused child, one with limited understanding who had abused Raymie herself when she could get away with it and who probably now believed that her mother had abandoned her and was angry about it. I had the feeling that she had no idea what she was doing.

When Karen attempted cross-examination, Tonette was sullen and silent, refusing to answer her questions and refusing to look at her mother or Karen. She sat, head hanging down, eyes on the floor, and Karen soon abandoned the effort.

Alice was next. At only ten years old, she was petite and fine-featured and had a quick alertness about her. Unlike Precious, Tonette, and Scoot, as well as Dorothy herself, sheseemed, so far, relatively unscathed by the insanity and suffering and poverty around her.

For months before the trial, Alice had defended her mother to the police. No, she had insisted, her mother hadn't burned Raymie with cigarettes, only touched him quickly, not leaving a mark. But Precious had, and Mister had. No, her mother did not beat Raymie. She spanked him on the buttocks once or twice, for misbehaving, as she did her other children. "You couldn't usually see marks from it afterward," she had insisted. Yes, her mother tied him by his ankle to the heating grate or to the couch, but only so he wouldn't set fire to the kitchen or run off into the street to be squashed like a bug on a windshield. "If you didn't tie him, he might could get hurt," she had said.

When Alice heard the loud thump and got up that night, she told the police initially, she saw that Raymie had put a pan on the stove. There was cornmeal and pepper in the pan. He was going to cook it, she thought, like he had tried to cook the dry cornmeal that time before, when he got burned. He was still lying on the floor, dazed, covered in sugar, several minutes after she heard the thud of him hitting the floor. She woke up her mother, who made him a sandwich, and they sat with him while he ate. And when he was finished, as Alice swept some of the sugar up with her hands and carefully put it back into the remnants of the tattered yellow bag, Dorothy hit him—on the buttocks and the back of his legs, she thought. Three times, or maybe five. With the wooden paddle. And she touched his arm with her lit cigarette, quickly, lightly.

"Ow," he said, scrunching up his face into a cry.

"That's so you remember next time to leave the stove alone," her mother said, according to Alice's statement to the police. Then she quick-marched him to the couch, holding him by the scruff of his pajamas. He stumbled a step or two and fell, according to Alice's initial account, once, twice; Alice wasn't sure, she said. "Did she throw him down?" a police officer asked. "No, only she was, like, pushing him and he might've lost his balance and fell." Or he might already have been losing his coordination from the head injury from the fall in the kitchen, I realized. But Alice couldn't know that, and I doubted Dorothy could, either.

This was what Alice had told them, over and over again, for the first few months. But when she took the stand, she couldn't meet her mother's eyes.

Gallo stood up and thrust his hands into the pockets of his suit coat.

"Tell us your name," Gallo said.

"Alice Ellen Dunn," she said.

"And how old are you, Alice?"

"Ten."

"Has somebody besides your mom and Tonette and Scoot stayed with you in the house for the last couple of months?" he asked.

"No," said Alice.

Gallo tried again: "Other than your brother, were there any other *kids* that lived in your house for the last year or half a year or months?"

"Yes," she said, getting it right this time.

"And who is that?"

"Raymie."

"How are you related to Raymie?" he asked.

"His niece," Alice said.

"You mean his aunt?"

"Yeah. Aunt."

"Alice, I want you to remember back to the sixth of September. Did you hear anything that night while you were in the house?"

"Yes."

"Where were you when you heard this noise?"

"I was upstairs laying down."

"And where were Tonette and Scoot?"

"They were both asleep."

"What did you hear?"

"I was upstairs and I heard a noise and I thought it was my mother because she usually gets up and cleans clothes."

"Where did the noise come from, and what did you do after you heard it?"

"From out in the pantry room," she said. "It was like a big bang on the floor in the pantry room."

"What happened after you heard that bang?"

"I stayed up there for a while because I thought it was my mother. Then I went downstairs because I didn't hear anybody. I looked for Raymie and I saw him on the floor in the pantry room."

"What did you do when you saw him?" Gallo asked.

"I scraped sugar off him and went and got my mother," Alice said.

"Did he say anything to you?" asked Gallo.

"He said he was hungry."

"What happened, you went to talk to your mom?"

"Yeah, she was laying on the couch in the dining room. I woke her up and told her Raymie was in the kitchen."

"Was Raymie allowed to be in the kitchen?" Gallo asked.

"No."

"What happened next?" he asked.

"She made him a sugar sandwich and gave him some hot jalapeños with the sugar."

"You say a sugar sandwich?" he asked.

"Yeah. She had dumped some of the sugar off on it."

"Did he like those peppers?"

"No," she said.

"Then what happened, Alice?"

"Then she told him to go in the room and stand up until she get in there."

"Then what?" asked Gallo.

"She had got the belt, and she was whipping him on his legs with it."

"Do you know how many times she did it?"

"About three, I think," Alice said.

"Then what did your mom do?" he asked.

"She was asking him why he went in the kitchen. She said, 'I told you don't go in the kitchen,' and then every time she asked him he put his head down and didn't say nothing so she hit him again."

"Then she stopped?"

"No. Then she started hitting him with the wooden paddle."

"Where was she hitting him, Alice?"

"On the legs and his butt and his back," she said, looking down at the floor.

"Did she do anything else to him?" Gallo asked.

"Umm. Yeah. She was, like, throwing him across the room."

"Throwing him across the room?"

"Yes."

"What was happening to Raymie when she threw him across the room?"

"Well, when she told him to get up, he kept falling and couldn't stand up. She was telling him to get up, and when he didn't get up, she hit him," Alice said.

"And then what did she do?" he asked.

"The last time she did it he was laying on the floor and she picked him up because he kept making noises, so she picked him up and his head kept falling, so then she gave him some water to drink and he spit it back out."

"What happened after that?" Gallo asked.

"She was trying to keep his eyes from closing. But his eyes had closed and then she laid him down in the dining room. She said that 'he'll be okay, he's just knocked out' and I went upstairs to bed."

"What happened the next day?"

"I couldn't feel no heartbeat," she said.

"And could you tell if Raymie was breathing?" Gallo asked.

"No," she said. "I couldn't tell. He was cold."

Tears rolled down her face, joining her mother's tears, though they would not look at each other.

I saw the looks on the faces of the jurors. "Poor baby," I imagined them thinking. "Look at what her mother has put her through." And, though they probably tried not to, they may have hated Dorothy just a little bit, for Alice's sake.

Dorothy wept silently, and when Karen rose to begin her cross-examination, Dorothy tugged on her shoulder. "She done gone through enough already," Dorothy whispered. "Let her be. It's not good for her to have to talk against me like that. She'll feel bad about it later. Just let it be. It's all right."

Karen sat down, reluctantly. She could not override her client's wish when so clearly expressed, even if it was a terrible mistake.

The prosecutor rested; he had completed his case against Dorothy Dunn. Alice's testimony was devastating, and significantly at odds with what she had told the police immediately after Raymie's death. She had described him as lying "dazed" on the pantry floor, staring at her, blinking, not speaking. She had described him stumbling and falling in the living room as his mother chastised him after his sugar sandwich, not a word about Mrs. Dunn's "throwing" him repeatedly to the ground.

But she and the other children had been separated from their mother for many months now, allowed no contact and surrounded by social workers and other people who probably firmly believed that Dorothy Dunn had killed Raymie and that the sooner the children accepted it, the better off they'd be.

For months, Alice and Tonette had both independently insisted to the phalanx of therapists that their mother had not killed Raymie. And for months, therapists had worked with them to accept the narrative propounded by the prosecution, a narrative seemingly confirmed by the fact that their mother was in jail, although they were too young to know anything about the presumption of innocence and the prosecution's burden of actually proving guilt beyond a reasonable doubt. By the time of the trial, the pump had been primed. And now, Alice had become her mother's unwitting executioner.

I gathered up my coat and my thoughts and left the courtroom. It had been a long day. I hated what this trial was doing to Dorothy's children. I wondered how they could recover from it. The newspaper headline that night was: "TINY VOICE DETAILS 'HORRIFIC' ABUSE."

CHAPTER 38

THE NEXT MORNING, Karen began Dorothy's defense. Criminal trials are like plays: first the prosecutor tells a story, then the defense gets a turn; each side must try to convince the jurors that their story is the true one. Karen needed to make the jurors see Dorothy as human again. She had to try to get them to understand, across the chasm of poverty, ignorance, mental illness, and race that divided her world from theirs, that Dorothy's actions, ill-conceived though they were, were the result not of cruelty or recklessly depraved indifference but of ignorance and mental illness. She would try to disprove the prosecutor's theory that Dorothy had inflicted the fatal injury; failing that, she would have to prove that it was probable that Dorothy had not known what she was doing or that it was wrong.

If the jurors understood Dorothy, they would convict her of nothing more than manslaughter—even that, I thought, would be too much—and she would spend no more than four years in prison. There would still be time for her and for her children. But I feared that the jurors would read "depraved indifference" into her blank expression rather than post-traumatic stress disorder, depression, a lifetime of abuse, poverty, mental retardation, and mental illness. And if they could not, or would not, identify with her, could they have empathy for her and see her suffering for what it was? Or would they see malice in place of pain, intent in place of imbalance?

Primo Levi wrote about the transformation of moral men into immoral ones under extraordinary circumstances. But I believe the acts, not the men, are immoral. Under conditions of exhaustion and fear, the remarkable can become unremarkable, and we all can turn into complacent savages, deaf to the humanity of others. As the Nazi menace advanced, my husband's grandmother was shot dead in her living room by her Lithuanian neighbors, who then moved into her home and live there happily still. Were they evil? I don't know; they were in evil times.

Do we sense this hidden secret of ours, that we are a murderous race under the surface? Is this why we need to pretend there are such stark moral differences between ourselves and the prisoner in the dock? Judging by humanity's history, we are in greater danger from the sane than the insane.

A child was dead, and someone had to be to blamed. Someone should have to pay; that feels like justice. Would the jurors be able to accept that Raymie's life had been taken by nameless poverty? By apathy, incompetence, and the lack of will to adequately staff and fund Child Protective Services? Could they accept something so mundane as the banality of evil, in Arendt's words, and with such shared guilt, as cause for a child's death?

Gallo had completed his case against Dorothy. Now Karen had to convince the jury that it was more likely than not that Dorothy was too impaired to have known the danger and to have been indifferent to it.

KAREN BEGAN HER CASE by calling CPS caseworker Charles Bremer to testify. He'd arrived with two attorneys, one for himself and one for the

Department of Social Services, which may have worried that some negligence on its part would be claimed to have contributed to the child's death.

He stepped up to the stand, was sworn to tell the whole truth, and
took his seat.

"Mr. Bremer, were you employed as a child protective caseworker?"

"Yes."

"And what were your duties?"

"Investigate alleged cases of child abuse and neglect," he said.

"Were you assigned to be the child protective caseworker for Precious Love James and her children the January before Raymie James's
death?"

"Yes."

"Why?" she asked.

"A referral was made that the children were left alone, unsupervised,
and hadn't been fed or properly clothed, and that Mom was taken to a
psychiatric hospital."

"What was the condition of the house?"

"I wasn't able to get into the house," he said.

"What was your responsibility as the child protective caseworker
assigned to the case?" Karen asked.

"To assess the safety situation for the children," he said. "And see
whether there's enough evidence that what is alleged happened."

"That's called an 'indication'?" Karen asked.

"Yeah."

"And there had been previous 'indications' of abuse or neglect involving Precious Love?"

"I believe so."

She had him review the case record to make sure, and he said that
previously the children had been found to have high levels of lead and the
mother wasn't getting the necessary medical care for them.

"As part of your duties as the caseworker," Karen asked, "did the law require you to make an assessment of child safety in regards to Precious's children?"

"Yes," he said.

"What was your assessment?"

"I don't remember."

She had him review his notes again.

"What was your safety assessment?"

"That Precious was unable to provide adequate supervision, unable to provide food, clothing, and shelter and that her mental illness was a concern," he said.

"So did you make a safety decision?"

"Yes."

"And what was the safety decision that you made?" Hughes asked.

"That the children would be unsafe without intervening factors," Bremer said.

"After her release from the hospital, where did Precious go to live?"

"With her mother, Dorothy Dunn, and her son, Raymie."

"Do you see Mrs. Dunn in the courtroom today?" Hughes asked.

"Not that I recognize, no."

"Did you make a home visit to Mrs. Dunn in February, approximately seven weeks after you received the referral, to see how Raymie was doing?"

"Yes," he said.

"Is that the first time you had actually seen Raymie?"

"I believe so."

"What observations of Raymie did you make, to determine his condition?" she asked.

"He appeared in good health and was fine. He was adequately clothed, properly clothed."

"Did you ever take his clothing off and conduct a visual examination of his body to look for bruises or scars?"

"Objection," Gallo called out.

"Overruled," said the judge.

"No," Bremer said.

"No?" Karen asked, turning toward the jury. "You never looked at his arms or legs, his back or his tummy, to see if there were any marks? Never weighed him to make sure he was adequately fed?"

"No."

"And, of course, you also never examined him physically before he got to Mrs. Dunn's house, is that right?"

"Yes," Bremer said.

"Six months later, in June, did you receive a new report naming Precious Love as a perpetrator of suspected abuse or neglect?" Hughes asked.

"Yes. From the director of the women's shelter."

Did you make a further home visit with Precious Love?"

"Yes, I saw her at a women's shelter."

"Did you ever discuss with Precious placing Raymie into foster care during that visit?"

"Objection," Gallo said.

"Overruled," said the judge.

"Yes," Bremer said.

"What did you tell Precious?" asked Hughes.

"Objection," Gallo called out.

"Sustained," the judge said.

"Mr. Bremer, three weeks later, was Precious still living at the shelter with Raymie?" asked Hughes.

"No. She had returned to her mother's house."

"How did you know that?"

"A phone call from Mrs. Dunn."

And is that when you closed the case?" she asked.

"Shortly after that," Bremer said.

"You closed it, in spite of the fact that Precious was still crazy, she still had no stable housing, and Mrs. Dunn had told you that she didn't think she could adequately care for the boy?"

"Objection," Gallo said.

"I withdraw the question," Hughes said. The jury had already heard the question, and already knew the answer.

"That's all," Hughes said and Gallo rose and approached the witness for cross-examination.

"Mr. Bremer," Gallo asked, "you didn't have any contact with Dorothy Dunn, Raymie James, Precious Love, after June?"

"Correct," Bremer said.

"And up to that time, there were no allegations of abuse on the part of Precious Love, just neglect. Is that correct?"

"Correct."

"When Mrs. Dunn called and told you that Precious and Raymie were at her house, she also told you that she didn't want them there very long; isn't that correct?" Gallo asked.

"Yes."

"She told you that they were going to have to find their own place to live, correct?"

"Yes."

"And did you ever see suspicious injuries on Raymie during the almost year and a half that you had contact with the family?"

"No."

"I have no more questions, Your Honor," Gallo said, taking his seat.

Hughes rose and asked, "Did you ever *look* for any injuries?"

"When I saw Raymie I would always—we always—look at the child,

but we don't do a strip search or we don't look for things that are not indicated in the report," Bremer said.

"I see," said Hughes, glaring at him, her voice rising. "In other words,
you're saying that there was not a report of physical abuse, so you weren't
obligated to take his shirt off, correct?"

"Correct," he answered.

CHAPTER 39

K AREN HAD FOUND NO character witnesses on Dorothy's behalf. No relatives willing to speak for her. No friends, no neighbors. No employers. And she hadn't had time to review the heaping mound of records that documented social workers' positive observations about Dorothy over the years, as well as her clear limitations. I didn't know whether she'd seen Raymie's medical records, showing that Dorothy had more than once gotten him needed medical care, including even saving him from almost certain starvation, or the records describing his difficult behaviors and impulsivity, his prenatal drug exposure and elevated lead levels. I hoped so. She had tried, but so far without success, to get access to Dante's old CPS file, documenting, Dorothy claimed, that a caseworker had told her to use harsher corporal punishment against the child.

Dorothy had probably not killed Raymie, but there was only Alice's word and Dorothy's own for that. Now Alice was vacillating and who would believe Dorothy? Karen couldn't even call Dorothy to testify on her own behalf; Gallo would destroy her on cross-exam, as limited and confused as she was. She didn't even really understand what she was charged with, and to make matters worse, she felt guilty for Raymie's death—she should have protected him better, she said—and was likely to say that it was her fault. Anyway, it was not up to me to decide whether she had inflicted the fatal injury; that was the jurors' call.

Karen's only defense, besides showing the weaknesses in Gallo's proof that Dorothy had caused the fatal injury, would be my psychiatric testimony that she had not had a "guilty mind."

I'D BEEN HAVING TROUBLE sleeping, tense and unsure where my duty lay. I thought about something legal scholar Richard Lowell Nygaard had written, that experts "are unable to make accurate and scientific determinations fit into the rigid legal definitions." It was not clear to me that I could swear, under oath, that Dorothy had not *known*, in the most basic meaning of the word, what she was doing, or that it was wrong, on the day of Raymie's death. And if I couldn't take a clear position, how the hell was the jury going to puzzle it out, legally and psychologically, with Gallo doing all he could to introduce doubt?

When you are an expert witness, you are in a vulnerable, delicate position. You are not an advocate for the side that has called you—truth doesn't have a side—though your data probably support their cause or they wouldn't be calling you to testify on their behalf. And though I had had no allegiance to Dorothy going in—had, in fact, at first glance judged her to be repulsive and probably guilty—after examining the psychological evidence, I had come to think that meting out severe punishment to her would be a miscarriage of justice.

I liked Karen; she was dedicated and sharp. But she was also badly overworked; as the *Report of the Sentencing Project to the U.N. Human*

Rights Committee found in 2013, "funding at both the state and federal levels indicates that effective indigent defense is not a priority in many jurisdictions in the United States. At the state and local level . . . each public defender handled 371 cases—more than one new case for each day of the year. . . . They must decide which of their cases will receive the bulk of their limited resources and attention—a process called 'triage.'" The report quotes an article from the *Yale Law Journal*: "For most [public defenders], the question is not 'how do I engage in zealous and effective advocacy,' but rather 'given that all my clients deserve aggressive advocacy, how do I choose among them?'" There is no possible way to do right by each of them.

Karen and I had had only two hours of time together on the case. I'd given her a crash course, or the bare outlines of it. But I'd also had to use a kind of triage: I couldn't possibly alert her to every specific small fact from the voluminous records that might somehow figure into Dorothy's defense. Had I chosen wisely in deciding what to bring to Karen's attention out of that mass of information? What if I'd inadvertently left out something crucial?

If Karen wasn't careful in questioning me, building the testimony brick by psychological brick, the jurors would not understand. And when they do not understand, they go with their guts and preconceptions. Many people think that O. J. Simpson was acquitted of two murders because the jury couldn't understand the DNA testimony, and so discounted it. And in this case, one look at Dorothy Dunn, with her blank, emotionless expression, was likely to convince them that she was cruel and without remorse. There was nothing endearing or appealing about her on the surface.

I needed Karen to ask questions skillfully, almost like a tutorial on mental illness, and in the right order. When you are an expert witness, it is somewhat like being a puppet controlled by the attorney—puppet master. You have to dance to their tune, and your dance is only as effective as their ability to work the strings.

I wasn't sure she could do it, under the circumstances.

THE TIME HAD COME for me to take the stand and swear to tell the truth, the whole truth, and nothing but the truth on behalf of Dorothy Dunn and the people of the state of New York. But while witnesses are questioned in a way that occasionally permits them to tell some of the truth, they almost never have the opportunity to tell the *whole* truth. In the many times I've testified, I've never been given the latitude during questioning to tell the whole truth, and partial truths can sometimes be as false as lies. To further complicate matters, I was being called as an "expert" witness, not a "fact" witness. This means that I could give my opinion on matters directly related to Dorothy's mental status and capacity, my area of special expertise and training, but I could not offer opinions about the facts of the case—what had happened to Raymie, and how. I would not be allowed to testify, for example, that I did not think Dorothy had struck Raymie in the head and caused the fatal injury. I could only offer the opinion that her personality was inconsistent with such cruelty and aggression.

Court is theater, and testifying is a performance when a jury is involved. I'd chosen conservative, understated attire that projected, I hoped, a sense of confidence and probity. Black pants and a white blouse, a simple strand of pearls, a pair of black pumps: boring but professional. I took one last look in the mirror and decided I had done what I could. I looked like my mother, ready for church, except for the pants and the absence of white cotton gloves.

Slipping into a seat in the back of the courtroom, I waited to be called, running through the details of Dorothy's evaluation in my head for the hundredth time, remembering the words of a colleague: "It takes courage to endure seeing your opinions deliberately distorted by a cross-examiner one day and incorrectly reported in the press the next." I was determined to do what little I could to prevent that. I focused on looking outwardly calm and emotionally disengaged, though my nerves were fraught, magnifying every little noise or touch. Mentally, I made a note to apologize to Jacob; he'd offered me a piece of burnt toast for breakfast, and I'd snapped at him. I felt the smoothness of the old wooden bench, which seemed to have been pirated from some Calvinist meetinghouse long ago, and concentrated on my breathing.

Karen was up at the defense table, also looking tense as she shuffled through a thick stack of notes. Dorothy, as always, sat stolidly beside her, glancing neither right nor left. I had spoken to her briefly in her cell the day before, telling her that I would probably say some things in court that might embarrass her or hurt her feelings and that I was sorry.

"'S'all right, then" was all she'd said. I had no idea whether she'd understood.

Karen swiveled around, and our eyes met for an instant just as the bailiff called out, "All rise."

"Counselor?" the judge said, looking at Karen.

"Ready, Your Honor," she replied.

"Then call your witness and let's get started."

"The defense calls Dr. Vinocour," Karen said.

I made my way up the long center aisle of the courtroom, past the curious eyes of spectators and reporters, past the tables for the prosecutor and his assistants, on the right, and Dorothy and Karen, on the left. I looked at Dorothy one last time, but she didn't return my gaze.

"Raise your right hand," the bailiff directed. "Do you swear to tell the truth, the whole truth, and nothing but the truth, so help you God?"

"I do," I said.

"You may be seated."

Karen began by asking me the usual questions about my qualifications and experience, and then asked about the conditions under which I had agreed to evaluate Dorothy Dunn.

"I pointed out to you that I had spent most of my career as a child advocate, in the area of child abuse," I said, "and that I had pretty strong feelings about parents who injure their children and didn't know whether I would be able to set that bias aside and objectively evaluate your client."

"Did I ever condition your hiring on your coming to a certain result in the case?" she asked.

"In no way, and I wouldn't have accepted the assignment if you had."

She had me go over the number of hours I'd spent interviewing Mrs. Dunn and watching the video of Dr. Kraft's interviews for the jury, the psychological testing I'd done, the thousand pages of documents I'd reviewed.

The jurors listened politely.

"Did you form an opinion as to whether Mrs. Dunn suffered from a psychiatric disorder at the time of Raymie James's death?"

"Yes, I did," I said. "My opinion is that she suffered from a psychotic break, as well as dissociative disorder and borderline intellectual functioning, at that time, perhaps brought on by her shock at Raymie's fall and head injury."

I glanced over at Dorothy to see if she understood, if she felt ashamed or upset at what I'd said.

"Were there other hypotheses you explored?"

"Yes, antisocial personality disorder would be the likely diagnosis if she actually inflicted all those injuries on Raymie herself," I said.

"Were you able to rule that in or out?" Hughes asked.

"Yes. She has no history, in her first forty years, of violent or aggressive behavior, rule breaking, cruelty, or a lack of empathy for others. She is not a sociopath."

"Were there other possibilities?"

"Yes. She could have just hated or resented this particular child and wished him harm. That happens in families at times. One child is abused, the others are left alone."

"So what about that," she asked. "Was there evidence for or against that hypothesis?"

"Yes," I said. "Mrs. Dunn loves Raymie's mother, her first child, very much. She has nothing against his father. When Raymie was a baby, she's the one that made sure he got the needed vaccinations. She got him to the doctor for treatment of his lead poisoning when his mother didn't. She's the one that discovered he was starving, out on the streets with his mother, and got him to the hospital in time to save him. She's the one who took care of him and his sisters time and time again when Precious Love was drugged out or otherwise missing in action. At one time, she told one of the girls that she wished she could have had him all the time since his birth, so she could have raised him more consistently."

"But didn't she also tell the CPS worker that she didn't want him?"

"Not exactly. What she said was she couldn't take him, toward the end, because her own three children were so needy and demanding, because she worried that Tonette might be bad to him, and because she herself was exhausted and depressed. It's similar to what happened when Scoot was born: it wasn't that she didn't want him, it was that she didn't think she could do right by him and he needed somebody better. As she told Tonette, who objected to his living there, 'by my taking him in, I thought that would help him. Raymie needs somebody to love him and do for him, so that's why he's here.' I don't believe that she hated this child. I think she loved him and cared for him in her own way."

"Did you consider other possibilities?" Hughes asked.

"Yes. I considered the possibility that she didn't cause all those injuries—that some of them were inflicted by Precious and the strangers and addicts she exposed Raymie to while they were homeless, and that she—Mrs. Dunn, that is—didn't cause his death. That it was caused by his fall."

"What about her intellectual ability?" Hughes asked.

"She's quite limited. In the bottom four or five percent of the population. Her thinking is very concrete and literal. She doesn't know much, and she's not a good problem solver, because she's not very bright."

"Is that relevant?"

"Yes, because in order to have reckless disregard for something or depraved indifference to it, you first have to be aware of it, to know it. And Dorothy Dunn knows very little. Much less than a mother of ordinary intelligence. For example, she knows nothing about child nutrition and what should a child normally weigh. Her academic skills are only at about a fourth grade level; she never passed a course after seventh grade, and that was only gym and home economics," I said.

I had a sinking feeling. Each one of these assertions was critical for the jury to understand if they were to get a true sense of Dorothy's state of mind, whether she knew what she was doing and acted with depraved indifference. I needed Karen to ask follow-up questions so I could expand on these issues, explain them further, drive them home. I felt a little like a note in a bottle, drifting at sea.

"Do you have an opinion about how she felt after she realized he was dead?" Karen asked.

"Yes. She expressed a tremendous feeling of responsibility that if only she had been able to teach him better, if only she'd been able to supervise him better, he would have stayed safe and he wouldn't have experienced his fatal injury. She was very tearful about his death and very perplexed as to what happened after she had gone to sleep that night that could have caused his death. At first, she thought he died because he got into the kitchen and ate something bad that made him sick. And she felt that was her fault for falling asleep and not watching him at night."

"Did she tie a rope around his ankle and tether him to things?"

"Yes, she said she did. He would get up in the middle of the night when everyone was sleeping and turn on the gas stove, and this scared her to death. In fact, she said it scared her so badly that the first time it happened she had to go and lay down because she was shaking so hard. And Alice said her mother would tie him because otherwise he ran out of the house and into the street." I explained that you or I might be able to think of a better, more effective way to corral Raymie, but that this was the best idea Dorothy could come up with.

"What supported your conclusion that she had a psychotic or dissociative episode, Doctor?" Hughes asked.

"Many things. First, she had very blunted affect, showing little emotion, other than profuse crying. Her speech was illogical and incoherent at times and ran off in unrelated tangents. Her hygiene was poor, the house was filthy and in disarray, she hadn't managed to get the kids registered for school yet, even though it had already started. Her memory for events around the time of Raymie's death was confused and illogical. The psychological testing suggested that her thinking and perception of reality were impaired. There's a long family history—her mother and her daughter and an aunt—of psychosis. And then, too, she slept with this little boy's corpse for two days, moving him off and on a heating grate to keep his body a life-like temperature, and then asked paramedics if they could fix him. That's not exactly an indication of normal thinking and reasoning."

"Can psychosis be brought on by stress?"

"Yes. If a person has an underlying genetic predisposition to psychosis, stress can trigger it. Stress and exhaustion."

"And was there any stress in Dorothy's life at the time of Raymie's death?" she asked.

"She was under considerable stress. Her beloved daughter Precious Love was schizophrenic and decompensating. Her son Dante had recently gone back to prison. Her father, who was severely abusive to Dorothy and who'd been living with her for nearly a year while she took care of him, died in her house the year before. Tonette was having significant behavioral and emotional problems at school, and Dorothy had begun to suspect that her girls had been sexually abused by a man. Then Raymie came into the household, and he was severely impulsive and hyperactive and unused to any rules. He'd been exposed to drugs and alcohol in utero and had toxic lead levels, so he was neurologically impaired and hard to manage. He really hadn't had much parenting. Dorothy tried to supervise him and she wasn't getting much sleep. She was exhausted."

I tried to convey to the jury a sense of her utter exhaustion, depletion, and feelings of helplessness. But I wasn't sure that the jurors, who did not live on the extreme margins of society like Dorothy, had ever really experienced this in their own lives. I explained how Dorothy had tried to help Tonette, who had become such an angry child that the school could not manage her. Tonette, with the "chipped shoulder," as Dorothy said. ("They told me she had a chip on her shoulder," she had told me, recalling her meeting at the school, "but I didn't see no chip. It looked all right to me.")

"Can all that make a person lose their bearings?" Hughes asked.

Who among us could keep our balance under such stress?

"It certainly can," I said. "Especially given the family history of psychosis."

"Thank you, Doctor. Now I ask you, do you have an opinion as to whether, at the time of Raymie's death, Mrs. Dunn was unable to be aware of and disregard the risk that her conduct would cause grave risk of death?"

And now the most difficult part: the leap of faith for the jurors. Faith in me, if not in Dorothy, I hoped. This was the moment of truth. What is the essence of insanity, and of guilt? What was the truth, and the whole truth, of this matter? Had Dorothy Dunn lost her ability to "know" in the days before Raymie's fall or just after, in reaction to it? How could I be sure?

I looked at Dorothy. The woman's life was at stake. I knew she might not meet the exact prevailing legal definition of insanity—no one could say for absolutely sure what her precise level of awareness had been the moment the boy suffered the fatal injury—but I also knew it was not in her to have intentionally, knowingly, done anything to endanger her grandson's life. I knew it for sure. The child had surely suffered, and the child was dead. There was no fixing that. But no malice had been involved on Dorothy's part.

I took a breath, squared my shoulders, and looked directly at the jury.

"Yes," I said. "I have an opinion."

"And what is your opinion, Doctor?"

"I think her limited intelligence, compounded with her exhaustion and mental illness, make it highly unlikely that she was able to identify a substantial risk to either regard or disregard the impact of her actions. If Dorothy Dunn did something wrong on the night of Raymie's death, in my opinion she did not know what she was doing, that it was wrong, or that it created a grave risk to him. She had no intent to harm him."

Well, that's done, then, I thought, heart racing. I knew Gallo would try to completely undermine my credibility and cast doubt on my conclusions on cross-exam.

When court ended for the day, I retreated to my office, wrung out from the eight hours of intense concentration that testifying requires. And I still had to prepare for Gallo's cross-examination in the morning. I checked my phone and saw that someone had left a message.

I hit Play, and a man's voice, dripping with menace and hate like hot venom, filled the room.

"I oughta tear your fucking lips off, you lying bitch. You fucking whore. Defending that murderer! It's like you killed him yourself! You deserve to die. I know where you live, you know; I can get you anytime."

I sighed and rubbed my eyes. Did he know what he was doing, and that it was wrong?

CHAPTER 40

ALLO'S CROSS-EXAMINATION the next day, and the next, was
brutal. It was aggressive and persistent. It was nothing personal.
He didn't rely on some of the clumsy old saws favored by lesser attorneys: "You're not a *real* doctor, are you?" And "You're getting paid for
your testimony, aren't you?" That's an especially ironic question, given
that attorneys are the ultimate mercenaries. There are legitimate questions that can be asked of an expert, but these are not among them. He
planted more subtle seeds: "During the course of your *employment* by
Mrs. Hughes . . ." and "When did you go to *medical* school, Doctor?"

Good attorneys, whether for the prosecution or the defense, ask questions as carefully and precisely as composers orchestrate musical scores,
controlling what instrument will have a voice and when. On cross-examination, a witness's responses are generally confined quite tightly to simple
yes or no answers, with no latitude allowed for explaining or expanding.

But Dorothy Dunn could not be explained in simple yeses and nos. I
tried to expand my answers, to give the jury a fuller picture of her, and

Gallo tried just as hard to prevent me from doing so. In the end, it's hard to say who ended up more frustrated, Gallo, me, or the judge. But I felt like I'd run a marathon.

It was part of the game, but should we really be playing these games in a situation like this? How can we expect psychologists and psychiatrists to provide their expertise to the court when this sort of treatment goes hand in hand with it? I'm an attorney, used to verbal combat. I can handle it. I even know that when an opposing attorney attacks me personally, it's because they have a weak case or I'm having a more powerful effect as a witness than they like. But my blood pressure still rises when I'm on the stand. Most expert witnesses are not used to being disrespected, suspected, and abused; they don't know how to deal with it. They become defensive and overstate their case, or they grow meek and compliant to soothe the cross-examiner. Neither outcome does justice to the case or to the mental health profession.

This is one of the reasons most mental health practitioners resist offering their services to attorneys and the court. They don't relish the certain prospect of having their words and opinions twisted and distorted, their motives, ethics, honesty, and competency questioned, or their reputations besmirched by an attorney waging an adversarial battle. I often feel that my testimony is misused, that I end up being an unwitting and unwilling collaborator in an injustice.

Gallo attacked relentlessly on every point: my credentials, my methodology, my data, then Dorothy's intellectual disability, her depression, her exhaustion, and her eventual collapse into a dissociative or psychotic loss of touch with reality, culminating in Raymie's death. I focused on his questions, and on the jury, and tried not to think about the phone call the night before.

"You have had an opportunity to evaluate the videotapes from Dr. Kraft?" he asked.

"Yes," I said.

"During the course of your interviews, you didn't videotape them; is that correct?"

"Yes, that's correct," I said.

"Wouldn't you agree that a better method of doing a forensic interview is to videotape that interview?"

"No," I said. "It distracts people and makes them nervous."

"Well, how can you observe Mrs. Dunn's affect and behavior if you're taking verbatim notes?"

"Practice," I said. "I have done it for years, as a matter of course."

"You can read a piece of paper and observe, at the same time?" he asked with an astonished tone.

"Of course," I said. "That's why I had to go to Dr. Kraft's office and read my notes to him; he couldn't decipher all the handwriting."

"Doctor, Doctor, you have to limit your answers to the question that's asked. Okay?" the judge interjected.

"Sorry," I said, which was my first lie of the day.

"Did you rely at all on the four hours of interviews videotaped by Dr. Kraft?" he asked.

"I considered that data along with all the other data I had available," I said.

"Doctor, then you must believe that Dr. Kraft did a better job interviewing Mrs. Dunn than you did?"

"No, I don't."

Gallo continued, focusing on my finding that Mrs. Dunn had limited cognitive ability.

"One of the things you indicated was that she had two at-home, unassisted child births; is that correct?"

"Yes."

"So you must have asked her why she gave birth to Scoot at home."

"No, I didn't."

"You never even asked her the question?"

"Nope."

"And what the medical records describe is that she thought she had to take a bowel movement and at some point Scoot was born; she was on the toilet and Scoot was born?"

"That's right," I said. I thought he was making my point pretty effectively.

"Does that tell you that she must have been borderline intellectually functioning?"

"Not necessarily, but it's one possibility."

"And you indicated a second issue was that Mrs. Dunn didn't receive prenatal care. Doctor, are you aware of what percentage of women in the world receives prenatal care?"

"In the *world*?" I asked.

"Women in the world," he answered.

"Mr. Gallo, I think there are pretty significant cultural differences in terms of access to and beliefs about prenatal care, and we really have to compare her to the norms in our own culture."

"So then your answer is no, you don't know the number."

"Right," I said. "I don't."

He then attacked the notion that letting a cellulitis infection go untreated for months was also an indication of her limited knowledge and judgment.

"The illness is just a skin disorder; isn't that correct?" he said.

"To say it's just a skin disorder, Mr. Gallo, is to trivialize the fact that it's a major staph infection that can become systemic and turn into a blood disorder and that she has permanent scarring from it," I said.

"When did you go to medical school, Dr. Vinocour?" he asked.

"About the same time you did, Mr. Gallo," I said. I couldn't help myself.

"Dr. Vinocour," the judge began.

"Sorry," I said, my second lie of the day. "I haven't gone to medical school, Mr. Gallo."

The judge called for a fifteen-minute recess. The bailiff escorted the jurors out, back to their little cubbyhole of a room with the dog-eared crossword puzzles and ancient big-print *Reader's Digests*. I headed out into the hallway for a breath of air and saw Karen headed for me.

"How are you doing?" she asked.

"Okay," I said, though my heart was running in a kind of irregular gallop, as it does sometimes under stress. I wondered, idly, what impact it would have on the jury if I dropped dead while on the stand. Would it make Gallo look like a reckless and depravedly indifferent murderer and be of any help to Dorothy's case?

"I think it's going pretty well," Karen said. "But be careful. You're sparring. Don't be too argumentative. It makes it sound as if you're not impartial."

She was right, I knew. I was being too defensive. But I was out there alone. She wasn't objecting to Gallo's tactics or offering me any cover. The judge, who sometimes intervened to protect expert witnesses from the disrespect and sarcasm from attorneys, was not going to throw me a rope, either. I imagined he figured, since I'd been an attorney in my dark past, I had the tools to protect myself. Maybe he was even enjoying seeing Gallo and me joust with each other.

Gallo and I were definitely bringing out the worst in each other, but I was gambling that the jury would like me better. Still, I'd have to tone it down, emotionally disengage, stay neutral, avoid making it personal.

We reassembled in the courtroom, I again took my seat in the witness box, and the jurors filed in. I made a mental note to be less argumentative.

Gallo rose and strode toward me.

"You know that the defendant, who you say was intellectually limited, was able to obtain a graduate equivalency degree?" he said.

"No, sir," I said. "There's no record of her having ever obtained any GED degree. She did tell me and Dr. Kraft that she obtained it, but there's no record of it, and I don't believe that she did."

"With respect to her ability to understand cause and effect," Gallo said, "she threw Precious Love out of the house at one point because she was fighting with Tonette and she knew it was bad for Tonette?"

"Yes."

"She also told you about Mr. Wilson, things that Mr. Wilson did in the home, about abusing the children? You understand that the defendant kicked Mr. Wilson out of the house because she believed he abused her children?" This was the man Dorothy referred to simply as "Mister."

"Yes."

"So it's your testimony, then, that the defendant could understand cause and effect."

He changed tacks before I could answer.

"You indicated that with respect to the defendant's talking with ambulance personnel, the police, that they reported her to appear evasive, but it was your opinion that it was a dissociative disorder that they were actually observing; correct?"

"Yes," I said. "It's my opinion that a part of what they thought was evasiveness in not supplying answers might have been that she truly did not have any clear memory and didn't have answers."

"Doctor," he said. "Please just answer the question."

"I'm trying to, Mr. Gallo," I said.

He next began trying to create doubt about whether Dorothy's behaviors really were disorganized and impaired in the weeks before Raymie's death. I had referred in my report to Dorothy's failure to keep food in the house or to fix meals for the children.

"Doctor, you have children. Did your boys ever prepare their own meals?"

"Yes," I said.

"So you are saying that because sometimes a child would make a meal it shows that a parent is incapable of organizing meals?"

"It depends on why they were doing it," I said. "Out of necessity or just because they liked to."

We continued to go around like that, Gallo testing whether I'd had an adequate basis to conclude that Mrs. Dunn had a significant mental illness. We circled each other, mentally, like wrestlers searching for a hold. His questions became more and more pointed, and he frequently cut off my answers, looking for the yes or no that would support his theory of her guilt.

"DSS was pressuring Dorothy Dunn to take responsibility for Raymie; is that correct?"

"Yes."

"And she said that she didn't want to take that on?"

"Right."

"This is the warm, caring woman who loved Raymie?"

"Yup."

He flashed one of the autopsy pictures up onto the screen, looked at it, then looked at the jury.

"Doctor, you told us that you felt that Dorothy Dunn loved Raymie. Showing you People's Exhibit 54, is *that* an example of her love?" he bellowed.

"I don't know how to answer that question, Mr. Gallo. I think a sane person, who loved a child, would not cause these injuries."

And with that, we were done.

CHAPTER 41

GALLO HAD ONE LAST card to play. When he'd received a copy of my evaluation of Dorothy Dunn, detailing her mental retardation and mental illness and putting him on notice that Karen would mount a psychological defense, he had enlisted the services of psychiatrist Dr. Merlin Kraft to give a second opinion.

Kraft was a longtime consultant to the district attorney's office. His assessment of Dorothy Dunn was based on four and a half hours spent with her, nearly six months after her arrest. By that time, she was in a very different condition than she had been at the time of Raymie's death. She had stabilized in prison, with sufficient sleep, nourishment, and routine.

According to Kraft's report, he did not read any of Dorothy's, or Precious Love's, school, psychiatric, medical, or Department of Social Services or child protective records. His information about Dorothy Dunn was thus limited.

GALLO NOW CALLED Dr. Kraft to the stand to rebut my testimony.

Kraft was trim, slight, and nattily dressed, and had a shock of distinguished white hair. He raised his right hand, swore to tell the whole truth, and settled into the witness chair.

After Gallo took him through his credentials, Kraft started by asserting that Mrs. Dunn was not psychotic, citing as proof, among other things, that she had no psychiatric history. "She's never had anyone else that's observed that she had any psychotic symptoms," he said.

"Do you have an opinion as to whether or not the defendant was capable of knowing her actions could create a grave risk of serious physical injury to Raymie on September sixth?" Gallo asked.

"Yes," said Kraft. "I did come to an opinion on that. I considered whether she has a 'mental defect,' that is, some form of retardation, and concluded that she doesn't, because she was able to get her GED, her graduate equivalence degree from high school. She also became certified as a health aide and certified in CPR."

"Did the defendant exhibit any signs of disorganized behavior or thinking on that occasion?" asked Gallo.

"Of course, I wasn't there that night to make a direct observation, but I was able to reconstruct that. She didn't demonstrate disorganized thinking or behavior around the time of the crime, in my opinion."

Crime, I thought. An interesting word to use. The jury had yet to decide that very thing: whether there had been a crime. But Kraft had evidently seen it that way.

"She was misrepresenting things to the 911 operator," he said. "That's a level of organized thinking and behavior, to be evasive."

"Doctor, do you have an opinion, to a reasonable degree of medical certainty," Gallo asked, "as to what the defendant's attitude toward Raymie was while he was in her home?"

Karen objected, but to no avail.

"Yes," said Kraft. "There's two contradictory pictures. One is the picture that she talks about how hard she tried, that he was a difficult-to-manage child, in her view. That she was trying to protect him. And then the other picture is the one that emerged during the interviews. She told Dr. Vinocour that the child protective services who placed Raymie with her, that she really didn't want that responsibility and she felt pressured into taking him. She told me, 'No child has no business plundering in my house for food.' That to me is her attitude about Raymie— she considered what he was doing 'plundering'—it was a challenge to her control."

He went on to offer opinions about the psychological testing, even though he did not seem to have a correct understanding of its use or interpretation. He did not have the training to interpret the testing I had done: psychological testing is the unique province of psychologists. Psychiatrists' training is as medical doctors; they generally have no special knowledge of testing theory, test construction, issues of reliability and validity, and other crucial aspects of psychological testing. As noted in the *Journal of Psychiatry and Law*, "When asked about psychological tests in court, most psychiatrists respond by saying that they have not been trained to administer, score, or interpret psychological tests and that it would be inappropriate and unethical for them to [do so] . . . due to their lack of expertise." When psychological testing is required, most competent forensic psychiatrists hire a psychologist to administer and interpret such tests. Nonetheless, Dr. Kraft offered the view that the psychological tests showed no intellectual or psychiatric impairment.

"Doctor," Gallo continued, "did you make any finding that showed in any way that the defendant was unable to appreciate the risk of striking Raymie or consciously disregarding that risk?"

"I did not find that she had a mental disease or defect that would preclude her understanding the risks of her behavior or appreciating the results of her actions."

"Thank you, Doctor. No further questions," said Gallo.

So, I thought. According to Kraft, Dorothy Dunn was, essentially, sound as a dollar. Unimpaired either intellectually or psychiatrically and guilty as sin. I was offended by his lack of regard for my findings or opinion. But then, to be fair, I had a similar disregard for his at this point.

Karen rose to begin her cross-examination of Kraft, flipping through her yellow pad of notes as she went.

"Didn't you testify two years ago that, I quote, 'videotaping is intrusive and puts the defendant ill at ease, it makes it hard to get a good picture of what's going on'—is that right?"

"I recall saying that," Kraft replied.

"One of the things that you relied on in assessing Mrs. Dunn's intellectual functioning was that she told you she got her GED, correct?" Hughes asked.

"Correct," he said, nodding.

"Now, you never actually verified that she got a high school diploma, did you?"

"No," he said.

"And there's no record of it, is there?"

"I don't know," Kraft said.

"You didn't check?" she asked.

"No," he said.

"Another thing you indicated was that she was bright enough to be able to hold a job as a nurse's aide, correct?"

"Yes," he said.

"In fact, she told you her job was to fix people's hair and make beds, correct?"

"Okay," he said.

"Well, did she say that?" Karen pressed.

"I don't remember," Kraft said.

"You believed she had received a CPR certificate, correct? That's what she told you?"

"I thought she indicated that she had studied CPR and was certified," he said.

"Okay. Well, you actually went through the CPR procedure with her, didn't you, to see how competent she was?"

"I was seeing what she'd retained from it."

"And she hadn't retained very much, had she?" Karen asked.

"Just the basic, the initial assessment for breathing."

"She didn't give you a satisfactory answer, did she?"

"She wouldn't pass a test on it," he said.

Karen moved on to the next problem.

"You often became very frustrated with Dorothy's inability to respond to you during your interview, didn't you?"

"She didn't respond promptly. She was very delayed. She wasn't always responding to what I was asking. She'd go off on tangents," he said.

"You often found it necessary to lead Mrs. Dunn through every single answer?" Karen asked.

"There were times that was necessary. I don't think she knew what I was asking and driving at."

Karen continued her questioning.

"The principle of whether a person knows or appreciates the consequence of their action is the legal principle specifically applicable to the defense of not guilty by reason of insanity, and that requires also that a defendant has a mental disease or defect, right?" she said.

"Right," he said.

"That's a different standard from the legal principle involved in reckless conduct, right?" she asked.

"Well, New York State doesn't really directly address that," Kraft said.

"Doctor, you do understand the legal principle of reckless conduct, don't you?" she pressed.

"I don't know that I'm clear about that," he said.

"Do you dispute that Mrs. Dunn has borderline intellectual functioning?"

"I think she's low normal," he said.

"At no time did you do an independent evaluation of any of the psychological tests that Dr. Vinocour performed, did you?" she asked.

"That's correct," he said.

"You listed a number of factors you considered in determining that Dorothy Dunn didn't exhibit disorganized thinking and behavior the night Raymie died?"

"Yes."

"And one of the factors was that Dorothy said she told Alice that Raymie was knocked out, correct?" Karen said.

"Yes."

"So that showed a level of awareness?"

"Yes."

"Now, in fact, are you aware that Alice testified that it was she who told Dorothy 'maybe he's knocked out'?" Karen asked.

"No, I didn't know that," he said.

She continued: "And you've said that, in determining to what degree dissociation was occurring to Dorothy, you needed to determine how intact her memory for the events was. But, in fact, you had to prompt her constantly during the entire interview, didn't you?"

"Yes," he acknowledged. " 'Spontaneous' is not a good adjective here. But it was in her memory!"

"Most of your questions were leading questions, weren't they?" she persisted.

"Well, she was crying and she wasn't speaking, not articulating, clearly. I just wasn't sure I was understanding her clearly."

"Because Mrs. Dunn told you that Raymie shouldn't be plundering in her pantry, it was your opinion that she had a negative attitude toward Raymie?"

"I didn't say she had a negative attitude," Kraft said. "I said it would be an indication of her attitude."

"There were other portions of that interview which indicated that Mrs. Dunn cared deeply for Raymie, wasn't that true?" Karen asked.

"I said so," he answered.

"In fact, she cried a lot. And said she loved the boy, didn't she?"

"Yes, she did."

"And one more thing, Doctor. A majority of your forensic testimony over the years has been for the prosecution, is that right?" Karen asked.

"Correct," he said.

Karen had done what she could with Dr. Kraft. Now Gallo got the opportunity to ask him a few more questions, on redirect exam, like batting cleanup in baseball.

Gallo rose.

"You talked about a number of things concerning Mrs. Dunn's evasiveness, Doctor?"

"Well," Kraft said. "It turns out Tonette went to a foster home and had trouble so then she went to a residential treatment center of children and she had a psychological evaluation and was seen by social workers and they talked to her about events. And it was evident to me, reading those records, that Tonette was very interested in being sure that her mother did not go to jail and she wasn't going to say things that might be detrimental to her mother. But then little Scoot started blabbing to the police. Scoot was going to talk! So I put this all together, that Tonette and her mother probably tried to figure out what—"

"Objection!" Karen said, rising to her feet and appealing to the judge.

"Overruled," the judge said.

"—how they were going to present this," Kraft continued, "and what their story would be. And Alice is a Goody Two-shoes; she always did what she's supposed to and didn't demonstrate that kind of guardedness in trying to protect her mother."

I was struck by his language: Scoot "blabbing," Alice "a Goody Two-shoes." Where was this coming from? Of one thing I was sure: if he didn't realize that Raymie was "a difficult-to-manage child" by some objective standard, and not just in Dorothy's mind, he didn't understand anything at all about Dorothy's situation and the stresses she'd been under at the time Raymie died.

"Thank you, Doctor," Gallo said. "That's all."

Karen rose for her one last chance at Kraft.

"Doctor," she said, "that little scenario you gave—about Tonette and Mrs. Dunn planning together and planning out how this injury occurred—is not something you have any evidence for, is it?" She looked at him stonily.

"It's speculation," he said. And it was done.

HOW ARE JURORS to know whom to believe when experts' opinions are diametrically opposed and each has been stated with certainty? How *can* they know? Would they defer to this white-haired eminence, with his professorial air and the MD after his name? Would they assume that as a male and a psychiatrist he knew more than I, a female and a psychologist? Would they rely on my findings or discount both of our testimonies because they were at odds or too confusing to sort out? Opposing testimonies on complex, technical matters beyond the jury's ken tend to cancel each other out.

In actuality, according to Dr. Park Dietz, a well-known forensic psychiatrist, "Psychiatric opinion as to a defendant's criminal responsibility is divided far less often than press coverage suggests." But in the intersection between law and psychiatry, things are never that simple. It is more accurate to say that opinions as to a defendant's psychiatric status are often consistent between experts, while their conclusions about "insanity" differ. This was true in the Holmes case: psychiatrists on both sides of the case agreed that Holmes was psychotic—schizophrenic—and suffering from paranoid delusions that twisted his judgment and reasoning and skewered his sense of reality at the time of the crime. They concurred on the diagnosis, the condition of the defendant, but could not agree on the legal application of "insanity" in Holmes's case. This sort of thing makes jurors, and the media, believe that the experts can't agree about when a person is crazy, and it makes the business of diagnosis seem arbitrary and too uncertain to be relied upon. It makes it look like there's not much expertise among experts.

Nygaard's work led him to conclude that "the contradictory testimony of experts . . . virtually assure arbitrary outcomes." He felt that "trained professionals should be the ones who determine a defendant's mental capacity, not lay persons who must sift through masses of often incomprehensible, or at least uncomprehended, data to make life and death decisions."

Of course, there is an alternative view, and professions often guard their territories zealously. In 1572, when physician Johan Weyer sought to challenge the English law regarding mental illness, the court ruled, "Weyer is not a lawyer, but a physician—consequently, his view on the relationship between mental disease and transgressions of the written law are of no moment." The court meant that final legal determinations of guilt or insanity must be left to the judges and jurors and not given over to mere physicians.

Surely the law has changed in the ensuing 450 years? No.

SUPREME COURT JUSTICE Felix Frankfurter recognized "the pathological processes which give rise to the conflict between so-called legal and medical insanity" in *Solesbee v. Balkcom*. He rejected the notion that there were "treacherous uncertainties in the present state of psychiatric knowledge." Our knowledge of mental illness and the workings of the brain has expanded exponentially in the ensuing decades. We accept this proposition readily when it comes to astronomy, biochemistry, physics, and the other so-called hard sciences, and certainly in medicine generally. Why are we so resistant to it when it comes to psychology?

In any event, the battle of experts in the Dunn case was now joined; Gallo had produced his own mental health expert, for his own reasons, to rebut my testimony and Kraft and I did surely disagree. The jury would have to somehow figure out where the truth lay.

IN AN EARLY CASE hinging on a defendant's sanity, Clarence Darrow railed against cynical and ignorant prosecutions of the mentally ill. In 1893, twenty-five-year-old Patrick Prendergast showed up on the front doorstep of Chicago's newly reelected mayor, Carter Harrison, politely asked to see him, and shot him dead. Prendergast, whom Harrison had never met, was laboring under the delusion that if the mayor's reelection campaign succeeded, he—Prendergast—would be appointed corporation counsel of the city of Chicago. This would have been an odd occurrence on a number of scores, not least of which was that Prendergast had not successfully completed high school, let alone law school.

Prendergast was tried for murder, and his attorneys produced a significant amount of evidence from reputable psychiatrists that he was insane. But the prosecutor had hastily arranged for his own "expert," a psychiatrist of questionable credentials and methods, to evaluate the defendant. This expert convinced the jury that Prendergast "knew" right from wrong, and he was convicted and sentenced to death. But legal errors during the trial entitled him to retrial, where he was represented by one of the most eminent criminal trial attorneys in American history, Clarence Darrow.

Darrow, an impassioned orator, was struck by the prosecutorial shenanigans in discrediting respected psychiatrists who testified for the defense and offering the testimony of a well-known mountebank in their place. Here is part of his closing argument on Prendergast's behalf (I always picture Spencer Tracy here in *Inherit the Wind*):

Before engaging in the present trial I had supposed that there were certain tried standards which the ethics of the profession had enjoined upon prosecutors that should be followed by honorable men. I had never believed that the State was so interested in taking the blood of any human being that lawyers should travel beyond the truth and beyond the record and beg the jury to violate their oath for the sake of "giving justice a victim," as these gentlemen put it. . . .

The only issue before you, gentlemen, is the condition of this man's mind. Nothing else. And yet counsel have paraded to you the horrible details of a horrible assassination. They have pictured the blood of the victim and the sorrow of the family . . . and they have done this, gentlemen, that you might be blinded by the sight of this blood and forget the question of the mind of this unfortunate being. . . .

Over and over again you have been advised by respectable men of this boy's condition, and in spite of that you [the prosecutors] have gone up and down through the sewers of the medical profession and searched for men [the prosecution's psychiatrists] who would be willing to tie the rope around this boy's neck; . . . These gentlemen know that the reason they have introduced in this case doctors without name and without reputation is that they could not get any other to seek to swear away this boy's life. . . ." They went [to the boy's jail cell] to find reasons for hanging, they went there to make excuses for your conscience, they went there to prejudice your judgment, they went there to extort reasons from this weak mind; not to investigate the case and to ascertain the truth. . . . They asked their questions as a hunter would set a snare to catch a bird. . . .

Alas for the humanity of men who, through some mysteri-

ous means become attached to the State, and to what they call
the administration of justice.

Darrow's argument failed, the images of blood and sorrow prevailed,
and Prendergast, the penniless Irish immigrant, was hanged before the
year was out.

"GOD HELP THE JURY," I said to Karen as we left the courtroom for
the day.

"God help Dorothy Dunn," she replied.

That evening, as I sat nursing a headache and a gin and tonic, Karen
called.

"Good news!" she said. "The judge has finally ordered the Department of Social Services to release Dante's Child Protective Services
records. You know how Dorothy has always maintained that the CPS
worker she had with Dante told her she should hit him harder? Well,
now we at least have a chance to see if there's any conceivable truth to
it. Can you take a look at them?"

Of course I could.

The courier arrived shortly and handed a heavy, rain-flecked, manila
envelope through the door. I made a cup of tea, shut off the phone, and
began to page through the stack of neatly typed reports and smudged,
hand-scrawled progress notes. It was at least two inches thick; this was
going to take several hours of close reading.

I went through the social worker's log very carefully. In it, she had
written: "Ms. Dunn continues to be invested in Dante, and seems most
appreciative of service." She described Dorothy as "disorganized" and
"lacking in practical parenting know-how" and noted that Dorothy's idea
of discipline was "whupping him with a broom to control his behavior,"
although this only made him laugh. Finally, she made note of Dorothy's
"clear limitations" and "her essential good nature."

And then, word for word, the social worker's advice to Dorothy when she'd protested that she didn't want to strike her children, didn't want to beat them:

"I advised her she had to do whatever it takes," the worker had written.

I called Karen.

"Karen, "I said, "The social worker from CPS as much as told Dorothy to beat the child."

"Are you sure?"

"Yep. Absolutely."

"So when she hit Raymie she was following their directions?"

"Yep. That's just how she would have understood it."

"My God," said Karen. "This means I've got to call you back to the stand tomorrow, you know, to testify about the contents of that file."

"I know. I'll be there."

I slept more peacefully that night than usual and woke feeling refreshed for the first time in weeks.

CHAPTER 42

"ALL RISE," THE BAILIFF INTONED as the judge strode into the courtroom the next morning.

"Be seated," said the judge. Karen rose. "Counselor?" he queried, arching one eyebrow.

"Your Honor, I would like to recall Dr. Vinocour to the stand for brief redirect examination."

"Objection," Gallo said, rising and pushing his glasses up onto his forehead.

"Overruled," the judge said, his curiosity perhaps piqued. He nodded his head in my direction, and I took the witness chair again.

"I remind you that you are still under oath," the judge admonished.

I nodded, the thick Social Services file on Dante in my lap like a delicate box of TNT, and turned my attention toward Karen.

"Doctor," she began, "have you now had an opportunity to review the Department of Social Services CPS case file regarding Ms. Dunn's son Dante and the advice the department gave Ms. Dunn about how she should use physical discipline on her son?"

"I have."

"Will you please tell the court if there was anything in that record that supports your clinical findings and opinion about Mrs. Dunn?"

"Yes, there—"

Gallo jumped up.

"Objection!" he barked, papers spilling off his lap and onto the floor.

He had not seen those records, but perhaps he divined their implication. The rules of evidence bar either prosecution or defense from springing evidence on their opponent without prior notice and the ability to review that evidence. He was entitled to object to the last-minute presentation of this evidence.

"Ms. Hughes failed to disclose those records to the people in a timely manner, Your Honor," Gallo said. "She didn't give notice. This is the first I'm hearing of them. We haven't had a chance to review this material. The time limit for disclosure has expired, and she is barred from introducing this evidence over my objection."

Law is about a system of rules, and the orderly application of those rules to each case that comes before the court. The rules were developed to try to maximize fairness and justice overall, but they don't always lead to the truth in individual cases.

"Ms. Hughes?" The judge peered at her over the tops of his reading glasses. "He has a point."

"Your Honor," Karen said. "This material is critical to shedding light on my client's intentions and motivations. It goes right to the heart of the matter of what she understood about right and wrong and whether she meant to be abusing the child or was making a good-faith effort to discipline him, following the advice of the Department of Social Services."

"Nevertheless," the judge said, "you did not give timely notice to the prosecution."

"I didn't know about it myself until last night, Your Honor," she protested. "The Department of Social Services wouldn't release the material to me. We only had a chance to review it within the last few hours."

He could order an adjournment to give the prosecutor time to review the files, but that would screw up his calendar and keep the jurors under obligation, away from their jobs and families longer.

"I'm sorry, counselor. I'm going to have to sustain the objection," the judge ruled.

"But—"

"Objection sustained. Move on. Do you have any other questions for this witness?"

"No, Your Honor," Karen said, running a hand through her hair.

"Very well, then. The witness is excused. Do you have anything else?"

"No, Your Honor. The defense rests," Karen said.

I felt stricken.

CHAPTER 43

DRESSED IN A SOMBER navy blue suit that accentuated the darkening circles under her eyes, Karen stood and faced the jury. She paced for a moment, head down, thoughtful. Then she looked up and began her closing argument.

"I just want to remind you all that Dorothy Dunn is not on trial for burning Raymie James with cigarettes or beating him with a switch or a belt or tying him up. The government has accused Dorothy Dunn of hitting Raymie in the head with a board, and that that's what killed him. She's on trial for one act, one act that should be the focus of what you have to decide. Mr. Gallo argues that by doing that, ladies and gentlemen, she did an evil act, one that was immoral. But the issue in this case that you're going to have to decide, first of all, is whether you are satisfied beyond a reasonable doubt that Mrs. Dunn committed this act.

"Alice is the eyewitness to this case, and she told you what happened: she heard a thump in the night and came downstairs and found Raymie lying on the pantry floor and that Mom was asleep, that Raymie was covered with sugar. That's what she saw, ladies and gentlemen. You saw evidence of where the sugar was kept in the pantry, way up on the shelf. A big heavy container of sugar that a twenty-eight-pound boy was trying to lift, I suggest to you, trying to put back.

"Remember that Alice is only ten years old, and she has the limited understanding of a ten-year-old. But she told you she woke up her mother and that Dorothy gave Raymie a butter and sugar sandwich, then some peppers, then took Raymie out into a room and started to yell at him and then she started to beat him with the board, with the paddle. That's not in dispute, but where did she say her mother hit Raymie? In the backside, in the butt, in the legs. Those are not the injuries that the government claims killed Raymie. Dr. Welch talked about a head injury so severe by a hit in the head with a board that it would compare to an automobile accident. Alice said that didn't happen, that was not her testimony.

"I ask you to evaluate the credibility of Dr. Welch's testimony. What empirical evidence did he have to draw the conclusion that the final head injury to Raymie was caused by a hit in the head with a board? I submit that when Dr. Welch first saw Raymie's body he was horrified and he let emotion cloud his investigation in this case. He decided that this was child abuse and he was going to make sure that that's what his final conclusion was. I suggest to you, ladies and gentlemen, that when Dr. Welch first got this case he already decided that he was going to find a cause of death that included child abuse, a shaken/struck baby case. But he acknowledged that to confirm this diagnosis, there would have to be retinal hemorrhages, so he sent those eyeballs out to be tested and they came back with no retinal hemorrhage.

"Ask yourself, didn't Dr. Welch fail to do an objective, scientific investigation because he was so overcome with emotion? Why did he so quickly discount the testimony of the only eyewitness, Alice Dunn? He let emotion get in the way of what his objective duty was; it affected him so deeply that he actually was tearful when he testified before the grand jury. He had already made up his mind before he began to examine the evidence.

"He said that this was 'the most horrific case of child abuse he had ever seen.' But he had only worked in the medical examiner's office for approximately twenty days at the time he did Raymie James's autopsy. His inexperience, ladies and gentlemen, certainly explains why he did not maintain a professional attitude in investigating the case.

"What if Mrs. Dunn really does not know or understand how or why Raymie died? In her limited way, she felt responsible because it happened in her house. It was a logical statement for her to make when she said, 'Am I going to prison?' when there were fifteen law enforcement personnel in and out of the house that morning. Is that an admission of guilt? No. Because something happened in her house which she feels responsible for and believes she will be held responsible for. Why else would she sign a 'consent to search' form? The investigator said to her, 'This will help us find out what happened to Raymie,' and she said, 'I'll sign it.'

"Dorothy Dunn is very limited, ladies and gentlemen. Nothing is obvious to Dorothy Dunn, and I want you to think about that. Nothing is obvious to her. These appear on the surface to be brutal acts, but I'm asking you to get in Mrs. Dunn's mind and think the way she thought. She didn't want to injure, she didn't want to hurt. She just wanted to discipline, to teach, to get Raymie to behave the way she thought a child should behave.

"She's limited in her understanding, and I'm asking you to remember that and try to understand who she is, because on the surface, it would be our natural reaction to think that this had to be a monster. But Mrs. Dunn was not a monster; she was a caring mother of limited capacity, overwhelmed, poor, poor, with children to support, an older daughter deteriorating, psychotic, not washing, wandering the streets. An older son who's been in and out of the prison system, and Mrs. Dunn's own abilities to function deteriorating at that time. You saw the videotape of her home. She has no phone. She hadn't even got the kids enrolled in school this year. I'm not suggesting to you that Mrs. Dunn couldn't appreciate the nature and consequence of her actions. She knows right from wrong; she's a moral person with a moral fiber.

"Every life involved in this case is such a tragedy. Think of Dorothy's children: Where is Precious Love, Raymie's mother? Where is Dante? Where is Tonette? What does Alice feel, knowing she came to court and testified for the government at her mother's murder trial? What about little Scoot? Raymie? Raymie?

"This whole case is such a human tragedy. And you're going to see photographs and you're going to feel the tragedy, and that's okay. I ask you to feel that, to feel it, but don't, ladies and gentlemen, let it get in the way of what the issues are, of what your role is.

"I'm asking you to find that Dorothy Dunn is not Raymie James's murderer. I'm asking you to find that Dorothy Dunn is not a monster, that her conduct is not so immoral that it makes her a murderer or that she showed no regard for human life. She's not a monster, and she cares about human life. She's not a murderer because she just didn't have, at the time of Raymie's death, the right understanding. Nothing is obvious to her. At the time of Raymie's death, she wasn't aware in a clear sense of her actions and what her actions could result in. And because she didn't have that bright, obvious, clear, knowing, awareness, she couldn't disregard anything. And if you find that she's not a murderer, ladies and gentlemen, it's an expression of hope, not just for humanity, but for Raymie."

Karen made eye contact with each juror in turn and then slowly walked back to the defense table, sat down, and put a comforting hand on Dorothy's arm.

THE JUDGE NODDED and Gallo rose to give his closing argument and walked over to the jurors, his hands clasped as if in prayer.

"Every child's life," he began, "is marked by the passing of milestones. We watch as children learn to walk and to talk. We celebrate his birthdays past. We watch as they go to school for the first time. Raymie James's life was also marked, but it wasn't marked by milestones, it was marked by systematic torture at the hands of one individual. The life of this little boy is not measured by the birthdays that passed, but by what part of his body is being struck and what implement is doing the damage on that particular day. This little boy was in a living hell. Raymie James was abused from head to toe, inside and out.

"This case is not about love, and it's not about teaching. It's about anger and resentment. Raymie James was not being punished for some safety issue about being in the kitchen. He knew that in order to get food, he would have to sneak up in the middle of the night and get whatever he could get his hands on. Raymie James was being tortured because he wanted to eat. He knew he had to risk the constant abuse, the constant torture that he faced, but he had to take that risk because that was the only way he was going to eat.

"Ladies and gentlemen, Ms. Hughes ended her comments with a cry toward what was suggested to you is sympathy. But the judge is going to talk to you about the definition of reckless conduct, and you're going to hear about the definition of depraved indifference to human life. What you're not going to hear is that you must find the defendant to be a monster or that she has antisocial behavior.

"We know that the person who touched him with a cigarette, who beat him with a spatula, who struck him with high-heeled shoes, beat him with a belt, an extension cord, a wooden paddle and tied him to the air conditioner are all the same person. We know that that person is the defendant. Little Alice has told us. . . . She describes her mother's actions. She doesn't describe merely a punishment, she describes a course of conduct that builds from the first point where the peppers are given to Raymie—'eat this'—to the point where she takes Raymie out into the living room and she's, once, 'Why are you doing this?' and strikes him and gets no answer and strikes him, and asks again and gets no answer and strikes him again and again and again. Now, Alice doesn't tell you she specifically sees Raymie get hit in the head, but we know that the house is dark and a three-year-old boy is not going to be standing at attention. And we know that the fatal blow is very likely to the back of his head and the blow in and of itself shows this depraved indifference. But striking him with a board as hard as she did wasn't enough. She throws him from room to room, to a point where Alice is able to describe Raymie is unable to walk. He can't keep his head level.

"Dorothy Dunn knew full well then and there what she had done. She understood the risk; she told Dr. Kraft, 'You don't hit a child in the head, that's abuse, you can mess up their brain.' She had perfect understanding of what the risk was and made a conscious decision to continue the assault. She doesn't call for help. She knows what condition Raymie is in, she's indifferent to that condition; she wants to go back to sleep. Is there some explanation other than indifference, other than malice, other than anger and spite that can explain the defendant's actions?

"Dr. Welch does not have an agenda, he has a heart and a soul. Ms. Hughes wants you to remember the other children. She cries out for humanity. But, ladies and gentlemen, I'm not going to cry, I'm going to ask you for justice. I'm going to ask you to return a verdict that tells Dorothy Dunn, Your actions on September sixth were brutal, were wanton, were callous, were devoid of caring to the life of a three-year-old boy who only wanted to eat. Dorothy resented this child, that's what all the proof points to. I'm asking you to decide whether taking a bread board to this child is brutal, whether it shows malice, whether it shows she was caring and loving or whether she was angry and resentful.

"The pictures of Raymie's body are not pictures that show someone's love. They are pictures that show us the horrors that this little boy lived with and that this little boy died from; it shows the defendant is guilty of murder!"

CHAPTER 44

T HE JURORS WENT TO deliberate without being told a crucial fact: if a defendant is found not guilty by reason of insanity, she is not simply released; she is involuntarily confined to a secure psychiatric facility until certified as no longer a danger, and many of the psychiatrists staffing these units are loath to stake their reputations on predicting safety, especially in high-visibility cases.

In some states, the law does not allow giving the jury any information at all about the consequence of a verdict of not guilty by reason of insanity. In New York, a cryptic statement is permitted during the charges to the jury:

> Where a defendant has raised the . . . defense of lack of crimi-
> nal responsibility by reason of mental disease or defect, . . . the
> court must, without elaboration, instruct the jury as follows: "a
> jury during its deliberations must never consider or speculate
> concerning matters relating to the consequence of its verdict.
> However, because of the lack of common knowledge regard-

ing the consequences of a verdict of not responsible by reason
of mental disease or defect, I charge you that if this verdict is
rendered by you there will be hearings as to the defendant's
present mental condition and, where appropriate, involuntary
commitment proceedings.

The average adult, and presumably the average juror, reads at a
ninth-grade level. Do they understand this legal instruction? Why is it
that we don't tell jurors what the result of an insanity verdict would be?
And would it make a difference to jurors in deciding whether to find a
defendant sane or insane if they knew?

In 1999, Andrew Goldstein shoved Kendra Webdale off a subway plat-
form in New York City, into the path of an onrushing train, and she was
killed in front of horrified onlookers. The defense attorneys argued that
Goldstein had been legally insane at the time of the act. As journalists sat
schmoozing during a break in the trial, *New York Times* writer Michael
Winerip related, "a TV reporter remarked 'I'd vote guilty. I'd want to
make sure Goldstein goes away for a long time.'" Winerip noted, "That
of course was not what the trial was supposed to be about. It was the
jurors' job to decide whether Goldstein knew right from wrong when he
pushed Kendra Webdale in front of the subway train or whether he was
insane at the time, and thus not responsible for what he did."

If found sane, Goldstein would be guilty of murder and sentenced
to at least twenty-five years in prison. But "if judged insane, he would
go to a secure state psychiatric hospital. There he would be re-evaluated
every two years to determine whether he was fit for discharge. And that,
I believe," said Winerip, "scared the hell out of many New Yorkers—the
possibility that Andrew Goldstein could be back on the streets in a few
years' time. It was, to my mind, the prosecutor's secret weapon." In fact,
Goldstein had admitted himself to a psychiatric hospital several months
before, suffering from delusions, extreme mental confusion, and violent

urges. But he was released after only a few weeks. Three weeks later, he murdered Webdale.

Winerip discovered that the jurors were roughly split on the question of insanity when they started their deliberations. "But," he added, "there was something else, several of them said in interviews, that kept eating at them, that they knew, as jurors, they were not supposed to consider, but that they could not help worrying about. 'I was thinking, What happens if he's found not guilty by reason of insanity and gets out in a short time,' [one juror] said. 'I know we weren't supposed to talk about it, but I brought it up once myself. I said, 'Let's talk about the ramifications of our judgment. . . . I know that people don't stay in mental institutions very long. I thought to myself, How am I going to feel in a year or two or five when he's killed somebody else? . . . It definitely had an influence on me.'"

Goldstein was convicted of murder and sentenced to prison for twenty-five years to life. Kendra Webdale's mother, who may have needed to believe there was some sense and reason to her daughter's murder, and that that reason was evil, said, "I thought of my daughter Kendra when I heard it [the verdict] and it was more than I hoped for. I felt like jumping for joy."

We have a term, *jury nullification*, for when a jury finds a defendant innocent although the evidence clearly proves guilt, because conviction does not seem just to the jury. What should we call it when a jury convicts a defendant clearly proven not guilty by reason of insanity to ensure that person's lengthy imprisonment? I don't think you can call it justice. The verdict amounted to the loss of another life, Goldstein's—hardly a cause for joy. His conviction was akin to shooting a rabid dog, who cannot help himself, for biting. We feel relief that the danger is past, but joy? That is vengeance, not justice.

The insanity defense is hardly the "get out of jail free" card of popular myth. Winerip went on to note that Goldstein would probably spend more time locked away in a psychiatric facility if found not guilty by reason of insanity than he would in jail once convicted. Citing a 1995 study from the journal *Law and Human Behavior*, he explained that "defendants who were judged insane actually wound up spending more time confined to psychiatric facilities than their guilty counterparts spent in prisons." In fact, the Supreme Court has ruled that committing insanity-verdict defendants involuntarily for an indefinite length of time is not a violation of their due process rights under the Constitution, as long as they are both mentally ill and dangerous.

Psychiatrists and psychologists are given responsibility for determining when an involuntarily admitted patient judged not guilty by reason of insanity can safely reenter society without posing a danger to others. Psychiatric experts almost always err on the side of caution, continuing to confine patients long after any evidence of danger has passed. In most states, New York among them, there is no limit to the potential length of time a patient can be confined.

Prison terms are finite; when the time is up, a convicted mentally ill defendant is released back into society, still dangerous or not. This usually occurs without their having received any meaningful treatment for any underlying psychiatric disorder and without any inquiry into whether they still constitute a danger to others. They have paid their debt; they are free to reoffend.

CHAPTER 45

THE HOURS CRAWLED BY, and still the Dunn jury was not back. I took it as a good sign that their deliberations were still going on. I was aware of the effects of implicit racial bias in our courts and the difficulty jurors have in feeling any emotional connection to a mentally ill defendant. But there was certainly a reasonable doubt as to whether Dorothy had inflicted the fatal injury or been aware that Raymie needed help. And a strong case had been made for the likelihood that Dorothy had not known what she was doing on the night of the child's death. I hoped it had been enough to overcome the jurors' visceral, emotional reaction to a child's death and the great divide between them and Dorothy as she'd sat, silent and unresponsive, never making eye contact, throughout the trial. To the jury, her depression, confusion, and sense of shame over Raymie's death might have looked like heartless indifference and even proof of guilt.

I knew that Karen was waiting anxiously, just as I was. Was Dorothy also waiting? It wasn't clear to me that she even understood that her future hung in the balance as those hours ticked by. Did she know what was going on? Did she realize that if the jury found her not guilty, she might soon be going back home to her children and her life, as miserable as it was? Did she understand that if she was found not guilty by reason of insanity, she would be going to a psychiatric hospital for an indeterminate period of time, perhaps as short as thirty days, but perhaps as long as any prison sentence could be or longer, even? And that if they returned a verdict of guilty, she would be remanded to a state prison, far from her children, for many years?

Standing in the solitude of my office, lost for a moment in my own thoughts, I was startled by the shrilling of the phone. I jumped and answered it.

"The jury's on its way back. They have a verdict," Karen said.

I realized I had been holding my breath.

I hurried over to the courthouse and slipped into the courtroom just as the judge was taking his seat. I felt strongly invested in the outcome of the case. It wasn't that I "liked" Dorothy Dunn; her mental illness and limited intellect made it difficult to establish any bond with her. But I liked justice. In Dorothy, I had found an abused child who had grown up with precious little help from anyone, a mentally deficient child inhabiting a woman's body and responsibilities, and a person for whom suffering had been the norm. I saw a woman who had done her best under impossible circumstances, resulting in tragedy, and who had never intentionally done anyone harm. I saw a woman who was not guilty. I hoped the jurors saw her, too.

As the jurors shuffled in, single file, I studied their faces. I did not envy them; I knew how much they didn't know, how much important evidence they had not been allowed to hear. Maybe they suspected it, as well. The rules of evidence that control what can be introduced at trial often keep things out that most of us, were we charged with getting to the truth of a matter, would want to know.

A murmur rippled through the gallery, and the judge rapped his gavel smartly on the bench. The journalists sat on edge, ready to spring for the door when a verdict was announced. This case was hanging in the air at every dinner table and coffee break in the community. People at local companies like Kodak and Bausch & Lomb and Xerox, at the medical centers and the colleges, at the muffler shops and Chinese restaurants, were waiting to see how it would end, like penny gamblers watching the spinning whirls of one-armed bandits.

"Silence!" the judge commanded, scanning the room with a threatening gaze. "We'll have silence or I'll clear the courtroom!" Then he turned to the jury. "Have you reached a verdict?" he asked.

"We have," the forewoman answered.

The judge motioned for her to stand. Then he turned to Dorothy and Karen.

"The defendant will rise and face the jury," he commanded.

Karen stood up, gently pulling Dorothy up beside her by the elbow, and faced the jury.

The bailiff walked over to the forewoman and took the folded ballot from her. He passed it to the judge, who opened it, glanced at it, betraying no trace of emotion, and handed it to his clerk.

"As to the charge of murder in the second degree, how say you?" the judge asked.

The clerk cleared her throat.

"We, the jury, find the defendant, Dorothy Dunn, guilty of murder in the second degree."

"So say you all?" the judge asked, following the ancient formula for justice.

"So say we all."

The reporters, hurrying to file their stories, stampeded for the exits, coats crumpled under their arms like broken wings. Spectators rumbled their approval and gathered up their things to leave.

I felt crushed and remained in the courtroom a long time. When I slowly made my way out of the now-deserted courtroom I found Karen standing in the marble hallway.

"I polled some of the jurors," she said. "They told me they liked you, and they wanted to believe you, but they just couldn't get past the pictures."

"I'm sorry," I said. And then, clumsily: "You did the best you could for her."

It wasn't much, but it was all I could do. It came from the awkward kinship of defense attorneys, the knowledge that they must console one another in defeat, as no one else will. Their cause is not a popular one.

As I walked down the broad granite courthouse steps, through the door, and into the chill air and the fading light of late afternoon, I felt as though we, and the system, had utterly failed Raymie and Dorothy Dunn.

PART III

The Punishment

CHAPTER 46

Nowhere are the effects of the concatenation of poverty, mental illness, and racial disparity more clear than in a comparison of Dorothy Dunn's case with the simultaneous story of Deirdre Hart Wilson, scion of Xerox founder Joseph Wilson.

At about the same time Dorothy Dunn was being tried for the death of her grandson Raymie, a nineteen-month-old child was found to have starved to death in a home occupied by "the Family," a group of five women, one man, and thirteen children out in Marin County, the land of plenty at the end of the Golden Gate Bridge. One of the women in the Family was Deirdre Hart Wilson, granddaughter of Joe Wilson, the founder of Xerox, and several of the children were hers.

The San Francisco paper *SF Weekly* reported:

At around 10:30 p.m., four women walked through the ER doors [at Kaiser Permanente] as casually as if they were entering a Safeway. One of them—a middle-aged woman wearing a head scarf—was cradling a baby in her arms. Meyer [the ER doctor] observed that the boy was limp and looked dead. "Our child isn't breathing," the woman calmly told an emergency medical technician. The women's facial expressions were weirdly "flat," remembers Meyer. They didn't, in any case, seem especially concerned.

The boy was nineteen months old but looked half that age. He had a bloated belly, and his legs were bowed, "like frog legs." Attempts to revive him failed, and the autopsy determined that the child, Ndigo, had died of severe malnutrition. He also had a number of broken bones.

"It seemed very bizarre to walk up with an obviously very dead child, and before that not realize that something very, very bad was going on, and not call an ambulance," said Meyer. When he told the women Ndigo was dead, there was no crying, no screaming.

"Their reaction was, 'Uh, OK,'" said Meyer.

The woman who had carried the boy into the hospital—who appeared to be in charge—asked if the coroner had arrived yet. Meyer told them he had.

"Good," she said, as if bored, "because we're ready to go home."

Investigators soon determined that the thirteen near-starving children, all fathered by the Family's sole man, Winnfred Wright, were forced to live by a "Book of Rules." Any child who broke a rule would be bent over a weight-lifting bench and whipped with a leather belt. They were forced to fast, to wear tape over their mouths, and to eat hot jalapeño peppers. One young girl said she had been tied to a playpen for two weeks because, during an enforced fast, she had snuck some food.

The children did not go to school, to doctors, or to dentists. They ate a strict diet that left them suffering from bones deformed by rickets, a vitamin-deficiency disease almost unheard of in the United States in modern times.

The *Marin Independent Journal* reported:

Two of the children with the worst injuries in the video were Wilson's. One five-year-old child walked toward the camera with extremely bowed legs, knees close together and feet far apart, resulting from rickets. Another child, two years old, was said to be unable to walk or stand because of rickets and erupted into tears when an older sibling had him sit up. . . . One of Wilson's children will have to have corrective surgery involving breaking both legs and resetting them.

THE FAMILY HAD first been investigated by San Francisco Child Protective Services a decade before, after the mysterious death of another infant. Subsequent investigations revealed allegations of abuse and starvation, but the children were never taken from the home, and no charges were brought against the parents.

The man and three of the women, including Deirdre Hart Wilson, were each charged with second-degree murder, manslaughter, and multiple counts of felony child endangerment. Ms. Wilson, whose family was well resourced, was represented by a private attorney, who requested, and was granted, a gag order on the press so that pretrial publicity would not prejudice the jury or sway public opinion. After some legal wrangling, Wilson was offered a deal: plead guilty to five counts of child endangerment, and the charges of manslaughter and second-degree murder would be dropped. She took the deal.

Wilson rose to speak on her own behalf at her sentencing hearing. She said her mind had been controlled by Wright, who had robbed her of her own judgment and will. Weeping, she told the court, "I've been living as a psychological amputee." Prosecutor Barry Borden rejected this contention, pointing out that Wilson had made her own entries to the Book of Rules and had "actively participated in the 'house of horrors.'" He asked the judge to impose a lengthy sentence, pointing out that Wilson was an educated woman and "had done nothing to help her two-year-old boy, who could not walk or talk, cried incessantly from pain and could only get around by pushing his head around on the floor like a wheelbarrow."

The judge, like many judges and juries, was put in the position of amateur psychologist, trying to gauge the defendant's degree of culpability and remorse, but without the least mental health training or expertise. He acknowledged that he struggled with an appropriate sentence for Wilson. He said he could not absolve her of responsibility but did believe she was remorseful. In consequence of the appearance of remorse, he quietly accepted her plea of guilty to the reduced charge of child endangerment. He sentenced Deirdre Hart Wilson, originally charged, like Dorothy Dunn, with second-degree murder, to a term of seven years and four months in prison. With credit for time served and good behavior, she was paroled two years later.

CHAPTER 47

WHAT WOULD BECOME of Dorothy and her children now? She had been convicted, and she, and they, would be punished. Philosopher Immanuel Kant tells us that to fail to punish a crime is to permit an injustice to exist. Others tell us that retribution is a less than lofty goal and urge safety and rehabilitation as legitimate aims. But what would their punishment be?

Some theorists have pointed out that, in reality, punishment tends to "reflect the dominant forms of social and political power—the power to threaten, coerce, suppress, destroy, transform—that prevail in any given" society and time. The *Report of the Sentencing Project to the United Nations Human Rights Committee* concluded that "the United States in effect operates two distinct criminal justice systems: one for wealthy people and another for poor people and minorities" and that "once minority defendants are convicted, they are likely to be sentenced more harshly than white defendants convicted for similar crimes." And public policy expert Tushar Kansal notes, "Race still exerts an undeniable presence in the sentencing process."

Disparity in sentencing is widespread, in spite of various sentencing guidelines, and as Kevin Clancy et al. observe, "substantial dissensus exists among judges about the sentences that convicted offenders should serve," i.e., there is little consistency in sentencing. According to Willard Gaylin and Daniel Callahan, "Each judge has a point of view, a set of standards and values, a bias, if you will, which will color, influence, and direct the nature of his verdicts independently of the specific conditions of the criminal being charged." They also note: "These sets of values constitute bias in a non-pejorative sense—but bias nonetheless, and a bias that will influence equality and fairness in exactly the same way as naked bigotry does."

Another issue also exerts a powerful pull on judges during sentencing: the appearance of remorse and contrition. Defendants perceived as bad or evil by jurors are much more likely to be convicted than those who are not, and they receive harsher sentences. Part of jurors' and judges' calculation is whether the defendant appears remorseful, has learned her lesson and is repentant, as though this is some reliable index of her likelihood of repeating the act. Here, mentally ill defendants are at a significant disadvantage; their dull gaze, flat affect, and lack of emotional response or flagrantly inappropriate response to what is going on around them is often interpreted by judges and juries as a lack of remorse, rather than a manifestation of their illness.

The common belief is that it doesn't take an expert to know if a defendant is remorseful. But this is not true. How would this judge know what was behind Dorothy's wooden expression? Rachel Aviv cites a study of cases of juveniles charged with violent crimes, described in a *Columbia Law Review* article by Martha Grace Duncan: "youths who failed to express their contrition promptly and appropriately . . . were often penalized for showing 'less grief than the system demands.'" Aviv notes that "prosecutors and judges interpreted their [the juveniles'] strange reactions—falling asleep after the crime, giggling, rapping—as signs of irreparable depravity" and that "Duncan found that courts looked for remorse in 'psychologically naïve ways without regard for defense mechanisms, developmental stages, or the ambiguity that inheres in human behavior.'" Studies have shown that the same is true when it comes to perceptions of mentally ill defendants, whose illness often makes them blank, flat, and disengaged, as though they don't care.

The question was, would the judge in the Dunn case value reason over outrage in sentencing Dorothy? Would he see her humanity first, in spite of the mental illness that hung between them like a thick curtain, or interpret her lack of affect as a sign of evil? Would her race or gender affect his view adversely?

To guide him in deciding on a sentence, he had the probation officer's presentence investigation report, describing Dorothy's compliant behavior in jail, her lack of any prior offenses, and the improbability that she constituted a danger to anyone in the community. The judge had my report, as well as Dr. Kraft's, though the two were grossly at odds with each other. And he had his own observations of Dorothy's wooden expression during the trial. He also had his predilections.

He could give whatever weight he wanted to each of those factors and would be answerable to no one in his decision. Judges are not schooled in the theory or efficacy of punishment. They're not taught how to filter out the effects of their own biases. They have no special understanding of the role their emotional reactions or implicit bias may play in shaping their proclivities toward any particular defendant. And, being elected officials, like the prosecutor, they may be swayed by political considerations or ambitions or even just the desire for public approval.

It was now May; it had been six weeks since Dorothy's conviction, and she was still being held in the county jail, pending sentencing. She had still not been allowed any contact with her children, and she had had no visitors at all, except Karen and officers from the probation department, there to prepare their sentencing report for the judge. No one else had asked to see her.

She didn't appear to pose a danger to anyone else, and a long sentence was unlikely to deter others like her. Her crime, if it was one, was a crime of impulse, not premeditation. People like Dorothy—mentally ill and mentally challenged—do not say to themselves, "I'd like to kill this child, but I don't want a long prison sentence, so I'd better not." Her behavior was not the product of a cost-benefit analysis amenable to modification by possible punishment.

Nor was any rehabilitation likely to be accomplished by a long prison term: Dorothy would be no smarter or more capable when released. And her life, far from being easier, was likely to be even harder after prison—her family broken up, her children unparented, and her ability to get a job all but vanished.

But punishment serves another purpose, as well; it is not just about deterrence or safety. It is also about revenge: it serves to discharge feelings of moral outrage toward a defendant and a crime, keeping that outrage within societal bounds. There is an inherent danger here, of the thirst for revenge run amok. It is part of the law's job to hold this in check. As Sir Francis Bacon said, "Revenge is a kind of wild justice, which the more man's nature runs to, the more ought law to weed it out."

The Supreme Court has recognized that "that which diminishes personal culpability reduces the legal justifications of deterrence and retribution," ruling that it is unconstitutional to subject a severely intellectually disabled defendant to capital punishment. And it has ruled that "punishment for crime should be graduated and proportioned to [the] offense." But it isn't clear whether it is proportionality to the act or to the actor that must be considered. In the words of Justice Sandra Day O'Connor, "Our precedents in this area [of which factors indicate gross disproportionality in sentencing] have not been a model of clarity." Where the crime is murder and the victim a helpless, innocent child, there is a great deal of outrage. Are we any less outraged if the defendant is cognitively compromised and mentally ill? The child is still dead, the harm still done.

Perhaps we would feel differently if we understood mental illness better. The Supreme Court tells us that it is not only the act that must be considered in levying punishment; we must also take into account characteristics of the actor. A defendant with "diminished moral culpability"—due, for example, to youth or impaired intellect—should be subject to less severe punishment. But because of discretionary and subjective sentencing guidelines, and judges' general lack of knowledge when it comes to intellectual deficits, developmental disabilities, and mental illness, defendants with diminished moral culpability are vulnerable to overly harsh punishment.

The psychiatric reality is that while sociopaths (people without empathy or internal conscience, predatory and opportunistic people motivated by immediate gratification) do make decisions based on a rational calculation of costs versus benefits, people like Dorothy Dunn—mentally ill, intellectually incapacitated, and exhausted—generally do not. For Dorothy, poverty, ignorance, stress, and exhaustion, not a fear of consequences, were the determinants of her behaviors. Giving her a prison sentence would do nothing to prevent another Raymie's death at the hands of another Dorothy.

I SAT IN THE COURTROOM as Dorothy was brought in for sentencing, ankles shackled and wrists manacled, wearing prison orange. Her hair was coarsely braided, sticking out in fat, graying tufts here and there. Karen was with her.

"All rise," the bailiff intoned as the judge, black robes rustling, took his seat.

I could read nothing from his expression, which was as flat and passive as Dorothy's.

"Be seated," the bailiff said. He crossed his thick brown arms over his chest and surveyed the spectators crowded onto the wooden benches, waiting until a hush settled over the room. When he was satisfied, he glanced at the judge and nodded.

The judge looked down at a paper before him and scowled.

"Dorothy Dunn," he said, "the jury has found you guilty of the crime of murder in the second degree in the death of your grandson, Raymie, whom you starved and beat, and on whom you inflicted a fatal head injury." He looked at her. "Have you anything to say to the court before sentencing?"

"I'm sorry," she said, tears coursing down her cheeks. "I tried my best, but I was a failure. I loved the boy. I never meant to hurt him. I'm sorry. I can ask for mercy, but I know I have to answer to God."

"Very well," the judge said. "Grandmas mean something. They mean cuddles and fairy tales. But for Raymie, it was a tale of terror. There weren't any cuddles for him. There were beatings and bruises and bruises and more bruises. There being nothing more for this court to consider, I hereby sentence you to the maximum sentence allowable under the law, a term of twenty-five years to life, to begin immediately."

"Well, that's done, then," Dorothy said, as she was led away. She never looked back.

CHAPTER 48

PERHAPS MENTAL ILLNESS and insanity are legal luxuries afforded only to the wealthy, the white, the educated. There is the story of Deirdre Hart Wilson, a white daughter of power and privilege, private schools and high-priced attorneys. And there is the story of Dorothy Dunn, mentally ill, mentally retarded, and represented by a public defender. Did they receive equal justice? Would Dorothy's story have come out differently if she had been white, or attractive, or educated, or wealthy enough to hire a private attorney?

Was justice done for Raymie? For Dorothy or her children or for us, the larger community? Is Dorothy really the sort of person we mean to condemn and consign to a lifetime in prison? Prosecutor Gerald Nora refers to what he calls "the criminal justice system's current regime of willful ignorance," regarding mental health issues, and says, "If we persist in prosecuting mentally ill defendants in willful ignorance of their medical problems, our system will stand as an asylum whose keepers are as deluded as the inmates." I recall the words of James Baldwin: "Ignorance allied with power is the most ferocious enemy justice can have."

And yet we continue to litigate the issue of sanity or insanity in the adversarial arena of trials, a wholly unsuitable venue for uncovering the complex truth of the matter in cases like Dorothy's, and to apply a legal definition of insanity that is without psychiatric validity. To use forensic scholar Homer Crotty's language, "It is time to bring law into alignment with reality and science. Science can help us to determine whether the offender presents as a moral problem or a medical problem we must rectify." This is true now, and it was true when he said it, nearly a century ago. Yet still we do not move forward to better marry psychiatric reality with legal rules about moral accountability.

I'm not sure we really believe in mental illness. If you haven't experienced it personally or in a close friend or family member, it is hard to understand the nature of a malfunctioning brain. We use the same standard for legal insanity that was in effect in the Middle Ages, when we thought those with schizophrenia and epilepsy were under demonic possession or were witches to be burned or drowned. A strong strain of seeing mental illness as moral weakness, weakness of character, continues to color our decisions.

The studies are clear: justice for the mentally ill is an elusive goal. Our prisons are full of people—many of whom are black, brown, and poor—with serious mental illness. Our prisons and jails have become warehouses for the mentally ill, especially those of color. Among the prisoners on death row are many men and women who barely know that they are to be executed or why, due to mental illness or intellectual disability.

In 2002, the American Psychiatric Association estimated that "on any given day, between 2.3 and 3.9 percent of inmates in state prisons are estimated to have schizophrenic or other psychotic disorders, between 13 and 18.6 percent have major depression, and between 2.1 and 4.3 percent suffer from bipolar disorder." Among jail inmates, suicide is the leading cause of death. Jamie Fellner, director of the U.S. Program of Human

Rights Watch, observed that "while the number of mentally ill inmates surges, prisons remain dangerous and damaging places for them." He wrote, "Prisons are woefully ill-equipped for their current role as the nation's primary mental health facilities. . . . People who suffer from mental illness need mental health interventions, not punishment for behavior that may be motivated by delusions and hallucinations."

There is plenty of blame to go around. The legal profession bears responsibility for not addressing the problem more effectively. Law students receive little or no training in mental health as part of their degree requirements. Defense attorneys, prosecutors, and judges should have a modicum of mental health training, awareness of what constitutes a competent evaluation, and knowledge of how to present mental health evidence in court to expose, rather than obscure, relevant data about a defendant's mental status. They should be "mental health qualified," just as they must be "death penalty qualified" in cases involving possible execution.

The mental health profession contributes to the problem. I have seen both psychiatrists and psychologists express opinions to the court about people they have not interviewed and give opinions with insufficient and contaminated data. I've heard them give opinions that lie outside their area of expertise. Too many of us are not sufficiently analytical in our reasoning and are too influenced by our personal philosophy or our biases or our desires to please or to maintain a lucrative relationship with an attorney or prosecutor. Why *should* a prosecutor or juror trust such opinions?

Mental health professionals who hold themselves out as forensic experts should be "forensically qualified": familiar with the laws and court processes, having special expertise in the evaluation of the mental health conditions disproportionately found among criminal defendants. These are special populations, in special circumstances, not the typical patient who voluntarily presents in one's office for treatment; they should be evaluated by practitioners who are familiar with their special circumstances and self-presentation.

Journalists, lawyers, professors, and pundits of all types expound about psychological issues as self-proclaimed experts, as if it is all just a matter of enlightened common sense, and potential jurors may be tempted to rely on their own common sense rather than listening to mental health testimony.

Perhaps we ask too much of jurors. I would not like to be in their shoes during a trial such as Dorothy Dunn's: never given all the facts, never allowed to hear the whole story, and not knowing all that I need to know about the mental health issues in a case. When confronted with two mental health experts, both apparently qualified but expressing diametrically opposed opinions, how can a juror determine whose opinion is sounder? Social scientists find that juries often do not trust mental health experts or make much use of their testimony in coming to a decision. Generally, they disregard both analyses and rely on their own impressions and biases, biases that tend to compound the injustices done to the mentally ill in our courts. Emotions—passions, fears, anger, and sympathy for the victim—hold sway.

In emotional cases, we are torn between our intellectual desire to be compassionate to the mentally ill and our impulse to avenge a wrong. The jurors were likely unable to identify or empathize with Mrs. Dunn. Perhaps where there was mental illness, they saw only the autopsy photos; where there was ignorance, they saw depraved indifference. They, like those who judged Charles Guiteau, may have decided that her acts were due to bad character, vice, and sin, not the illness for which she was not responsible.

Change won't come easily. As Attorney Jeffrey Toobin notes, "One of the difficulties of criminal-justice reform is that power is spread so diffusely through the system." He references Alfred Blumstein, a professor at Carnegie Mellon University: "You have legislators who decide what's a crime and establish the range of penalties. You have judges who impose the sentences. You have police who decide whom to arrest. And you have prosecutors who have wide discretion in what cases to bring, what charges to call for, and what sentences to agree to in plea bargains." He left out the impact an aroused media can have on the players in sensational cases and the element of caprice added when mental health experts come to differing conclusions about a defendant's mental state and how to shoehorn it into the arcane definition of legal insanity.

Where should we go from here? How do we chart a better course across the no-man's-land between law and psychiatry, justice and mercy, good and evil? Just as responsibility for the problem lies in multiple hands, so must the solution.

EPILOGUE

I'D LIKE TO BE ABLE TO TELL YOU that things have changed in the years since Dorothy Dunn's conviction and sentencing, but four states still have no insanity defense. In New York, it is still not enough to have severe mental illness, delusions, or psychosis; to be deemed legally insane, a defendant must also prove that he or she lacked the general ability to know right and wrong. As defense attorney Martin Goldberg says, "The problem is, being crazy isn't enough." Prosecutors still argue that insanity is a ruse and that a defendant who has engaged in any rational behavior at all in planning the attack or escaping detection must therefore be sane. Attorneys on opposing sides still shop for an expert who will support their cause. And jurors are still left to sort it all out.

We still focus on the act and not the actor, the effect rather than the intent; if the consequences for the victim were horrible, we want the consequences for the defendant to be horrible, too. Regardless of whether the defendant was sane, rational, or foresaw or intended those consequences, we want to "teach them a lesson."

In 2012, Manhattan nanny Yoselyn Ortega stabbed two-year-old Leo and six-year-old Lucia Krim to death after caring for them well for two years. Their mother returned home from an errand and found the children and Ortega, who had slashed her wrists and plunged a butcher knife into her throat, shut in the bathroom.

Ortega made no attempt to hide her crime or flee. Nor did she deny that she had done it. Why had she done it? The prosecution contended that she was angry about her workload and had killed the children vengefully, to spite their mother. In other words, she was a consummately evil person who had killed wantonly and intentionally. The defense attorney offered an insanity defense, providing psychiatric evidence that Ortega had a history of significant mental illness, including depression with psychotic features—paranoia and auditory and visual hallucinations—going back to adolescence, waxing and waning over time and reemerging in the weeks preceding the stabbings.

Mental health experts still have difficulty squaring the psychiatric facts with the legal definitions and conveying psychiatric realities to lay jurors effectively within the confines of a criminal trial. After hearing apparently conflicting mental health testimony, the jury at Ortega's 2018 trial was asked to decide whether she had known what she was doing and that it was wrong or whether she'd been "legally insane" at the time of the children's deaths. The jurors concluded that she "knew" that she was killing the children and convicted her of first- and second-degree murder. The judge sentenced her to life in prison, though he acknowledged that "there was no doubt that Ms. Ortega's untreated mental illness played a significant role." The judge asserted that she was "pure evil"—echoes of earlier judges in other times—and the children's father said she should "live and rot and die in a concrete and metal cage," which she most likely will.

What happened to the Krim children, like what happened to Raymie James, is a terrible tragedy, the magnitude of which the jury may have sought to acknowledge with its verdict. And what's more, Ortega *had* clearly known what she was doing at some point in the chain of events;

she appears to have planned to kill herself since the early morning of that day.

But do we really find it believable that this woman who had kindly cared for Leo and Lucia murdered them out of spite or malice or for any rational reason? Or is it more rational to believe, as the defense attorney argued, that she "did not possess or exhibit the faculties of understanding and liberty of will" because of mental illness? Don't get me wrong; I have known truly evil people. I believe in the existence of pure evil. I just don't believe that it often shows its ugly head for the first time in a fifty-five-year-old woman with no previous history of malfeasance, malice, or evildoing.

As *New York Times* reporters James C. McKinley and Jan Ransom noted, trials still come down to a battle between mental health experts who, "using the same set of facts, come to opposite conclusions about the defendant's capacity to understand his acts at the moment of the crime." And juries are still skeptical of insanity claims and have preconceived notions, expecting an insane defendant to be "incoherent, mumbling, almost catatonic," in the experience of defense attorney Frederick Sosinsky.

When is a person so mentally ill, so delusional and incapable of rationality, so unable to do any differently than they have done, as to qualify for humane treatment, for mercy rather than rotting in prison? Will we ever be able to separate our anger and need for combatting our sense of powerlessness when an awful event occurs from our legitimate need to protect society from those whose illness makes them a danger?

DOROTHY DUNN IS STILL IN PRISON—her earliest possible release date is September 5, 2022. In an odd way, prison might be the kindest place for Dorothy, if she isn't abused by the staff or other inmates, as often happens. For the first time in her life she has a guaranteed place to live, three square meals a day, and basic medical and dental care. She has no decisions to make, no problems to solve, no one but herself to take care of. She doesn't even have to think. In fact, it is better if she doesn't. And all it cost her was her children and her freedom. But then, she has never really been free.

Ironically, although the court had decided that Dorothy had no significant mitigating mental illness, prison officials came to disagree when they got to know her. She ended up being sent to the Bedford Hills Correctional Facility, a maximum-security prison where women who require intensive mental health services are kept. (Bedford is the only prison in New York State equipped to deal with female inmates with significant mental health issues.)

And what of her children?

It wasn't clear if Precious Love realized that Raymie was dead. She was told, while in the psychiatric hospital, but showed no reaction. It is likely her remaining children have been raised by someone else, on the margins of the system, out of sight and out of mind unless they cause trouble for the rest of us.

Dante was in prison at the time of Dorothy's trial. His history suggests that he is a sociopath, likely to remain on the wrong side of the law and potentially a danger to others for the forseeable future.

The Department of Social Services found a family member to foster Tonette and Alice: "a suitable person related to the child(ren) with whom such child may appropriately reside," as the New York Family Court Act calls it. It is doubtful whether a careful background check of this person was conducted, or that the children's well-being was looked into in any more useful way than when the CPS worker left Raymie with Dorothy. There was a rumor that Tonette ran away shortly after her mother's trial and got pregnant. One can only wonder what kind of mother she could have been, given the lack of stable role models in her life.

And then there was Alice. Alice alone, among all Dorothy's children,

had had a chance at life. A chance to escape the cycle of poverty, ignorance, and insanity that bedeviled her family. But Alice loved her mother
and had believed that her mother loved her. Despite the fact that she
clearly had been under tremendous pressure to testify for the prosecution, she was just a ten-year-old child, a child who might very well feel
that she had put her mother in prison for life. What a burden to carry
forward.

Scoot went into foster care, too, and he was too young to run away,
as Tonette reportedly had. He'd probably be in a series of foster homes
until he was old enough to run away. If they held true to history, some
would be good, and some abusive. He wouldn't have been eligible for
adoption and a permanent home unless his mother signed away her
rights—which is unlikely—or died. A parent's life sentence in prison
doesn't automatically free a child up for new parents and a permanent
home. A social worker friend of mine confided some months after the
trial that Scoot didn't seem to remember his mother or his sisters or Raymie; he never asked after them.

One day in a restaurant a few months after the trial, I saw a black boy
about Scoot's age with an older white woman who seemed to be his foster
mother. I watched him shyly draw a picture with crayons on his paper
place mat. He presented the picture to the woman, anxious to please. His
eyes, open and unguarded, searched hers as she contemplated it.

Her face contorted in a spasm of displeasure.

"That's just nasty, ugly scribbling!" she spat, with something like satisfaction at the pain in his face. "That's not coloring in the lines, all pretty
and neat like you've been taught. Why would you do such an ugly thing?
You're just a bad, bad boy!" Then she turned away from him.

I saw the boy wilt, like a crumpled flower. He hung his head and put
down his crayons, and I could see the light leaving his eyes. How many
more times would he try before giving up forever, I wondered, and my
thoughts went to Scoot—alone, confused, and too young to know why.

I would like to know where Dorothy's children are now, but their files are confidential, their futures sealed. I've not been able to find any trace of them. It's as if their footsteps, left in sand, vanished with the waves that washed over them.

THE MEDICAL EXAMINER declared himself a specialist in child abuse cases for a while, then left the area.

Denny Gallo remained in the prosecutor's office for several years, rising to chief of the Domestic Violence and Child Abuse Bureau. Then he was finally elected as a judge, running on a record of "over seventy-five successful felony convictions" and billing himself in electoral ads as "Monroe County's most experienced felony trial prosecutor, protecting our citizenry, fighting for crime victims, all the while maintaining the highest standards of the criminal justice system." I did not vote for him.

Karen left the public defender's office a few years ago, discouraged by the heavy workload, the long hours and short pay, and the stacked deck, but she continues in private practice as a defense attorney and is well respected.

The judge in Dorothy's case died suddenly of a heart attack, too young, at age sixty-two, and much praised by his family and colleagues as a man of fairness and compassion.

And me? Haunted by Dorothy's case and the murky no-man's-land between psychology and the law, between justice and mercy, I wrote this book.

ACKNOWLEDGMENTS

A WRITER WRITES ALONE, but no one could ever be a writer without the generosity and help of others, those who share their time, talents, and support. My path to this book has been a long and winding one, and I've been fortunate in those I've met along the way.

I was lucky enough to live in Rochester, where Joe Flaherty has birthed and nurtured Writers & Books, a literary center that fosters and promotes reading and writing. Undying thanks go to Dr. Lawrence Belle, who invited me to join a writing group where he, Cathy Salibian, and Joseph Callan, all fine writers in their own right, gave wise and kind feedback.

Cathy encouraged me to apply to the Bennington Writing Seminars MFA program, where I found invaluable teachers and lovers of the written word—Ben Anastas, Susan Cheever, Dinah Lenney, Bret Anthony Johnston, and also David Gates, James Wood, Jo Ann Beard, Alice Mattison, Lynne Sharon Schwartz, and others too numerous to list.

Special thanks go to my excellent agent, Jennifer Herrera, at the David Black Agency, for championing a tough story and helping me make it much better. If not for Jennifer's belief in the story, and her skill, strength, and support, it would never have seen the light of day. Plus, she's just delightful to work with.

I had the great good fortune to work with editor Alane Mason at W. W. Norton. Alane is a wise soul, and her expertise, guidance, and patience were invaluable. Thanks are also due to her excellent team: Bonnie Thompson, and artists Sarahmay Wilkinson and Amy Shire.

Court reporter Mary Jane Yaeger graciously transcribed large portions of the trial transcript for me, from notes that look to me like Babylonian cuneiform. I also owe thanks to the Monroe County public defender's office.

The folks at the Nieman Foundation for Journalism at Harvard and Columbia Journalism School who administer the J. Anthony Lukas Prize for a work in progress offered their support for the project, short-listing it for the prize and confirming my belief that people will care about this story. To be mentioned was an honor, and their encouragement is more valuable than they know.

Reading this story can be emotionally challenging. So was writing it. I am blessed to have sons who are unfailingly kind and thoughtful and a husband with infinite patience and good humor who kept me fed and watered for the duration. Good and true friends, better than I deserved while preoccupied with this project, offered encouragement and welcome diversion. My brother Paul, a gentle, wise, and talented soul, graciously allowed a part of his story to be told.

Finally, I must thank my mother and father for making me who I am, a person who felt compelled to tell this story and to work with the abused, the unheard, and the downtrodden. My father taught me the love of words, and together they taught me to work hard, always do my best, and never give up. My mother's dying wish—she was herself a talented artist struggling to find her way—was for me to realize my dream of being a writer.

Here you go, Mom. Thanks.

A NOTE ON SOURCES

THE FOLLOWING NOTES are for readers who might wish to delve further into some of the issues and authors that have informed parts of *Nobody's Child*. It is a far from exhaustive or complete list of important works and thinkers, but offers a start.

There are many wonderful resources for people who wish to know more about early English law and jurisprudence. The origins of much English law lie in early Roman law, and Aristotle's *Ethica Nicomachea* and the *Justinian Digest* are excellent places to begin. One of the best sources of insight into early English law is William Blackstone's *Commentaries on the Laws of England* (ed. William Carey Jones, San Francisco: Bancroft-Whitney, 1916). Another excellent reference is *De Legibus et Consuetudinibus Angliae* (*On the Laws and Customs of England*) by Henri de Bracton, from 1220. Written some two hundred years after the Norman conquest of England, it reflects the influences of Gallic law on the development of English common law. William Lambarde's *Archeio: A Discourse upon the High Courts of Justice in England*, written in 1591, demonstrates a very conservative perspective. J. F. Stephen's *A History of the Criminal Law of England*, from 1883, is a good overview. Contemporaneously, Dr. Oliver

Wendell Holmes Jr., was writing *The Common Law* (1881), profiling the development of American law and legal custom in the United States up to that time.

A number of eminent thinkers and writers from the fields of medicine and law have written on the development of the insanity defense in particular. An early example is the work of Homer D. Crotty, especially "The History of Insanity in Criminal Law," which can be found in the *California Law Review* (12, no.2 [1924]). Another is Edwin R. Keedy's "Report on Insanity and Criminal Responsibility," in the *Journal of the American Institute of Criminal Law and Criminology*. A good overview can be found in "The Origins of the 'Right and Wrong' Test of Criminal Responsibility and Its Subsequent Development in the United States: An Historical Survey," by Anthony Platt and Bernard L. Diamond (*California Law Review* 54, no. 3 [1966]). Psychiatrist Jacques M. Quen contributed his thoughts in "Anglo-American Criminal Insanity: An Historical Perspective," which can be found in the *Journal of the History of the Behavioral Sciences* (10 [July 1974]). Across the Channel, Daniel N. Robinson provided "Wild Beasts and Idle Humors: Legal Insanity and the Finding of Fault" (*Royal Institute of Philosophy Supplements* 37 [1994]). On the recent American side, see *Modern Histories of Crime and Punishment*, edited by Markus D. Dubber and Lindsay Farmer (Stanford, CA: Stanford University Press, 2007). Another useful resource is *The Encyclopedia of Forensic and Legal Medicine*, edited by Jason Payne James and Roger W. Byard (2nd ed., Amsterdam: Elsevier, 2015).

Many attorneys, psychiatrists, and psychologists have grappled with the difficult challenge of how to meld the legal and moral aims of an insanity defense with the psychiatric realities of what we know about mental illnesses. One of the earliest commentators from the mental health perspective was the eminent psychiatrist Dr. Isaac Ray. He wrote *A Treatise on the Medical Jurisprudence of Insanity* (Boston: Little, Brown, 1853), identifying the basic mismatch between the legal and psychiatric concepts of insanity and challenging the legitimacy of legal definitions of insanity. Nearly a hundred years later, another influential voice appeared in the form of Gregory Zilboorg, who tackled the problem in *Mind, Medicine, and Man* (New York: Harcourt, Brace, 1943). H. Fingarette made a notable contribution in "Disabilities of Mind and Criminal Responsibility: A Unitary Doctrine" (*Columbia Law Review* 76, no.2 [1976]). I have found Richard Lowell Nygaard's work particularly to provide much valuable insight into the issue; a representative piece is "On Responsibility: Or, the Insanity of Mental Defenses and Punishment," in the *Villanova Law Review* (41, no. 4 [1996]). Gerald Noa, a former prosecutor, is also a respected commentator on the mismatch between the legal definition of insanity and the original intent of the insanity defense. See, for example, "Prosecutor as 'Nurse Ratched'? Misusing Criminal Justice as Alternative Medicine" (*Criminal Justice* 22, no. 3 [2007]). A thought-provoking approach is offered by Christopher R. Williams and Bruce A. Arrigo; see *Law, Psychology, and Justice: Chaos Theory and the New (Dis)order* (Albany: State University of New York, 2001). Dave Cullen reflects on psychopathology and criminal responsibility in *Columbine* (New York: Twelve, 2009). And "How Much Agency Do We Have Over Our Behavior?", a *TED Radio Hour* NPR presentation by Robert Sapolsky from 2017, provides a unique perspective on criminal responsibility and intent, incorporating recent developments in neuroscience. Any interested reader would also do well to read the work of Bruce Winick, a professor of law and psychiatry and behavioral science, and a well-respected scholar in the area of mental health law and law and psychology.

Gary Melton's work is an excellent resource for insight into the intricacies of forensic mental health evaluations and testimony. I recommend especially *Psychological Evaluations for the Courts: A Handbook for Mental Health Professionals and Lawyers* by Gary Melton, John Petrila, Norman Poythress, Christopher Slobogin, Randy Otto, Douglas Mossman, and Lois Condie (3rd ed., New York: Guilford Press, 2007). The Association for Psychological Science article "Myth #4: Many Criminals Use the Insanity Defense to Escape Punishment," provides perspective on the issue of public distrust of mental health evidence and testimony. Another seminal contributor to the field is Phillip Resnick, past president of the American Academy of Psychiatry and the Law. An example of his thinking can be found in "Perceptions of Psychiatric Testimony: A Historical Perspective on the Hysterical Invective" (in the *Bulletin of the American Academy of Psychiatry and Law* 14, no. 3 [1986]). Well-known psychiatrist Park Elliott Dietz, writing in the *Annals of the American Academy of Political and Social Science* in 1985, considers "Why the Experts Disagree: Variations in the Psychiatric Evaluation of Criminal Insanity."

For insight into racial disparities in criminal justice, including legal representation and sentencing, see "Sentence Decision Making: The Logic of Sentence Decisions and the Extent and Sources of Sentence Disparity," by Kevin Clancy, John Bartolomeo, David Richardson, and Charles Wellford, in the *Journal of Criminal Law and Criminology* (72, no. 2 [1981]). Another excellent source is *No Equal Justice: Race and Class in the American Criminal Justice System* by David Cole (New York: New Press, 1999). Tushar Kansal offers an overview of the issue in "Racial Disparity in Sentencing: A Review of the Literature" (2005), part of the Sentencing Project. And the "Report of the Sentencing Project of the United Nations Human Rights committee: Regarding Racial Disparities in the United States Criminal Justice System" (2013) is a thorough and well researched document lending insight into racial disparity in sentencing. Dean Aufderheide's *Health Affairs* blog post from April 2014, titled, "Mental Illness in America's Jails and Prisons: Toward Public Safety/ Public Health Model" is a good entry point to the growing problem of mass incarceration of the mentally ill.

I am indebted to the *Rochester Democrat and Chronicle* for media accounts of the trial on which this book is based. I am indebted to the *Marin Independent Journal* and the *San Francisco Chronicle* for media accounts of the case of Deirdre Hart Wilson. Clarence Darrow's closing argument in the Prendergast case is reprinted in the *Chicago Law Journal*, 1894. The story of Dr. William Minor is recounted in *The Professor and the Madman: A Tale of Murder, Insanity, and the Makings of the Oxford English Dictionary*, by Simon Winchester (New York: HarperCollins, 1998).

Relevant statutes in New York include the New York Penal Law, New York Criminal Procedure Law, and New York Social Services Law. The ALI Model Proposal can be found in the American Law Institute Archives.

NOTES

EPIGRAPH

vii **"Tell me . . . and sanity begins?":** Dry Nurse [pseud.], *Monomania* (London: Saunders and Otley, 1843).

CHAPTER 2

8 **far above national standards:** Tim Donaher, *Office of the Public Defender Annual Report* (Monroe County, NY, 2012). Richard Meryhew, "State to Pare the Ranks of Public Defenders by 23," *Star Tribune* (Minneapolis), June 5, 2008; quoted in the Constitution Project, *Justice Denied: America's Continuing Neglect of Our Constitutional Right to Counsel; Report of the National Right to Counsel Committee,* April 2009.

8 **"There is a vast gulf":** Andrew Cohen, "How Americans Lost the Right to Counsel, 50 Years After 'Gideon,'" *Atlantic*, March 13, 2013.

8 **"to choose among clients":** Spangenberg Group and Center for Justice, Law and Society at George Mason University, *Assessment of the Missouri State Public Defender System* (Fairfax, VA: George Mason University, 2005), citing the Missouri State Public Defender Commission's Findings and Directive on Caseload Standards in Accordance with Professional and Statutory Obligations, Finding 9 (Adapted June 10, 2005; draft copy).

CHAPTER 6

28   **"Prosecutors decide whether":** Jeffrey Toobin, "The Milwaukee Experiment," *New Yorker*, May 11, 2015.

28   **"would 'indict a ham sandwich'":** Tom Wolfe, *The Bonfire of the Vanities* (New York: Farrar, Straus and Giroux, 1987), p. 624. See also Barry Popik, "Indict a Ham Sandwich," The Big Apple, July 15, 2004, https://www.barrypopik.com/index.php/new_york_city/entry/indict_a_ham_sandwich/.

29   **"The U.S. attorney is the representative":** *Berger v. U.S.*, 295 U.S. 78 (1935), p. 88.

29   **"have a biased view":** Gerald E. Nora, "Prosecutor as 'Nurse Ratched'? Misusing Criminal Justice as Alternative Medicine," *Criminal Justice* 22, no. 3 (Fall 2007).

30   **"was not an individual":** Mark I. Levenstein, "Authorities Probe Nursing Home Death," Forward.com, June 3, 2005.

32   **"GRANDMOTHER HELD FOR MURDER":** Michael Zeigler, "Grandmother Held for Murder in Death of Young Grandson, Found Beaten and Starved," *Rochester Democrat and Chronicle*, September 11, 1997.

CHAPTER 7

35   **"the application of the science":** "What Is Forensic Psychology?," American Board of Forensic Psychology, http://abfp.com.

35   **"Knowing and proving":** James Comey, *A Higher Loyalty: Truth, Lies, and Leadership* (New York: Flatiron Books, 2018), 163.

38   **"It is not uncommon":** Rachel Aviv, "Memories of a Murder," *New Yorker*, June 19, 2017, p. 44.

39   **"He is a person":** Karl Ove Knausgaard, "The Inexplicable: Inside the Mind of a Mass Killer," *New Yorker*, May 25, 2015, pp. 28, 33.

40   **"the application of":** "What Is Forensic Psychology?," American Board of Forensic Psychology.

40   **"The psychiatrist is the only":** Phillip Resnick, revision of Presidential Address to the American Academy of Psychiatry and the Law, October 1955, in "Perceptions of Psychiatric Testimony: A Historical Perspective on the Historical Invective," citing S. L. Halleck, "A Critique of Current Psychiatric Roles in the Legal Process," *Wisconsin Law Review* (1966): 379.

40   **"to choose a career":** Alan Stone, "The Ethical Boundaries of Forensic Psychiatry: A View from the Ivory Tower," *Journal of the American Academy of Psychiatry and the Law* 36 (2008): 167–74.

CHAPTER 8

41 **"Crimes are not":** *Bartlett's Familiar Quotations*, 13th ed. (Boston: Little, Brown, 1955).

41 **"A man who killed":** Code of Hammurabi, translation from Rev. C.H.W. Johns, "Babylonian Law," *Encyclopaedia Britannica*, 11th ed. (New York: 1910), p. 120.

42 **"that which is done in ignorance":** Aristotelis, *Ethica Nicomachea*, ed. I. Bywater (Oxford, UK: Oxford University Press, 1993).

42 **"with knowledge of the circumstances":** K. D. DeFreitas and S. J. Hucker, "Forensic Psychiatry and Forensic Psychology: Criminal Responsibility," in *Encyclopedia of Forensic and Legal Medicine*, 2nd ed., ed. Jason Payne-James and Roger W. Byard (Boston: Elsevier Academic Press, 2015).

42 **"such persons were regarded":** R. D. Melville, *The Principles of Roman Law: A Manual of the Principles of Roman Law Relating to Persons, Property, and Obligations, with a Historical Introduction for the Use of Students*, 3rd ed. (Edinburgh: W. Green and Son, 1921) (citing the Justinian Digest).

42 **"the one is excused":** *The Psychiatrist in the Courtroom: Selected Papers of Bernard C. Diamond, M.D.*, ed. Jacques M. Quen (Hillsdale, NJ: Analytic Press, 1994).

42 **"To make a complete crime":** William Blackstone, *Commentaries on the Laws of England*, ed. William Carey Jones, vol. 2 (1765; repr., San Francisco: Bancroft-Whitney, 1916), p. 2175.

43 **"We must consider":** Henri de Bracton, *De Legibus et Consuetudinibus Angliae* [On the laws and customs of England], circa 1220, in Jacques M. Quen, "Insanity Defense: How Far Have We Strayed?" *Cornell Journal of Law and Public Policy*, vol. 5, no. 1 (1955): article 3.

43 **Some neuroscientists:** Robert Sapolsky, "How Much Agency Do We Have Over Our Behavior?," *TED Radio Hour*, National Public Radio, August 25, 2017.

CHAPTER 9

49 **"The life of the law":** Oliver Wendell Holmes Jr., *The Common Law* (1881; repr., New York: Little, Brown, 1984), 1.

49 **basic standard for competency:** *Dusky v. United States*, 362 U.S. 402 (1960).

CHAPTER 10

53 **"grey steel cages":** Blake F. McKelvey, "A History of Penal and Correctional Institutions in the Rochester Area," *Rochester History* 34, no. 1 (January 1972).

CHAPTER 12

63   **"There is no present without the past":** Orhan Pamuk, "Memory and For-
getting" (lecture, Humanities Center Public Lecture Series, University of
Rochester, October 25, 2017).

CHAPTER 14

75   **"general ignorance":** Homer D. Crotty, "The History of Insanity as a Defence to
Crime in English Criminal Law," *California Law Review* 12, no. 2 (January 1924):
113.

75   **"men's freedom is restrained":** *The Psychiatrist in the Courtroom: Selected
Papers of Bernard L. Diamond, M.D.* ed. Jacques M. Quen (Hillsdale, NJ: Analytic Press, 1994).

76   **"If a madman or a natural fool":** Jacques M. Quen, "Anglo-American Criminal Insanity: An Historical Perspective," accessed through Semantic Scholar
(https://pdfs.semanticscholar.org/27c1/bd68ce34740966d827bbc70b5365abe55
26b.pdf); originally from *Journal of the History of the Behavioral Sciences* 10 (July
1974). Quen is quoting from William Lambarde, *Archeion; or, A Discourse upon
the High Courts of Justice in England*, published in 1635 (but written in 1591).

76   **"If one that is '*non compos mentis*' ":** Michael Dalton, quoted in Anthony
Platt and Bernard L. Diamond, "The Origins of the 'Right and Wrong' Test
of Criminal Responsibility and Its Subsequent Development in the United
States: An Historical Survey," *California Law Review* 54, no. 3 (August 1966):
1235

78   **"a wicked person":** Devin Dwyer, Kevin Dolak, Dean Schabner, and Emily
Friedman, "Cops Hunt Second Man Believed to Be Involved in Congresswoman Giffords Shooting," ABCNews.Go.com, January 8, 2011.

78   **"That is moral clarity":** Cal Thomas, "The Arizona Shootings: Place the
Blame for Evil Where It Belongs," *Milwaukee Journal Sentinel*, January 10, 2011.

78   **"The schizophrenic's complaint":** Oliver Sacks, *The Man Who Mistook His
Wife for a Hat* (New York: Simon & Schuster, 1970).

78   **Author Primo Levi:** Primo Levi, *Survival in Auschwitz* (Charleston, SC:
Important Books, 2012), and Primo Levi, *The Drowned and the Saved* (New
York: Vintage International, 1987).

80   **"*Is this a dagger which I see before me*":** William Shakespeare, *Macbeth*, in *The
Complete Works of Shakespeare* (New York: Walter J. Black, 1937), act 2, scene 1,
lines 33–41.

80   **"*wholly* loseth their memory and understanding":** Quoted in Gary B.
Melton, John Petrila, Norman G. Poythress, Christopher Slobogin, Randy
K. Otto, Douglas Mossman, and Lois Condie, *Psychological Evaluations for the*

Courts: A Handbook for Mental Health Professionals and Lawyers, 4th ed. (New York: Guilford Press, 2018), p. 201.

80 **"it is very difficult to define":** Quoted in W. H. Parry, "Insanity in Criminal Cases," *Albany Law Journal* 63 (1901–2): 433.

80 **Children age seven or younger:** James P. Snell, "History of Hunterdon and Somerset Counties," p. 200, quoted in Marfy Goodspeed, *Goodspeed Histories*, https://goodspeedhistories.com, 2013, and Watt Espy, "Death for Juvenile Crimes: Execution, a Practice Dating to 1642, May Continue This Week," *Los Angeles Times*, January 7, 1986.

81 **"Surely no two states of mind":** James Fitzjames Stephen, *A History of the Criminal Law of England*, vol. 2 (London: Macmillan, 1883), p. 150.

81 **Hale reduced:** Homer D. Crotty, "The History of Insanity as a Defence to Crime in English Criminal Law," *California Law Review* 12, no. 2 (January 1924): 105.

81 **Some courts have defined:** H. Fingarette, "Disabilities of Mind and Criminal Responsibility: A Unitary Doctrine," *Columbia Law Review* 76, no. 2 (1976): 236, 255n49, and *State v. Hamann*, 285 N.W.2d 180, 183, Iowa, 1979.

81 **while others:** *People v. Schmidt*, 110 N.E. 945, 946, New York 1915. So, for example, if A kills B, knowing he is killing B, and knowing it's illegal to kill B, but under the insane delusion that God commanded him to kill B because the salvation of the human race depends on it, then A is guilty if "wrong" is taken in its legal sense but not guilty by reason of insanity if "wrong" is understood in its moral sense.

82 **the "right and wrong" test:** A test with origins in Aristotle, endorsed by the eyre of Kent in 1313, by Lambarde in 1591, and by William Hawkins in his *A Treatise of Pleas of the Crown*, vol. 1, section 1: "In respect of their want of reason . . . it is to be observed that those who are under a natural disability of distinguishing between good and evil, as infants under the age of discretion, ideots, and lunaticks, are not punishable by any criminal prosecution" (1716; repr. London: S. Sweet, 1824).

82 **"crude and imperfect notions":** Isaac Ray, *A Treatise on the Medical Jurisprudence of Insanity* (Boston: Little, Brown, 1853).

82 **Of 5,111 murder cases:** "Nanny Faces Tough Insanity Test," *New York Times*, March 27, 2018 (citing the New York State Division of Criminal Justice Services Report).

82 **long, documented histories:** Sean Lahman and Gary Craig, "Will Mental Health Issues Factor in Holly Colino's Defense?," *Rochester Democrat and Chronicle*, September 3, 2017.

CHAPTER 16

91 **The fundamental question:** William E. Mikell, "McNaghten's Case and Beyond," *American Law Register* 50, no. 5 (May 1902), 267.

91 **"had been of good esteem":** John Winthrop, *The Journal of John Winthrop, 1630–1649*, ed. Richard S. Dunn, James Savage, and Laetitia Yeandle (Cambridge, MA: Belknap Press of Harvard University Press, 1996), p. 272.

92 **"see poor Dorothy Talbye":** Oliver Wendell Holmes, *The Writings of Oliver Wendell Holmes*, vol. 9, *Medical Essays, 1842–1882* (Cambridge, MA: Riverside Press, 1891), p. 356.

92 **"devils and imps" that had "invaded his belly":** *Rex v. Arnold*, 16 St. Tr. 695, 763 (1724).

93 **"it is agreed by all jurists":** Quoted in Daniel N. Robinson, "Wild Beasts and Idle Humours: Legal Insanity and the Finding of Fault," *Royal Institute of Philosophy Supplements* 37 (March 1994).

95 **"and as the sparing this boy":** William Blackstone, *Commentaries on the Laws of England*, ed. William Carey Jones, vol. 2 (1765; repr., San Francisco: Bancroft-Whitney, 1916), p. 2179.

95 **"the rule of law":** Ibid., p. 2180.

95 **"In criminal cases":** Ibid.; also quoted in Samuel Polsky, "Present Insanity—from Common Law to the Mental Health Act and Back," *Villanova Law Review* 2, no. 4 (1957): 509n20.

96 **"The chief criticism":** Quoted in Blackstone, *Commentaries on the Laws of England*, 2182.

97 **"Punishment deters not only sane men":** Markus D. Dubber and Lindsay Farmer, eds., *Modern Histories of Crime and Punishment* (Stanford, CA: Stanford University Press, 2007), quoting from Nigel Walker, *Crime and Insanity in England*, vol. 1, *The Historical Perspective* (Edinburgh: Edinburgh University Press, 1968), p. 189.

97 **"Punishment is intended for example":** *Kinloch's Case*, 25 How. St. Tr. 1001 (1795).

CHAPTER 21

121 **In one inner-city:** Edward J. Doherty, *Benchmarking Rochester's Poverty: A 2015 Update and Deeper Analysis of Poverty in the City of Rochester* (Rochester: Rochester Area Community Foundation and ACT for Rochester, 2015).

CHAPTER 22

124 **"it is not every degree":** *Clark's Case*, 1 City H. Rec. 176 (1816).

126 **"Hallucination of mind was evident":** Thomas Hart Benton, *Thirty Years' View; or, A History of the Working of the American Government for Thirty Years, from 1820 to 1850*, vol. 1 (New York: Appleton, 1858), p. 524.

126 **Nearly forty years later:** Simon Winchester, *The Professor and the Madman: A*

Tale of Murder, Insanity, and the Making of the "Oxford English Dictionary" (New York: Harper Perennial, 1998), p. 21.

CHAPTER 23

129   **"Mad or not"**: Alfred Swaine Taylor, *A Manual of Medical Jurisprudence*, ed. Thomas Stevenson, 12th ed. (New York: Lea Brothers, 1897), p. 760.

129   **"jurors ought to be told"**: Homer D. Crotty, "The History of Insanity as a Defence to Crime in English Criminal Law," *California Law Review* 12, no. 2 (January 1924): 117–18.

131   **"I have just shot the President"**: Charles Guiteau Collection, Georgetown University Library Special Collections Research Center 2/28/94, and "Excerpts from the Trial Transcript: Cross-Examination of Charles Guiteau." See also *United States v. Charles Guiteau*, 1 Mackey 498, 47 Am. Rep. 247, and James C. Clark, "The Murder of President Garfield," p. 134; available at https://www.archives.gov/files/publications/prologue/1992/summer/garfield.pdf.

132   **"As society has gained more knowledge"**: Douglas O. Linder, "The Trial of Charles Guiteau: An Account," www.famous-trials.com/guiteau/2197-home, working from *Report of the Proceedings in the Case of the United States vs. Charles J. Guiteau*, Part 3, H. H. Alexander and Edward D. Easton, stenographers (Washington, DC: Government Printing Office, 1882).

132   **"It is very hard to conceive"**: *Report of the Proceedings in the Case of the United States vs. Charles J. Guiteau*, Part 3, H. H. Alexander and Edward D. Easton, stenographers (Washington, DC: Government Printing Office, 1882), p. 1865.

133   **"I'm going to ask you"**: CBS/AP, "Knowing Right from Wrong: James Holmes Trial Begins," CBS News, April 27, 2015; https://www.cbsnews.com/news/opening-statements-in-james-holmes-trial/.

134   **"We are very happy"**: Sandy Phillips, mother of victim Jessica Ghawi, quoted in Anna Cabrera, Greg Botelho, and Dana Ford, "James Holmes Found Guilty of Murder in Colorado Theater Shooting," July 17, 2015; https://www.cnn.com/2015/07/16/us/james-holmes-trial-colorado-movie-theater-shooting-verdict/index.html.

134   **"If there was ever a case"**: Judge Carlos Samour quoted by Ann O'Neill, "Theater Shooter Holmes Gets 12 Life Sentences, Plus 3,318 Years," August 27, 2015; https://www.cnn.com/2015/08/26/us/james-holmes-aurora-massacre-sentencing/index.html.

134   **"The more horrendous"**: J. Reid Meloy quoted in "Should the Trial of James Holmes Be the Beginning of the End for Use of Psychiatric Testimony in Court to Judge Guilt or Innocence?," *fpamed* blog, May 31, 2015; www.fpamed.com/should-the-trial-of-james-holmes-be-the-beginning-of-the-end-for-use-of-psychiatric-testimony-in-court-to-judge-guilt-or-innocence.

134 **"The inadequacy of this formula":** Homer D. Crotty, "The History of Insanity as a Defence to Crime in English Criminal Law," *California Law Review* 12, no. 2 (January 1924): 118, citing Dr. Morton Prince's discussion of Edwin R. Keedy's "Report on Insanity and Criminal Responsibility," *Journal of the American Institute of Criminal Law and Criminology* 2, no. 538 (1912), p. 539.

135 **"Except for totally deteriorated":** Gregory Zilboorg, *Mind, Medicine, and Man* (New York: Harcourt, Brace, 1943), p. 274.

135 **"Whilst we are tenderly alive"":** William Wood, *Remarks on the Plea of Insanity and on the Management of Criminal Lunatics*, 2nd ed. (London: Longman, Brown, Green, and Longmans, 1852), p. 4.

135 **"O, let me not be mad":** William Shakespeare, *King Lear* (1605; rpt. Baltimore: Pelican, 1958), act 1, scene 5, lines 40–41.

CHAPTER 24

137 **"I didn't want to harm the man":** Truman Capote, *In Cold Blood* (1965; repr. New York: Vintage International, 2012), p. 244

138 **"I think it's a helluva thing":** Ibid., p. 340.

139 **Harris was armed:** Dave Cullen, "The Depressive and the Psychopath," *Slate*, April 20, 2004.

140 **"Isnt America supposed to be":** Dave Cullen, *Columbine* (New York: Twelve, 2009), p. 260.

140 **"cold-blooded, predatory psychopath":** Ibid., p. 234.

140 **"unlike psychotic individuals":** Cullen, "The Depressive and the Psychopath," *Slate*, April 20, 2004.

CHAPTER 25

143 **"sunk wholly below":** Francis Galton, "Psychometric Experiments," *Brain* 2, no. 2 (July 1, 1879).

CHAPTER 26

155 **"deep enough into family histories":** Meaghan M. McDermott, "Despite Reform Effort, Child Protective Services Remains Mired in Disarray," *Rochester Democrat and Chronicle*, May 4, 2018.

156 **"issues with Monroe County's agency":** Meaghan M. McDermott, "Little Girl Lost: The Questions Left Behind by Brook Stagles' Death," *Rochester Democrat and Chronicle*, September 23, 2017. The text of the law can be found here: New York State Social Services Laws, Article 6, Title 2: Powers and Duties of Public Welfare Officials, Section 397, 2(a); https://www.nysenate.gov/legislation/laws/SOS/397.

CHAPTER 27

159 **"Lawyers have never been receptive":** Phillip J. Resnick, "Perceptions of Psychiatric Testimony: A Historical Perspective on the Hysterical Invective," *Bulletin of the American Academy of Psychiatry and the Law*, 14, no. 3 (February 1986): 213, quoting G. Zilboorg.

159 **"insuring the public safety":** New York Penal Law, Part I, Section 1.05.6.

160 **"I have decided to take this method":** Oliver E. Remey, Henry F. Cochems, and Wheeler P. Bloodgood, *The Attempted Assassination of Ex-President Theodore Roosevelt*, chapter 22, "Unusual Court Precedent"; accessed at www.gutenberg.org/files/21261/21261-h/21261-h.html.

CHAPTER 28

162 **"moral blame shall not attach":** *Durham v. U.S.*, 214 F. 2d 862 (D.C. Cir. 1954).

163 **"lacks substantial capacity":** Model Penal Code records, American Law Institute Archives, ALI.04.005, Biddle Law Library, University of Pennsylvania Law School, Philadelphia, PA.

163 **"mental disease or defect":** Ibid.

164 **"At one time Miss Foster":** Stuart Taylor Jr., "Hinckley Hails 'Historical' Shooting to Win Love," *New York Times*, July 9, 1982; https://www.nytimes.com/1982/07/09/us/hinckley-hails-historical-shooting-to-win-love.html.

165 **"If you start thinking about":** Howell Raines, "Reagan Hails Proposal for New Insanity Law," *New York Times*, July 2, 1982.

165 **"mental condition shall not":** Idaho Code, Section 18-207(1).

165 **"pampered criminals":** "From Daniel M'Naughten to John Hinckley: A Brief History of the Insanity Defense," *Frontline*, PBS, www.pbs.org/wgbh/pages/frontline/shows/crime/trial/history.html.

165 **"nebulous and often psychologically":** Richard Lowell Nygaard, "On Responsibility; Or, the Insanity of Mental Defenses and Punishment," *Villanova Law Review* 41, no. 4 (1996): 977, 981.

165 **"the imprecision of legislative attempts":** Christopher R. Williams and Bruce A. Arrigo, *Law, Psychology, and Justice: Chaos Theory and the New (Dis)order* (Albany: State University of New York Press, 2002), p. 85, citing Bruce J. Winick.

166 **"Based on what I've seen":** Dan Barry et al., "Looking Behind the Mug-Shot Grin," *New York Times*, January 15, 2011.

CHAPTER 29

172 **"reflects a wicked":** *People v. Russell*, 91 NY2d 280, 287 (1998).

172 **"When the defendant intends":** *People v. Suarez*, 6 NY39 212 (2005).

CHAPTER 30

174   **"The paradox of an illness":** Oliver Sacks, *The Man Who Mistook His Wife for a Hat* (New York: Simon & Schuster, 1970), p. 89.

174   **" 'Yes, Father' ":** Ibid., p. 116.

175   **"It is precisely the downfall":** Ibid., p. 19.

175   **"Schizophrenia chose him":** Ted Johnson, "Aurora Theater Shooting Trial: James Holmes' Mother Says 'Schizophrenia Chose Him,'" *Variety*, July 29, 2015; https://variety.com/2015/biz/news/james-holmes-aurora-theater-shooting -trial-mother-1201552903/.

175   **"intensely vivid hallucinations":** Sacks, *The Man Who Mistook His Wife for a Hat*, p. 137.

176   **"If a man has lost a leg":** Ibid., p. 35.

177   **"One survey revealed":** Association for Psychological Science, "Myth #4: Many Criminals Use the Insanity Defense to Escape Punishment"; https:// www.psychologicalscience.org/media/myths/myth_4.cfm.

177   **"If a madman were to come":** James Boswell, *Life of Samuel Johnson, LL.D.*, April 3, 1776 (originally published in 1791); quote found at the Samuel Johnson Sound Bite Page, "Quotes on Self-Preservation," 1,574, http:// www.samueljohnson.com/selfpres.html.

177   **"A law that punishes a man":** William H. Parry, "Insanity in Criminal Cases," *Albany Law Journal* 63 (December 1901): 460.

CHAPTER 32

185   **"when, under circumstances":** NYS Penal Code § 125.25 murder in the second degree.

185   **"an utter disregard":** *People v. Maldonado*, NYS (2014).

185   **"simply does not care":** *People v. Spears*, NY Court of Appeals (2014).

185   **"reflects a wicked":** *People v. Suarez*, 748 NYS 2d 312 (2005).

CHAPTER 33

189   **"knew" in the most elemental way:** New York State Penal Law, Article 40.15: "In any prosecution for an offense, it is an affirmative defense that when the defendant engaged in the proscribed conduct, he lacked criminal responsibility by reason of mental disease or defect. Such lack of criminal responsibility means that at the time of such conduct, as a result of mental disease or defect, he lacked substantial capacity to know or appreciate either: 1. The nature and consequences of such conduct; or 2. That such conduct was wrong."

189   **"imperfect fit":** American Psychiatric Association, *Diagnostic and Statistical*

Manual of Mental Disorders: DSM-IV-TR (Washington, DC: American Psychiatric Association, 2000).

189 **"law virtually has stood still"**: Richard Lowell Nygaard, "On Responsibility; Or, the Insanity of Mental Defenses and Punishment," *Villanova Law Review* 41, no. 4 (1996): 966, 971.

CHAPTER 34

200 **"TESTIMONY TODAY"**: Michael Zeigler, "Testimony Today in Child's Beating Death," *Rochester Democrat and Chronicle*, March 3, 1998.

CHAPTER 35

209 **"PROSECUTION PLAYS TAPE"**: Michael Zeigler, "Prosecution Plays Tape of 911 Call," *Rochester Democrat and Chronicle*, March 5, 1998.

CHAPTER 36

211 **"When the ambulance crew arrived"**: Michael Zeigler, "Ambulance Tech Testifies . . ." *Rochester Democrat and Chronicle*, December 19, 1997.

CHAPTER 37

225 **The newspaper headline that night:** Michael Zeigler, "Tiny Voice Details 'Horrific' Abuse," *Rochester Democrat and Chronicle*, March 3, 1998.

CHAPTER 38

227 **Primo Levi wrote:** Primo Levi, *The Drowned and the Saved* (New York: Summit, 1988).

CHAPTER 39

234 **"are unable to make accurate"**: Richard Lowell Nygaard, "On Responsibility; Or, the Insanity of Mental Defenses and Punishment," *Villanova Law Review* 41, no. 4 (1996): 971.

235 **"funding at both the state"**: The Sentencing Project, *Report of the Sentencing Project to the United Nations Human Rights Committee: Regarding Racial Disparities in the United States Criminal Justice System* (Washington, DC, August 2013). The report cites L. Song Richardson and Phillip Atiba Goff, "Implicit Racial Bias in Public Defender Triage," *Yale Law Journal* 122, no. 8 (June 2013): 2626, 2632.

CHAPTER 41

253 **"When asked about psychological tests"**: Frank Dattilio, Bob Sadoff, Eric Drogin, and Tom Gautheil, "Should Forensic Psychiatrists Conduct Psychological Testing?" *Journal of Psychiatry and Law* 39, no. 3 (Spring 2012); https://www.ethicalpsychology.com/2012/01/should-forensic-psychiatrists-conduct.html.

258 **"Psychiatric opinion"**: Park Elliott Dietz, "Why the Experts Disagree: Variations in the Psychiatric Evaluation of Criminal Insanity," *Annals of the American Academy of Political and Social Science* 477, no. 1 (January 1, 1985): 84–95.

259 **"the contradictory testimony"**: Richard Lowell Nygaard, "On Responsibility; Or, the Insanity of Mental Defenses and Punishment," *Villanova Law Review* 41, no. 4 (1996): 971, 970.

259 **"Weyer is not a lawyer"**: Phillip J. Resnick, "Perceptions of Psychiatric Testimony: A Historical Perspective on the Hysterical Invective," *Bulletin of the American Academy of Psychiatry and the Law*, 14, no. 3 (February 1986): 163.

259 **"the pathological processes"**: Justice Frankfurter, in dissent, in *Solesbee v. Balkcom*, 339 U.S. 9 (1950).

259 **"treacherous uncertainties"**: Majority opinion in *Solesbee v. Balkcom*, 339 U.S. 9 (1950).

260 **most eminent criminal trial attorneys:** Andrew E. Kersten, *Clarence Darrow: American Iconoclast* (New York: Hill and Wang, 2011).

261 **"Before engaging"**: "The Prendergast Case: Mr. C. S. Darrow's Closing Argument," *Chicago Law Journal* 5, no. 8 (August 1894): 363–90.

CHAPTER 44

273 **if a defendant is found not guilty:** Stephen Seager, *Behind the Gates of Gomorrah: A Year with the Criminally Insane* (New York: Gallery Books, 2014).

273 **"When a defendant has raised the"**: New York State Criminal Procedure Law, Article 300, Section 10.3.

274 **"A TV reporter remarked"**: Michael Winerip, "The Jurors' Dilemma," *New York Times Magazine*, November 21, 1999.

275 **"I thought of my daughter Kendra"**: Laura Italiano, " 'Nightmare' over for Kendra's Kin," *New York Post*, March 23, 2000.

276 **committing insanity-verdict defendants involuntarily:** *Jones v. U.S.*, 463 U.S. 354 (1983).

276 **both mentally ill and dangerous:** *Foucha v. Louisiana*, 504 U.S. 71 (1992).

276 **no limit to the potential length:** Mac McClellan, "When 'Not Guilty' Is a Life Sentence," *New York Times*, September 27, 2017.

CHAPTER 46

283 **"At around 10:30 p.m."**: Lessley Anderson, "Death in the Family," *SF Weekly*, October 13, 2004.

285 **"Two of the children"**: Con Garretson, "Woman Sentenced in Death of Toddler," *Marin Independent Journal*, April 19, 2003.

285 **"I've been living as a psychological amputee"**: Peter Fimrite, "Last of Marinwood Cult Sentenced," *SFGate*, April 19, 2003.

CHAPTER 47

287 **to permit an injustice to exist:** Jamie L. Anderson, "Reciprocity as a Justification for Retributivism," *Criminal Justice Ethics* 16, no. 1 (1997).

287 **"reflect the dominant forms"**: Hugo Adam Bedau and Erin Kelly, "Punishment," *Stanford Encyclopedia of Philosophy*, revised July 31, 2015, referring to ideas from Michel Foucault, *Discipline and Punish: The Birth of the Prison* (New York: Pantheon, 1977).

287 **"the United States in effect"**: The Sentencing Project, *Report of the Sentencing Project to the United Nations Human Rights Committee: Regarding Racial Disparities in the United States Criminal Justice System* (Washington, DC, August 2013), citing David Cole, *No Equal Justice: Race and Class in the American Criminal Justice System* (New York: New Press, 1999), pp. 1, 12.

287 **"Race still exerts"**: Tushar Kansal, *Racial Disparity in Sentencing: A Review of the Literature*, ed. Marc Mauer (Washington, DC: The Sentencing Project, January 2005).

288 **"substantial dissensus exists"**: Kevin Clancy, John Bartolomeo, David Richardson, and Charles Wellford, "Sentence Decisionmaking: The Logic of Sentence Decisions and the Extent and Sources of Sentence Disparity," *Journal of Criminal Law and Criminology* 72, no. 2 (Summer 1981).

288 **"Each judge"**: Willard Gaylin and Daniel Callahan, "The Psychiatrist as Double Agent," *Hastings Center Report* 4, no. 1 (February 1974): pp. 12–14.

288 **"youths who failed"**: Rachel Aviv, "No Remorse," *New Yorker*, January 2, 2012.

290 **it serves to discharge feelings:** R. A. Duff, *Trials and Punishments* (Cambridge: Cambridge University Press, 1986).

290 **"Revenge is a kind of wild justice"**: Francis Bacon, "Of Revenge," *Essays* (originally published in 1625); quote taken from *Bartlett's Familiar Quotations*, 13th ed. (Boston: Little, Brown, 1955).

290 **"that which diminishes"**: *Atkins v. Virginia*, 536 U.S. 304 (2002).

290 **"punishment for crime"**: *Weems v. United States*, 217 U.S. 349 (1910), and *Roper v. Simmons*, 543 U.S. 551 (2005).

290 **"Our precedents in this area":** *Lockyer v. Andrade,* 538 U.S. 63, 72 (2003).

291 **"diminished moral culpability":** *Graham v. Florida,* 560 U.S. 48 (2010).

CHAPTER 48

293 **"the criminal justice system's":** Gerald E. Nora, "Prosecutor as 'Nurse Ratched'? Misusing Criminal Justice as Alternative Medicine," *Criminal Justice* 22, no. 3 (Fall 2007).

293 **"Ignorance allied with power":** James Baldwin, *No Name in the Street* (New York: Vintage, 1972), p. 149.

294 **"It is time to bring law":** Richard Lowell Nygaard, "On Responsibility; Or, the Insanity of Mental Defenses and Punishment," *Villanova Law Review* 41, no. 4 (1996): 973–74.

294 **"on any given day":** Dean Aufderheide, "Mental Illness in America's Jails and Prisons: Toward a Public Safety/Public Health Model," *Health Affairs Blog*, April 1, 2014.

294 **suicide is the leading cause:** Margaret Noonan, "Mortality in Local Jails and State Prisons, 2000–2010," U.S. Department of Justice, Bureau of Justice Statistics, August 2015.

295 **"while the number of mentally ill":** Human Rights Watch, "U.S.: Number of Mentally Ill in Prisons Quadrupled; Prisons Ill Equipped to Cope," September 5, 2006, https://www.hrw.org/news/2006/09/05/us-number-mentally-ill-prisons-quadrupled#, quoting Jamie Fellner and Sasha Abramsky from *Ill-Equipped: U.S. Prisoners and Offenders with Mental Illness* (New York: Human Rights Watch, 2003).

296 **"One of the difficulties":** Jeffrey Toobin, "The Milwaukee Experiment," *New Yorker*, May 11, 2015, p. 26.

EPILOGUE

299 **"The problem is":** James C. McKinley Jr. and Jan Ransom, "An Uphill Battle: The Insanity Defense," *New York Times*, March 27, 2018.

300 **"there was no doubt that Ms. Ortega's":** Jan Ransom, "Yoselyn Ortega, Nanny Who Killed 2 Children, Is Sentenced to Life in Prison," *New York Times*, May 14, 2018.

301 **"did not possess or exhibit":** Ibid.

301 **"using the same set of facts":** James C. McKinley and Jan Ransom, "An Uphill Battle," *New York Times*, March 27, 2018.

INDEX